TAHOE
CAMPING & HIKING

TOM STIENSTRA

Mount Tallac affords a view across Lake Tahoe

like no other: a cobalt-blue expanse of water bordered by mountains that span miles of Sierra wildlands. The beauty is stunning. Lake Tahoe is one of the few places on earth where people feel an emotional response just by looking at it. Yosemite Valley, the giant sequoias, the Grand Canyon, a perfect sunset on the Pacific Ocean . . . these are a few other sights that occasionally can evoke the same response. But Tahoe often seems to strike the deepest chord. It can resonate inside you for weeks, even after a short visit.

"What about all the people?" you ask. It's true that people come here in droves. But I found many spots that I shared only with the chipmunks. You can enjoy these spots, too, if you're willing to read my books, hunt a bit, and, most important, time your trip to span Monday through Thursday.

This area has the widest range and number of campgrounds in California.

Tahoe and the Northern Sierra feature hundreds of lakes, including dozens you can drive to. The best for scenic beauty are Echo Lakes, Donner, Fallen Leaf, Sardine, Caples, Loon, Union Valley — well, I could go on and on. It is one of the most beautiful regions anywhere on earth.

The north end of the Northern Sierra starts near Bucks Lake, a great lake for trout fishing, and extends to Bear River Canyon (and Caples Lake, Silver Lake, and Bear River Reservoir). In between are the Lakes Basin Recreation Area (containing Gold, Sardine, Packer, and other lakes) in southern Plumas County; the Crystal Basin (featuring Union Valley Reservoir and Loon Lake, among others) in the Sierra foothills west of Tahoe; Lake Davis (with the highest catch rates for trout) near Portola; and the Carson River Canyon and Hope Valley south of Tahoe.

You could spend weeks exploring any of these places, having the time of your life, and still not get to Tahoe's magic. But it is Tahoe where the adventure starts for many, especially in the surrounding Tahoe National Forest and Desolation Wilderness.

One of California's greatest day trips from Tahoe is to Echo Lakes, where you can take a hikers shuttle boat across the two lakes to the Pacific Crest Trail, then hike a few miles into Desolation Wilderness and Aloha Lakes. Yet with so many wonderful ways to spend a day in this area, this day trip is hardly a blip on the radar.

With so many places and so little time, this region offers what can be the ultimate adventureland.

How to Use This Book

ABOUT THE CAMPGROUND PROFILES

The campgrounds are listed in a consistent, easy-to-read format to help you choose the ideal camping spot. Here is a sample profile:

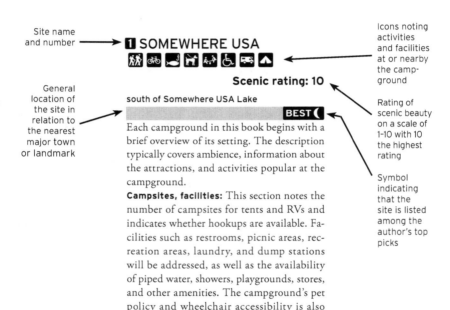

Site name and number

General location of the site in relation to the nearest major town or landmark

Icons noting activities and facilities at or nearby the campground

Rating of scenic beauty on a scale of 1-10 with 10 the highest rating

Symbol indicating that the site is listed among the author's top picks

1 SOMEWHERE USA

Scenic rating: 10

south of Somewhere USA Lake

BEST

Each campground in this book begins with a brief overview of its setting. The description typically covers ambience, information about the attractions, and activities popular at the campground.

Campsites, facilities: This section notes the number of campsites for tents and RVs and indicates whether hookups are available. Facilities such as restrooms, picnic areas, recreation areas, laundry, and dump stations will be addressed, as well as the availability of piped water, showers, playgrounds, stores, and other amenities. The campground's pet policy and wheelchair accessibility is also mentioned here.

Reservations, fees: This section notes whether reservations are accepted, and provides rates for tent sites and RV sites. If there are additional fees for parking or pets, or discounted weekly or seasonal rates, they will also be noted here.

Directions: This section provides mile-by-mile driving directions to the site from the nearest major town or highway.

Contact: This section provides an address, phone number, and website, if available, for each site.

ABOUT THE ICONS

The camping icons are designed to provide at-a-glance information on activities, facilities, and services available on-site or within walking distance of each campground.

- 🏃 Hiking trails
- 🚲 Biking trails
- 🏊 Swimming
- 🎣 Fishing
- 🚤 Boating
- 🛶 Canoeing and/or kayaking
- ❄ Winter sports

- ♨ Hot Springs
- 🐾 Pets permitted
- 🛝 Playground
- ♿ Wheelchair accessible
- 🚐 RV sites
- ⛺ Tent sites

ABOUT THE SCENIC RATING

Each campground profile employs a scenic rating on a scale of 1 to 10, with 1 being the least scenic and 10 being the most scenic. A scenic rating measures only the overall beauty of the campground and environs; it does not take into account noise level, facilities, maintenance, recreation options, or campground management. The setting of a campground with a lower scenic rating may simply not be as picturesque that of as a higher rated campground, however other factors that can influence a trip, such as noise or recreation access, can still affect or enhance your camping trip. Consider both the scenic rating and the profile description before deciding which campground is perfect for you.

ABOUT THE TRAIL PROFILES

Each hike in this book is listed in a consistent, easy-to-read format to help you choose the ideal hike. From a general overview of the setting to detailed driving directions, the profile will provide all the information you need. Here is a sample profile:

Map number and hike number →

Round-trip mileage (unless otherwise noted) and the approximate amount of time needed to complete the hike (actual times can vary widely, especially on longer hikes) →

1 SOMEWHERE USA HIKE
9.0 mi/5.0 hrs   🚶3 ⛰8

← Difficulty and quality ratings

at the mouth of the Somewhere River ←

← General location of the trail, named by its proximity to the nearest major town or landmark

BEST ←

Symbol indicating that the hike is listed among the author's top picks

Each hike in this book begins with a brief overview of its setting. The description typically covers what kind of terrain to expect, what might be seen, and any conditions that may make the hike difficult to navigate. Side trips, such as to waterfalls or panoramic vistas, in addition to ways to combine the trail with others nearby for a longer outing, are also noted here. In many cases, mile-by-mile trail directions are included.

User Groups: This section notes the types of users that are permitted on the trail, including hikers, mountain bikers, horseback riders, and dogs. Wheelchair access is also noted here.

Permits: This section notes whether a permit is required for hiking, or, if the hike spans more than one day, whether one is required for camping. Any fees, such as for parking, day use, or entrance, are also noted here.

Maps: This section provides information on how to obtain detailed trail maps of the hike and its environs. Whenever applicable, names of U.S. Geologic Survey (USGS) topographic maps and national forest maps are also included.

Directions: This section provides mile-by-mile driving directions to the trailhead from the nearest major town.

Contact: This section provides an address and phone number for each hike. The contact is usually the agency maintaining the trail but may also be a trail club or other organization.

ABOUT THE ICONS

The hiking icons are designed to provide at-a-glance information on the difficulty and quality of each hike.

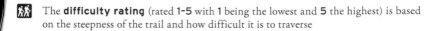

The **difficulty rating** (rated **1-5** with **1** being the lowest and **5** the highest) is based on the steepness of the trail and how difficult it is to traverse

The **quality rating** (rated **1-10** with **1** being the lowest and **10** the highest) is based largely on scenic beauty, but also takes into account how crowded the trail is and whether noise of nearby civilization is audible

ABOUT THE DIFFICULTY RATINGS

Trails rated 1 are very easy and suitable for hikers of all abilities, including young children.

Trails rated 2 are easy-to-moderate and suitable for most hikers, including families with active children 6 and older.

Trails rated 3 are moderately challenging and suitable for reasonably fit adults and older children who are very active.

Trails rated 4 are very challenging and suitable for physically fit hikers who are seeking a workout.

Trails rated 5 are extremely challenging and suitable only for experienced hikers who are in top physical condition.

MAP SYMBOLS

....	Expressway	(80)	Interstate Freeway	✗	Airfield
....	Primary Road	(101)	U.S. Highway	✗	Airport
....	Secondary Road	(21)	State Highway	○	City/Town
- - - - - - -	Unpaved Road	66	County Highway	▲	Mountain
....	Ferry	🌑	Lake	♦	Park
—— ■ —— ●	National Border	☁	Dry Lake	⟩ᵣ	Pass
—— - - ——	State Border	☁	Seasonal Lake	◉	State Capital

ABOUT THE MAPS

This book is divided into chapters based on major regions in the state; an overview map of these regions precedes the table of contents. Each chapter begins with a map of the region, which is further broken down into detail maps. Sites are noted on the detail maps by number.

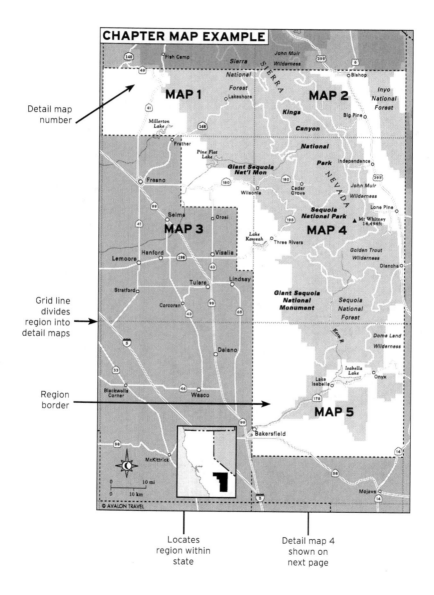

Locates detail
map within
region

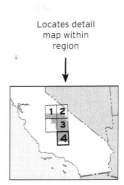

Map
number ➝ **Map 4**

Sites shown
on detail map ➝ **Sites 105-117**

Site
number ➝

Region
border ➝

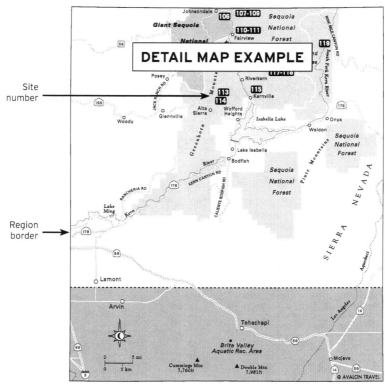

DETAIL MAP EXAMPLE

TAHOE CAMPING

© 123RF.COM/ANNA PARCIAK

BEST CAMPGROUNDS

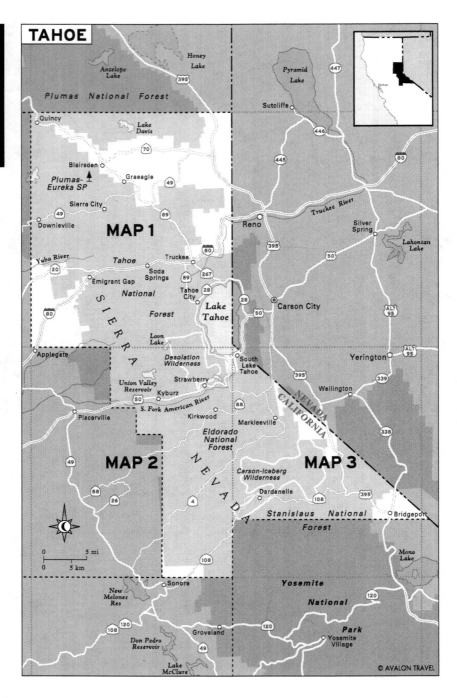

Map 1

Campgrounds 1-115

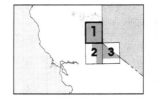

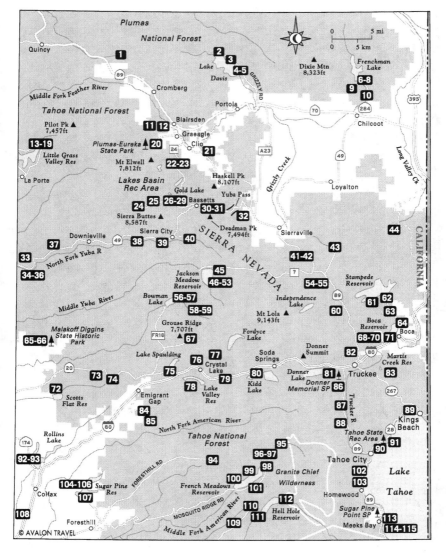

Map 2

Campgrounds 116-176

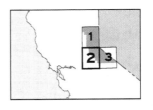

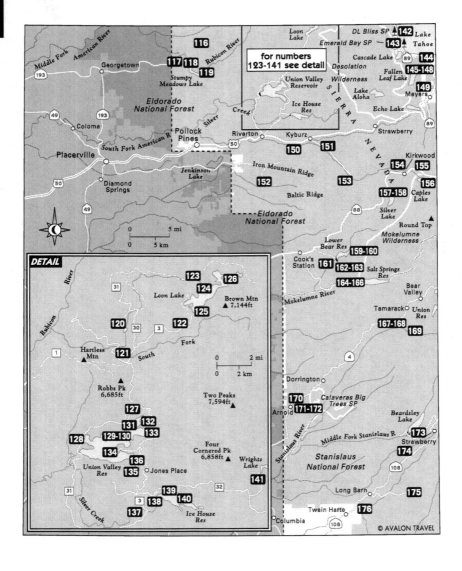

Map 3

Campgrounds 177-220

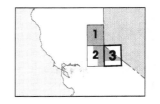

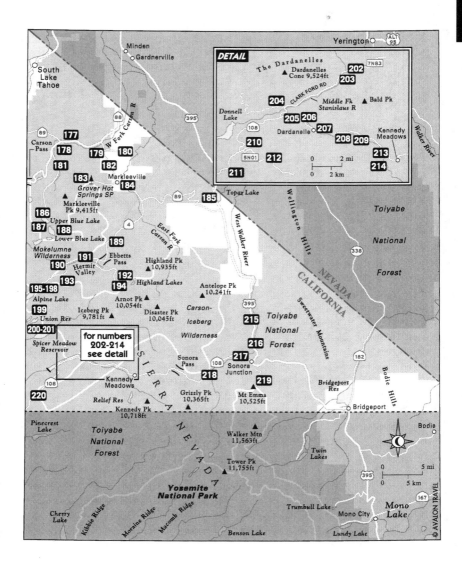

❶ BRADY'S CAMP

🏃 🛶 🐾 5% ⛺

Scenic rating: 4

on Pine Creek in Plumas National Forest

Don't expect much company here. This is a tiny, little-known, primitive camp near Pine Creek, at roughly 7,000 feet elevation. A side trip is to make the half-mile drive up to Argentine Rock (7,209 feet) for a lookout onto this remote forest country. To the east are many miles of national forest accessible by vehicle.

Campsites, facilities: There are four tent sites. Picnic tables and fire grills are provided. Vault toilets are available. No drinking water is available. Garbage must be packed out. Leashed pets are permitted.

Reservations, fees: Reservations are not accepted. There is no fee for camping. Open May through October, weather permitting.

Directions: From Oroville, drive north on Highway 70 to the junction with Highway 89. Turn south on Highway 89/70 and drive 11 miles to Quincy. In Quincy, continue on Highway 89/70 for six miles to Squirrel Creek Road. Turn left and drive seven miles (after two miles bear right at the Y) to Forest Road 25N29. Turn left and drive one mile to the campground on the right side of the road.

Contact: Plumas National Forest, Mount Hough Ranger District, 530/283-0555, fax 530/283-1821.

❷ LIGHTNING TREE

🏊 🛶 🛥 🐾 ♿ 🚐 ⛺

Scenic rating: 7

on Lake Davis in Plumas National Forest

Lightning Tree campground is set near the shore of Lake Davis. Davis is a good-sized lake, with 32 miles of shoreline, set high in the northern Sierra at 5,775 feet. Lake Davis is one of the top mountain lakes in California for fishing, with large rainbow trout in the early summer and fall. This camp is perfectly situated for a fishing trip. It is at Lightning Tree Point on the lake's remote northeast shore, directly across the lake from Freeman Creek, one of the better spots for big trout. This lake is famous for pike; the Department of Fish and Game has twice poisoned the lake to kill them. In turn, the biggest trout plants in California history have been made here, with more than one million trout in 2008! There are three boat ramps on the lake.

Campsites, facilities: There are 40 sites for tents or RVs up to 50 feet (no hookups). Vault toilets and drinking water are available. Garbage must be packed out. A dump station and a car-top boat launch are nearby. Some facilities are wheelchair-accessible. Leashed pets are permitted.

Reservations, fees: Reservations are accepted at 877/444-6777 or www.recreation.gov ($10 reservation fee). Sites are $9 per night, $18 per night for a double site. Open May through October, weather permitting.

Directions: From Truckee, turn north on Highway 89 and drive to Sattley and County Road A23. Turn right on County Road A23 and drive 13 miles to Highway 70. Turn left on Highway 70 and drive one mile to Grizzly Road. Turn right on Grizzly Road and drive about six miles to Lake Davis. Continue north on Lake Davis Road along the lake's east shore and drive about five miles to the campground entrance on the left side of the road.

Contact: Plumas National Forest, Beckwourth Ranger District, 530/836-2575, fax 530/836-0493; Thousand Trails, 530/832-1076.

❸ GRASSHOPPER FLAT

🏊 🛶 🛥 🐾 ♿ 🚐 ⛺

Scenic rating: 7

on Lake Davis in Plumas National Forest

Grasshopper Flat provides a nearby alternative to Grizzly at Lake Davis, with the boat ramp at adjacent Honker Cove a primary attraction for campers with trailered boats for fishing. The camp is on the southeast end of the lake, at 5,800 feet elevation. Lake Davis is known for its large rainbow trout that bite best in early summer and fall. Swimming and powerboats are allowed, but no waterskiing or personal watercraft are permitted.

Campsites, facilities: There are 70 sites for tents or RVs up to 35 feet (no hookups). Picnic tables and fire grills are provided. Drinking water and restrooms with flush toilets and coin showers are available. A boat ramp, grocery store, and a dump station are nearby. Some facilities are wheelchair-accessible. Leashed pets are permitted.

Reservations, fees: Reservations are accepted at 877/444-6777 or www.recreation.gov ($10 reservation fee). Sites are $18 per night. Open May through October, weather permitting.

Directions: From Truckee, turn north on Highway 89 and drive to Sattley and County Road A23. Turn right on County Road A23 and drive 13 miles to Highway 70. Turn left on Highway 70 and drive one mile to Grizzly Road. Turn right on Grizzly Road and drive about six miles to Lake Davis. Continue north on Lake Davis Road for a mile (just past Grizzly) to the campground entrance on the left side of the road.

Contact: Plumas National Forest, Beckwourth Ranger District, 530/836-2575, fax 530/836-0493; Thousand Trails, 530/832-1076.

4 CROCKER

Scenic rating: 5

in Plumas National Forest

Even though this camp is just four miles east of Lake Davis, it is little known and little used since there are three lakeside camps close by. This camp is set in Plumas National Forest at 5,900 feet elevation, and it is about a 15-minute drive north to the border of the Dixie Mountain State Game Refuge.

Campsites, facilities: There are 10 sites for tents or RVs up to 16 feet (no hookups). Picnic tables and fire grills are provided. Vault toilets are available. No drinking water is available. Garbage must be packed out. Leashed pets are permitted.

Reservations, fees: Reservations are not accepted. There is no fee for camping. Open May through October, weather permitting.

Directions: From Reno, drive north on U.S. 395 to the junction with Highway 70. Turn west on Highway 70 and drive to Beckwourth and County Road 111/Beckwourth-Genessee Road. Turn right on County Road 111 and drive six miles to the campground on the left side of the road.

Contact: Plumas National Forest, Beckwourth Ranger District, 530/836-2575, fax 530/836-0493; Thousand Trails, 530/832-1076.

5 GRIZZLY

Scenic rating: 7

on Lake Davis in Plumas National Forest

This is one of the better developed campgrounds at Lake Davis and is a popular spot for camping anglers. Its proximity to the Grizzly Store, just over the dam to the south, makes getting last-minute supplies a snap. In addition, a boat ramp is to the north in Honker Cove, providing access to the southern reaches of the lake, including the island area, where trout trolling is good in early summer and fall. The elevation is 5,800 feet.

Campsites, facilities: There are 55 sites for tents or RVs up to 35 feet (no hookups). Picnic tables and fire grills are provided. Drinking water and flush toilets are available. A boat ramp, grocery store, and a dump station are nearby. Some facilities are wheelchair-accessible. Leashed pets are permitted.

Reservations, fees: Reservations are accepted at 877/444-6777 or www.recreation.gov ($10 reservation fee). Sites are $18 per night. Open May through October, weather permitting.

Directions: From Truckee, turn north on Highway 89 and drive to Sattley and County Road A23. Turn right on County Road A23 and drive 13 miles to Highway 70. Turn left on Highway 70 and drive one mile to Grizzly Road. Turn right on Grizzly Road and drive about six miles to Lake Davis. Continue north on Lake Davis Road for less than a mile to the campground entrance on the left side of the road.

Contact: Plumas National Forest, Beckwourth Ranger District, 530/836-2575, fax 530/836-0493; Thousand Trails, 530/832-1076.

6 BIG COVE

🏃 🏊 🚣 🛶 🐴 ♿ 🚐 ⛺

Scenic rating: 7

at Frenchman Lake in Plumas National Forest

Big Cove is one of four camps at the southeastern end of Frenchman Lake, with a boat ramp available about a mile away near the Frenchman and Spring Creek camps. (For more information, see the *Frenchman* listing in this chapter.) A trail from the campground leads to the lakeshore. Another trail connects to the Spring Creek campground, a walk of 0.5 mile. The elevation is 5,800 feet.

Campsites, facilities: There are 38 sites for tents or RVs up to 50 feet (no hookups). Picnic tables and fire rings are provided. Drinking water and flush toilets are available. Some facilities are wheelchair-accessible. A boat ramp and dump station are nearby. A grocery store and propane gas are available seven miles away. Leashed pets are permitted.

Reservations, fees: Reservations are accepted at 877/444-6777 or www.recreation.gov ($10 reservation fee). Sites are $18–36 per night. Open May through October, weather permitting.

Directions: From Reno, drive north on U.S. 395 to the junction with Highway 70. Turn west on Highway 70 and drive to Chilcoot and the junction with Frenchman Lake Road. Turn right on Frenchman Lake Road and drive nine miles to the lake and to a Y. At the Y, turn right and drive two miles to Forest Road 24N01. Turn left and drive a short distance to the campground entrance on the left side of the road (on the east side of the lake).

Contact: Plumas National Forest, Beckwourth Ranger District, 530/836-2575, fax 530/836-0493; Thousand Trails, 530/832-1076.

7 SPRING CREEK

🏃 🏊 🚣 🛶 🐴 ♿ 🚐 ⛺

Scenic rating: 7

on Frenchman Lake in Plumas National Forest

Frenchman Lake is set at 5,800 feet elevation, on the edge of high desert to the east and forest to the west. The lake has 21 miles of shoreline and is surrounded by a mix of sage and pines. All water sports are allowed. This camp is on the southeast end of the lake, where there are three other campgrounds, including a group camp and a boat ramp. The lake provides good fishing for stocked rainbow trout—best in the cove near the campgrounds. Trails lead out from the campground: One heads 0.25 mile to the Frenchman campground; the other a 0.5-mile route to Big Cove campground.

Campsites, facilities: There are 35 sites for tents or RVs up to 35 feet (no hookups). Picnic tables and fire grills are provided. Drinking water and vault toilets are available. Some facilities are wheelchair-accessible. A boat ramp and dump station are nearby. Leashed pets are permitted.

Reservations, fees: Reservations are accepted at 877/444-6777 or www.recreation.gov ($10 reservation fee). Sites are $18 per night. Open May through October, weather permitting.

Directions: From Reno, drive north on U.S.

395 to the junction with Highway 70. Turn west on Highway 70 and drive to Chilcoot and the junction with Frenchman Lake Road. Turn right on Frenchman Lake Road and drive nine miles to the lake and to a Y. At the Y, turn right and drive two miles to the campground on the left side of the road.

Contact: Plumas National Forest, Beckwourth Ranger District, 530/836-2575, fax 530/836-0493; Thousand Trails, 530/832-1076.

8 FRENCHMAN

Scenic rating: 7

on Frenchman Lake in Plumas National Forest

This camp is on the southeast end of the lake, where there are three other campgrounds, including a group camp and a boat ramp. The best trout fishing is in the cove near the campgrounds and the two inlets, one along the west shore and one at the head of the lake. The proximity to Reno, only 35 miles away, keeps gambling in the back of the minds of many anglers. Because of water demands downstream, the lake often drops significantly by the end of summer. A trail from camp is routed 0.25 mile to the Spring Creek campground.

Campsites, facilities: There are 38 sites for tents or RVs up to 35 feet (no hookups). Picnic tables and fire grills are provided. Drinking water and vault toilets are available. A dump station and boat ramp are nearby. Leashed pets are permitted.

Reservations, fees: Reservations are accepted at 877/444-6777 or www.recreation.gov ($10 reservation fee). Sites are $18 per night. Open May through October, weather permitting.

Directions: From Reno, drive north on U.S. 395 to the junction with Highway 70. Turn west on Highway 70 and drive to Chilcoot and the junction with Frenchman Lake Road. Turn right on Frenchman Lake Road and drive nine miles to the lake and to a Y. At the Y, turn

right and drive 1.5 miles to the campground on the left side of the road.

Contact: Plumas National Forest, Beckwourth Ranger District, 530/836-2575, fax 530/836-0493; Thousand Trails, 530/259-7606.

9 COTTONWOOD SPRINGS

Scenic rating: 7

near Frenchman Lake in Plumas National Forest

Cottonwood Springs, elevation 5,800 feet, is largely an overflow camp at Frenchman Lake. It is the only camp at the lake with a group site. The more popular Frenchman, Big Cove, and Spring Creek camps are along the southeast shore of the lake near a boat ramp.

Campsites, facilities: There are 20 sites for tents or RVs up to 50 feet (no hookups), and two group sites for tents or RVs up to 35 feet that can accommodate 25–50 people each. Picnic tables and fire rings are provided. Drinking water and flush toilets are available. Some facilities are wheelchair-accessible. A boat ramp and dump station are nearby. Leashed pets are permitted.

Reservations, fees: Reservations are accepted for individual sites and are required for group sites at 877/444-6777 or www.recreation.gov ($10 reservation fee). Sites are $18 per night, $70–110 per night for groups. Open May through October, weather permitting.

Directions: From Reno, drive north on U.S. 395 to the junction with Highway 70. Turn west on Highway 70 and drive to Chilcoot and the junction with Frenchman Lake Road. Turn right on Frenchman Lake Road and drive nine miles to the lake and to a Y. At the Y, turn left and drive 1.5 miles to the campground on the right side of the road.

Contact: Plumas National Forest, Beckwourth Ranger District, 530/836-2575, fax 530/836-0493; Thousand Trails, 530/832-1076.

🔟 CHILCOOT

🏃 🏊 🎣 🏕 ♿ 🚐 ⛺

Scenic rating: 7

on Little Last Chance Creek in Plumas
National Forest

This small camp is set along Little Last
Chance Creek at 5,400 feet elevation, about
three miles downstream from Frenchman
Lake. The stream provides good trout fishing, but access can be difficult at some spots
because of brush.

Campsites, facilities: There are 40 sites for
tents or RVs up to 35 feet (no hookups), and
five walk-in sites for tents only. Picnic tables
and fire rings are provided. Drinking water
and flush toilets are available. Some facilities are wheelchair-accessible. A boat ramp,
grocery store, and dump station are nearby.
Leashed pets are permitted.

Reservations, fees: Reservations are accepted
at 877/444-6777 or www.recreation.gov ($10
reservation fee). Sites are $18 per night. Open
May through October, weather permitting.

Directions: From Reno, drive north on U.S.
395 to the junction with Highway 70. Turn
west on Highway 70 and drive to Chilcoot
and the junction with Frenchman Lake Road.
Turn right on Frenchman Lake Road and drive
six miles to the campground on the left side
of the road.

Contact: Plumas National Forest, Beckwourth Ranger District, 530/836-2575,
fax 530/836-0493; Thousand Trails,
530/832-1076.

🔟🔟 LITTLE BEAR RV PARK

🏊 🎣 🏕 🚐

Scenic rating: 7

on the Feather River

This is a privately operated RV park set near
the Feather River. Nearby destinations include
Plumas-Eureka State Park and the Lakes Basin

Recreation Area. The elevation is 4,300 feet.
About half of the sites are taken by full-season
rentals.

Campsites, facilities: There are 97 sites with
full or partial hookups (30 amps) for RVs of
any length, and 10 sleeping cabins. No tents
are allowed. Picnic tables and fire rings are
provided. Drinking water, restrooms with
showers and flush toilets, coin laundry, convenience store, satellite TV, modem access, RV
storage, propane, and ice are available. A dump
station, clubhouse, table tennis, shuffleboard,
and horseshoes are also available. Leashed pets
are permitted at campsites; but no pets in the
cabins.

Reservations, fees: Reservations are recommended. Sites are $27–29 per night, $4–8 per
person per night for more than two people,
$1 per pet per night. Weekly and monthly
rates available. Open mid-April through late
October.

Directions: In Truckee, drive north on Highway 89 to Graeagle. Continue north on Highway 89 for one mile to Little Bear Road. Turn
left on Little Bear Road and drive a short distance to the campground on the right.

Contact: Little Bear RV Park, tel.
530/836-2774, fax 530/836-1810, www.
littlebearrvpark.com.

🔟🔟 MOVIN' WEST RV PARK

🏃 🏊 🏕 🚐 ⛺

Scenic rating: 5

in Graeagle

This RV park began life as a mobile home
park. Approximately half of the sites are for
permanent residents; the other half are for
vacationers, with about half of those rented
for the summer. The park has also become
very popular with golfers. A nine-hole golf
course is across the road and five other golf
courses are within five miles. The elevation
is 4,300 feet.

Campsites, facilities: There are 51 sites for

RVs of any length with full (30 amps), partial, or no hookups, including five pull-through sites. There are also three tent sites and two cabins. Picnic tables and fire rings are provided. Drinking water, restrooms with flush toilets and showers, pay phone, cable TV, Wi-Fi, and a coin laundry are available. Propane gas, a nine-hole golf course, swimming pond, horse stable, and mini golf are nearby. Leashed pets are permitted.

Reservations, fees: Reservations are recommended. RV sites with full hookups are $29 per night or $25 per night with no hookups, tent sites are $25 per night, cabins are $40 per night, $5 per person per night for more than two people. Open May through October.

Directions: From Truckee, drive northwest on Highway 89 about 50 miles to Graeagle. Continue just past Graeagle to County Road A14 (Graeagle-Johnsville Road). Turn left and drive 0.25 mile northwest to the campground on the left.

Contact: Movin' West RV Park, 530/836-2614.

13 BLACK ROCK WALK-IN AND OVERFLOW
🚶🏊🛶🎣🐴🏕️⛺

Scenic rating: 7

on Little Grass Valley Reservoir in Plumas National Forest

This is the only campground on the west shore of Little Grass Valley Reservoir, with an adjacent boat ramp making it an attractive choice for anglers. The lake is set at 5,060 feet elevation in Plumas National Forest and provides lakeside camping and decent fishing for rainbow trout and kokanee salmon. If you don't like the company, there are seven other camps to choose from at the lake, all on the opposite eastern shore.

Campsites, facilities: There are 20 walk-in sites (a walk of a few yards to 0.1 mile) for tents or RVs up to 22 feet (no hookups). There

is a parking lot for overflow camping for RVs up to 35 feet. Picnic tables and fire grills are provided. Drinking water, vault toilets, and a fish-cleaning station are available. A dump station, boat ramp, and grocery store are nearby. Leashed pets are permitted.

Reservations, fees: Reservations are not accepted. Sites are $20 per night. Open May through September, weather permitting.

Directions: From Oroville, drive east on Highway 162/Oroville Dam Boulevard for about eight miles (becomes the Olive Highway) to Forbestown Road. Turn right and drive through Forbestown to Challenge and LaPorte Road. Turn left on LaPorte Road and drive to LaPorte. Continue two miles past LaPorte to the junction with County Road 514/Little Grass Valley Road. Turn left and drive about five miles to the campground access road on the west side of the lake. Turn right on the access road and drive 0.25 mile to the campground.

Contact: Plumas National Forest, Feather River Ranger District, 530/534-6500, fax 530/532-1210; Northwest Management, 530/283-5559.

14 HORSE CAMP
🚶🏊🛶🎣🐴♿🚐⛺

Scenic rating: 7

on Little Grass Valley Reservoir in Plumas National Forest

This camp is reserved for equestrians only and thus it gets low use. This is a high-country forested campground set near Little Grass Valley Reservoir, but there is no lake view because of tree cover. Several trails are accessible from the campground, including the Pacific Crest Trail and Lakeshore Trail, as well as access to Bald Mountain (6,255 feet). The elevation at camp is 5,060 feet.

Campsites, facilities: There are 10 sites for tents or RVs up to 25 feet (no hookups) available for equestrian campers only. Picnic tables and fire grills are provided. Vault toilets are available. No drinking water is available. Hitching posts and a wheelchair-accessible mounting rack are available. A restaurant and deli are available five miles away in LaPorte. Leashed pets are permitted.

Reservations, fees: Reservations are accepted at 877/444-6777 or www.recreation.gov ($10 reservation fee). Sites are $20 per night. Open June through September.

Directions: From Oroville, drive east on Highway 162/Oroville Dam Boulevard for about eight miles (becomes the Olive Highway) to Forbestown Road. Turn right and drive through Forbestown to Challenge and LaPorte Road. Turn left on LaPorte Road and drive to LaPorte. Continue on County Road 512 (which becomes County Road 514/Little Grass Valley Road) for three miles to Forest Road 22N57. Turn right and drive four miles (cross the bridge) to the campground on the left.

Contact: Plumas National Forest, Feather River Ranger District, 530/534-6500, fax 530/532-1210; Northwest Management, 530/283-5559.

water and flush toilets are available. A boat launch, fish-cleaning station, and a swimming beach are nearby. Leashed pets are permitted.

Reservations, fees: Reservations are not accepted. Sites are $20 per night. Open Memorial Day weekend through September, weather permitting.

Directions: From Oroville, drive east on Highway 162/Oroville Dam Boulevard for about eight miles (becomes the Olive Highway) to Forbestown Road. Turn right and drive through Forbestown to Challenge and LaPorte Road. Turn left on LaPorte Road and drive to LaPorte. Continue on County Road 512 (which becomes County Road 514/Little Grass Valley Road) for three miles to Forest Road 22N57. Continue on Forest Road 514 for one mile to the campground entrance on right. Turn right and drive 0.25 mile to the campground.

Contact: Plumas National Forest, Feather River Ranger District, 530/534-6500, fax 530/532-1210; Northwest Management, 530/283-5559.

15 PENINSULA TENT
🚶 🏊 🛶 🎣 🐕 🚐 ⛺

Scenic rating: 9

on Little Grass Valley Reservoir in Plumas National Forest

This camp, at 5,060 feet in elevation, is exceptional in that most of the campsites provide views of Little Grass Valley Reservoir, a pretty lake in national forest. The fishing can be excellent, especially for rainbow trout, brown trout, and kokanee salmon. The camp gets moderate use, and it is a pretty site with tents sprinkled amid white fir and pine. This is a good family campground. A 13.5-mile hiking trail circles the lake.

Campsites, facilities: There are 25 sites for tents or RVs up to 25 feet (no hookups). Picnic tables and fire rings are provided. Drinking

16 RUNNING DEER
🚶 🏊 🛶 🎣 🐕 🚐 ⛺

Scenic rating: 7

on Little Grass Valley Reservoir in Plumas National Forest

Little Grass Valley Reservoir is a pretty mountain lake set at 5,060 feet elevation in Plumas National Forest, providing lakeside camping, boating, and fishing for rainbow trout and kokanee salmon. Looking straight north from the camp is a spectacular view, gazing across the water and up at Bald Mountain, at 6,255 feet elevation. One of seven campgrounds on the eastern shore, this one is on the far northeastern end of the lake. A trailhead for the Pacific Crest Trail is nearby at little Fowler Lake about four miles north of Little Grass Valley Reservoir. Note that fish-cleaning stations are not available at Running Deer, but there is one nearby at Little Beaver.

Campsites, facilities: There are 40 sites for tents or RVs up to 40 feet (no hookups). Picnic tables and fire rings are provided. Drinking water and flush toilets are available. A fish-cleaning station, boat ramp, grocery store, and a dump station are nearby. Leashed pets are permitted.

Reservations, fees: Reservations are accepted at 877/444-6777 or www.recreation.gov ($10 reservation fee). Sites are $20–22 per night. Open late May through September.

Directions: From Oroville, drive east on Highway 162/Oroville Dam Boulevard for about eight miles (becomes the Olive Highway) to Forbestown Road. Turn right and drive through Forbestown to Challenge and LaPorte Road. Turn left on LaPorte Road and drive to LaPorte. Continue on County Road 512 (which becomes County Road 514/Little Grass Valley Road) for three miles to Forest Road 22N57. Turn right and drive three miles to the campground on the left.

Contact: Plumas National Forest, Feather River Ranger District, 530/534-6500, fax 530/532-1210; Northwest Management, 530/283-5559.

17 WYANDOTTE

Scenic rating: 8

on Little Grass Valley Reservoir in Plumas National Forest

Of the eight camps on Little Grass Valley Reservoir, this is the favorite. It is set at 5,100 feet elevation on a small peninsula that extends well into the lake, with a boat ramp nearby. All water sports are allowed. (For more information, see the *Running Deer* listing in this chapter.)

Campsites, facilities: There are 28 individual sites and two double sites for tents or RVs up to 40 feet (no hookups). Picnic tables and fire

rings are provided. Drinking water and flush toilets are available. A dump station, boat ramp, fish-cleaning station, and grocery store are nearby. Leashed pets are permitted.

Reservations, fees: Reservations are not accepted. Sites are $20 per night, $35 per night for a double site. Open late May through mid-October, weather permitting.

Directions: From Oroville, drive east on Highway 162/Oroville Dam Boulevard for about eight miles (becomes the Olive Highway) to Forbestown Road. Turn right and drive through Forbestown to Challenge and LaPorte Road. Turn left on LaPorte Road and drive to LaPorte. Continue two miles past LaPorte to the junction with County Road 514/Little Grass Valley Road. Turn left and drive one mile to a junction. Turn left and drive one mile to the campground entrance road on the right.

Contact: Plumas National Forest, Feather River Ranger District, 530/534-6500, fax 530/532-1210; Northwest Management, 530/283-5559.

18 LITTLE BEAVER

Scenic rating: 7

on Little Grass Valley Reservoir in Plumas National Forest

This is one of eight campgrounds on Little Grass Valley Reservoir, set at 5,060 feet elevation. Take your pick. (For more information, see the *Running Deer* listing in this chapter.)

Campsites, facilities: There are 120 sites for tents or RVs up to 40 feet (no hookups). Picnic tables and fire rings are provided. Drinking water and flush toilets are available. A grocery store, dump station, fish-cleaning station, and boat ramp are nearby. Some facilities are wheelchair-accessible. Leashed pets are permitted.

Reservations, fees: Reservations are not accepted. Sites are $20–22 per night. Open

June through mid-September, weather permitting.

Directions: From Oroville, drive east on Highway 162/Oroville Dam Boulevard for about eight miles (becomes the Olive Highway) to Forbestown Road. Turn right and drive through Forbestown to Challenge and LaPorte Road. Turn left on LaPorte Road and drive to LaPorte. Continue two miles past LaPorte to the junction with County Road 514/Little Grass Valley Road. Turn left and drive one mile to a junction. Turn right and drive two miles to the campground entrance road on the left.

Contact: Plumas National Forest, Feather River Ranger District, 530/534-6500, fax 530/532-1210; Northwest Management, 530/283-5559.

19 RED FEATHER CAMP

🏃 ♨ 🛶 🎣 🐕 🚐 ⛺

Scenic rating: 7

on Little Grass Valley Reservoir in Plumas National Forest

This camp is well developed and popular, set on the eastern shore of Little Grass Valley Reservoir, just south of Running Deer and just north of Little Beaver. Bears frequent this area, so be sure to properly store your food and avoid scented products. (For more information, see the *Running Deer* listing in this chapter.)

Campsites, facilities: There are 60 sites for tents or RVs up to 40 feet (no hookups). Picnic tables and fire rings are provided. Drinking water and flush toilets are available. A dump station, boat ramp, fish-cleaning station, and grocery store are nearby. Leashed pets are permitted.

Reservations, fees: Reservations are accepted at 877/444-6777 or www.recreation.gov ($10 reservation fee). Sites are $20–22 per night. Open late June through September, weather permitting.

Directions: From Oroville, drive east on Highway 162/Oroville Dam Boulevard for about eight miles (becomes the Olive Highway) to Forbestown Road. Turn right and drive through Forbestown to Challenge and LaPorte Road. Turn left on LaPorte Road and drive to LaPorte. Continue two miles past LaPorte to the junction with County Road 514/Little Grass Valley Road. Turn left and drive one mile to a junction. Turn right and drive three miles to the campground entrance road on the left.

Contact: Plumas National Forest, Feather River Ranger District, 530/534-6500, fax 530/532-1210; Northwest Management, 530/283-5559.

20 PLUMAS-EUREKA STATE PARK

🏃 ♨ 🎣 ♿ 🚐 ⛺

Scenic rating: 9

near Graeagle

Plumas-Eureka State Park is a beautiful chunk of parkland, featuring great hiking, a pretty lake, and this well-maintained campground. For newcomers to the area, Jamison Camp at the southern end of the park makes for an excellent first stop. So does the nearby hike to Grass Lake, a first-class tromp that takes about two hours and features a streamside walk along Little Jamison Creek, with the chance to take a five-minute cutoff to see 40-foot Jamison Falls. A historic mine, park museum, blacksmith shop, stable, and stamp mill are also here, with campers allowed free admission to the museum. Other must-see destinations in the park include Eureka Lake, and from there, the 1,100-foot climb to Eureka Peak (formerly known as Gold Mountain), at 7,447 feet, for a dramatic view of all the famous peaks in this region. Camp elevation is 5,200 feet. The park covers 5,500 acres. Fishing opportunities feature Madora and Eureka Lakes and Jamison Creek, best in May and June. The visitors center was originally constructed as a bunkhouse for miners. More than $8 million of gold was mined here.

Campsites, facilities: Upper Jamison Creek Campground has 67 sites for tents or RVs up to 30 feet (no hookups). At Camp Lisa, there is one group tent site for up to 50 people. Picnic tables, food lockers, and fire rings are provided. Drinking water and restrooms with flush toilets and free showers are available. Some facilities are wheelchair-accessible. A dump station is nearby, and a grocery store, coin laundry, and propane gas are available within five miles. Leashed pets are permitted.

Reservations, fees: Reservations are accepted at 800/444-7275 or www.reserveamerica.com ($7.50 reservation fee). (Note that Reserve America lists both camps under "Plumas-Eureka State Park" and not their camp names.) Sites are $20 per night, $6 per night for each additional vehicle, $200 per night for the group site. Open mid-May through mid-October, weather permitting.

Directions: In Truckee, drive north on Highway 89 to Graeagle. Just after passing Graeagle (one mile from the junction of Highway 70) turn left on County Road A14/Graeagle-Johnsville Road and drive west for about five miles to the park entrance on the left.

Contact: Plumas-Eureka State Park, 530/836-2380, fax 530/836-0498, www.parks.ca.gov.

21 CLIO'S RIVER'S EDGE RV PARK

🏊 🛶 🐕 ♿ 🚐

Scenic rating: 7

on the Feather River

This is a giant RV park set adjacent to a pretty and easily accessible stretch of the Feather River. There are many possible side-trip destinations, including Plumas-Eureka State Park, Lakes Basin Recreation Area, and several nearby golf courses and a horseback-riding facility. The elevation is about 4,500 feet. Many of the sites are rented for the entire summer season.

Campsites, facilities: There are 220 sites with full hookups (50 amps) for RVs of any length. Some sites are pull-through. Picnic tables are provided. Drinking water, restrooms with flush toilets and coin showers, coin laundry, Wi-Fi, modem access, and cable TV are available. Some facilities are wheelchair-accessible. A grocery store is within three miles. Leashed pets are permitted, with certain restrictions.

Reservations, fees: Reservations are accepted. Sites are $30–35 per night, $5 per person per night for more than two people. Weekly and monthly rates are available. Some credit cards accepted. Open mid-April through October.

Directions: From Truckee, drive north on Highway 89 toward Graeagle and Blairsden. Near Clio (4.5 miles south of Highway 70 at Blairsden), look for the campground entrance on the right (0.2 mile south of Graeagle).

Contact: Clio's River's Edge, tel./fax 530/836-2375, www.riversedgervpark.net.

22 LAKES BASIN GROUP CAMP

🏃 🛖 ⛰

Scenic rating: 8

in Plumas National Forest

This is a Forest Service group camp that is ideal for Boy and Girl Scouts. It is set at 6,400 feet elevation, just a short drive from the trailhead to beautiful Frazier Falls, and also near Gold Lake, Little Bear Lake, and 15 lakes set below nearby Mount Elwell.

Campsites, facilities: This group camp is for tents only and can accommodate up to 25 people. Picnic tables and fire grills are provided. Drinking water and vault toilets are available. Supplies are available in Graeagle. Leashed pets are permitted.

Reservations, fees: Reservations are required at 877/444-6777 or www.recreation.gov

($10 reservation fee). The camp is $60 per night. Open June through October, weather permitting.

Directions: From Truckee, drive north on Highway 89 toward Graeagle to the Gold Lake Highway (one mile before reaching Graeagle). Turn left on the Gold Lake Highway and drive about seven miles to the campground.

Contact: Plumas National Forest, Beckwourth Ranger District, 530/836-2575, fax 530/836-0493; Thousand Trails, 530/832-1076.

23 LAKES BASIN

Scenic rating: 8

in Plumas National Forest

This camp is a great location for a base camp to explore the surrounding Lakes Basin Recreation Area. From nearby Gold Lake or Elwell Lodge, there are many short hikes to small pristine lakes. A must-do trip is the easy hike to Frazier Falls, only a mile round-trip to see the spectacular 176-foot waterfall, though the trail is crowded during the middle of the day. The trail to this waterfall is paved and is wheelchair-accessible. The camp elevation is 6,400 feet.

Campsites, facilities: There are 23 sites for tents or RVs up to 30 feet (no hookups). Picnic tables and fire grills are provided. Drinking water and vault toilets are available. Some facilities are wheelchair-accessible. Supplies are available in Graeagle. Leashed pets are permitted.

Reservations, fees: Reservations are accepted at 877/444-6777 or www.recreation.gov ($10 reservation fee). Sites are $16 per night and double sites are $32 per night. Open June through October, weather permitting.

Directions: From Truckee, drive north on Highway 89 toward Graeagle to the Gold Lake Highway (one mile before reaching Graeagle). Turn left on the Gold Lake Highway and drive about seven miles to the campground.

Contact: Plumas National Forest, Beckwourth Ranger District, 530/836-2575, fax 530/836-0493; Thousand Trails, 530/832-1076.

24 PACKSADDLE

Scenic rating: 6

near Packer Lake in Tahoe National Forest

Packsaddle is a Forest Service site about a half mile from Packer Lake, with an additional 15 lakes within a five-mile radius, and one of America's truly great hiking trails nearby. The trail to the Sierra Buttes features a climb of 2,369 feet over the course of five miles. It is highlighted by a stairway with 176 steps that literally juts into open space, and crowned by an astounding view for hundreds of miles in all directions. Packer Lake, at 6,218 feet elevation, is at the foot of the dramatic Sierra Buttes and has lakefront log cabins, good trout fishing, and low-speed boating. The campground elevation is 6,000 feet.

Campsites, facilities: There are 15 sites for tents or RVs up to 35 feet (no hookups). Vault toilets and drinking water are available. Pack and saddle animals are permitted and corrals and hitching rails are available. Supplies are available in Bassetts and Sierra City. Some facilities are wheelchair-accessible. Leashed pets are permitted.

Reservations, fees: Reservations are accepted at 877/444-6777 or www.recreation.gov ($10 reservation fee). Sites are $20 per night, $5 per night for each additional vehicle. Open late May through September, weather permitting.

Directions: From Truckee, turn north on Highway 89 and drive 20 miles to Sierraville. At Sierraville, turn left on Highway 49 and drive about 10 miles to the Bassetts Store. Turn right on Gold Lake Road and drive 1.5 miles to Packer Lake Road. Turn left, drive a short distance, bear right at the fork, and drive 2.5 miles to the campground on the left.

CAMPING

Contact: Tahoe National Forest, Yuba River Ranger District, North, 530/288-3231, fax 530/288-0727; California Land Management, 530/587-9281 or 650/322-1181.

25 BERGER CREEK

Scenic rating: 6

in Tahoe National Forest

Berger Creek provides an overflow alternative to nearby Diablo, which is also extremely primitive. On busy summer weekends, when an open campsite can be difficult to find at a premium location in the Lakes Basin Recreation Area, these two camps provide a safety valve to keep you from being stuck for the night. Nearby are Packer Lake, the trail to the Sierra Buttes, Sardine Lakes, and Sand Pond, all excellent destinations. The elevation is 5,900 feet.

Campsites, facilities: There are 10 sites for tents or RVs up to 16 feet (no hookups). Picnic tables and fire grills are provided. Vault toilets are available. No drinking water is available. Garbage must be packed out. Supplies are available in Bassetts and Sierra City. Leashed pets are permitted.

Reservations, fees: Reservations are not accepted. Sites are $16 per night, $5 per night for each additional vehicle. Open June through October, weather permitting.

Directions: From Truckee, turn north on Highway 89 and drive 20 miles to Sierraville. At Sierraville, turn left on Highway 49 and drive about 10 miles to the Bassetts Store. Turn right on Gold Lake Road and drive 1.5 miles to Packer Lake Road. Turn left, drive a short distance, bear right at the fork, and drive two miles to the campground on the left.

Contact: Tahoe National Forest, Yuba River Ranger District, North, 530/288-3231, fax 530/288-0727; California Land Management, 530/587-9281 or 650/322-1181.

26 SNAG LAKE

Scenic rating: 8

in Tahoe National Forest

Snag Lake is an ideal little lake for camping anglers with canoes. There are no boat ramps and you can have the place virtually to yourself. It is set at 6,000 feet in elevation, an easy-to-reach lake in the Lakes Basin Recreation Area. Trout fishing is only fair, as in fair numbers and fair size, mainly rainbow trout in the 10- to 12-inch class. Note that campers here must provide their own drinking water.

Campsites, facilities: There are 12 sites for tents or RVs up to 16 feet (no hookups). Picnic tables and fire grills are provided. Vault toilets are available. No drinking water is available. Garbage must be packed out. Only hand boat launching is allowed. Supplies are available in Bassetts and Sierra City. Leashed pets are permitted.

Reservations, fees: Reservations are not accepted. There is no fee for camping. Open June through October, weather permitting.

Directions: From Truckee, turn north on Highway 89 and drive 20 miles to Sierraville. At Sierraville, turn left on Highway 49 and drive about 10 miles to the Bassetts Store. Turn right on Gold Lake Road and drive five miles to the campground on the left.

Contact: Tahoe National Forest, Yuba River Ranger District, North, 530/288-3231, fax 530/288-0727; California Land Management, 530/587-9281 or 650/322-1181.

27 DIABLO

Scenic rating: 8

on Packer Creek in Tahoe National Forest

This is a developed camping area set on Packer Creek, about two miles from Packer Lake. This area is extremely beautiful with several lakes nearby, including the Sardine Lakes and Packer Lake, and this camp provides an overflow area when the more developed campgrounds have filled.

Campsites, facilities: There are eight sites for tents or RVs up to 30 feet (no hookups). Picnic tables and fire rings are provided. Vault toilets are available. No drinking water is available. Supplies are available in Bassetts and Sierra City. Leashed pets are permitted.

Reservations, fees: Reservations are accepted at 877/444-6777 or www.recreation.gov ($10 reservation fee). Sites are $16 per night, $5 per night for each additional vehicle. Open June through October, weather permitting.

Directions: From Truckee, turn north on Highway 89 and drive 20 miles to Sierraville. At Sierraville, turn left on Highway 49 and drive about 10 miles to the Bassetts Store. Turn right on Gold Lake Road and drive 1.5 miles to Packer Lake Road. Turn left, drive a short distance, bear right at the fork, and drive one mile to the campground on the right side of the road.

Contact: Tahoe National Forest, Yuba River Ranger District, North, 530/288-3231, fax 530/288-0727; California Land Management, 530/587-9281 or 650/322-1181.

28 SALMON CREEK

Scenic rating: 9

in Tahoe National Forest

This campground is set at the confluence of Packer and Salmon Creeks, at 5,800 feet elevation, with easy access off the Gold Lakes Highway. It is near the Lakes Basin Recreation Area, with literally dozens of small lakes within five miles, plus great hiking, fishing, and low-speed boating.

Campsites, facilities: There are 31 sites for tents or RVs up to 30 feet (no hookups). Picnic tables and fire grills are provided. Drinking water and vault toilets are available. Supplies

and a coin laundry are available in Sierra City. Leashed pets are permitted.

Reservations, fees: Reservations are accepted at 877/444-6777 or www.recreation.gov ($10 reservation fee). Sites are $20 per night, $5 per night for each additional vehicle. Open June through October.

Directions: From Truckee, turn north on Highway 89 and drive 20 miles to Sierraville and Highway 49. Turn left on Highway 49 and drive about 10 miles to the Bassetts Store and Gold Lake Road. Turn right on Gold Lake Road and drive two miles to the campground on the left side of the road.

Contact: Tahoe National Forest, Yuba River Ranger District, North, 530/288-3231, fax 530/288-0727; California Land Management, 530/587-9281 or 650/322-1181.

29 SARDINE LAKE

Scenic rating: 8

in Tahoe National Forest

BEST (

Lower Sardine Lake is a jewel set below the Sierra Buttes, one of the prettiest settings in California. The campground is actually about a mile east of the lake. Nearby is beautiful Sand Pond Interpretive Trail. A great hike is routed along the shore of Lower Sardine Lake to a hidden waterfall (in spring) that feeds the lake, and ambitious hikers can explore beyond and discover Upper Sardine Lake. Trout fishing is excellent in Lower Sardine Lake, with a primitive boat ramp available for small boats. The speed limit and small size of the lake keeps boaters slow and quiet. A small marina and boat rentals are available.

Campsites, facilities: There are 29 sites for tents or RVs up to 22 feet (no hookups). Picnic tables and fire grills are provided. Drinking water and vault toilets are available. Some facilities are wheelchair-accessible. Limited supplies are available at the Sardine

Lake Lodge or in Bassetts. Leashed pets are permitted.

Reservations, fees: Reservations are accepted at 877/444-6777 or www.recreation.gov ($10 reservation fee). Sites are $20 per night, $5 per night for each additional vehicle, $40 per night for double sites. Open June through October, weather permitting.

Directions: From Truckee, drive north on Highway 89 for 20 miles to Sierraville. Turn left on Highway 49 and drive about 10 miles to the Bassetts Store. Turn right on Gold Lake Road and drive 1.5 miles to Packer Lake Road. Turn left, drive a short distance, then bear left at the fork (signed) and drive 0.5 mile to the campground on the left.

Contact: Tahoe National Forest, Yuba River Ranger District, North, 530/288-3231, fax 530/288-0727.

30 CHAPMAN CREEK
🚶 🏊 ✒️ 🐕 🚐 ⛺

Scenic rating: 8

on the North Yuba River in Tahoe National Forest

This campground is set along Chapman Creek at 6,000 feet, just across the highway from where it enters the North Yuba River. A good side trip is to hike Chapman Creek Trail, which leads out of camp to Beartrap Meadow or to Haskell Peak (8,107 feet).

Campsites, facilities: There are 29 sites for tents or RVs up to 22 feet (no hookups). Picnic tables and fire grills are provided. Drinking water and vault toilets are available. Supplies are available in Bassetts. Leashed pets are permitted.

Reservations, fees: Reservations are not accepted. Sites are $20 per night, $5 per night for each additional vehicle. Open June through October, weather permitting.

Directions: From Truckee, turn north on Highway 89 and drive 20 miles to Sierraville. At Sierraville, turn left on Highway 49, drive

over Yuba Pass, and continue for four miles to the campground on the right.

Contact: Tahoe National Forest, Yuba River Ranger District, North, 530/288-3231, fax 530/288-0727; California Land Management, 530/587-9281 or 650/322-1181.

31 SIERRA
🚶 🏊 ✒️ 🐕 🚐 ⛺

Scenic rating: 7

on the North Yuba River in Tahoe National Forest

This is an easy-to-reach spot set along the North Yuba River, used primarily as an overflow area from nearby Chapman Creek (a mile upstream). Nearby recreation options include Chapman Creek Trail, several waterfalls (see the *Wild Plum* listing in this chapter), and the nearby Lakes Basin Recreation Area to the north off the Gold Lake Highway. The elevation is 5,600 feet. Note: Bring your own drinking water.

Campsites, facilities: There are 16 sites for tents or RVs up to 22 feet (no hookups). Picnic tables and fire rings are provided. Vault toilets are available. No drinking water is available. Supplies are available in Bassetts. Leashed pets are permitted.

Reservations, fees: Reservations are accepted at 877/444-6777 or www.recreation.gov ($10 reservation fee). Sites are $16 per night, $5 per night for each additional vehicle. Open June through October, weather permitting.

Directions: From Truckee, turn north on Highway 89 and drive 20 miles to Sierraville. At Sierraville, turn left on Highway 49 and drive over Yuba Pass. Continue for five miles to the campground on the left side of the road.

Contact: Tahoe National Forest, Yuba River Ranger District, North, 530/288-3231, fax 530/288-0727; California Land Management, 530/587-9281 or 650/322-1181.

CAMPING

32 YUBA PASS

Scenic rating: 6

in Tahoe National Forest

This camp is set right at Yuba Pass at an elevation of 6,700 feet. In the winter, the surrounding area is a Sno-Park, which gives it an unusual look in summer. Yuba Pass is a popular bird-watching area in the summer.

Campsites, facilities: There are 20 sites for tents or RVs up to 22 feet (no hookups). Picnic tables and fire grills are provided. Vault toilets are available. There is no drinking water. Supplies are available at Bassetts. Leashed pets are permitted.

Reservations, fees: Reservations are accepted at 877/444-6777 or www.recreation.gov ($10 reservation fee). Sites are $20 per night, $5 per night for each additional vehicle. Open late June through October, weather permitting.

Directions: From Truckee, drive north on Highway 89 past Sattley to the junction with Highway 49. Turn west on Highway 49 and drive about six miles to the campground on the left side of the road.

Contact: Tahoe National Forest, Yuba River Ranger District, North, 530/288-3231, fax 530/288-0727; California Land Management, 530/587-9281 or 650/322-1181.

33 CARLTON/CAL-IDA

Scenic rating: 7

on the North Yuba River in Tahoe National Forest

Carlton is on the North Yuba River, and Cal-Ida is across the road. Both are right next door to Fiddle Creek. (For more information, see the *Fiddle Creek* listing in this chapter.)

Campsites, facilities: There are 30 sites at Carlton and 20 sites at Cal-Ida for tents or RVs up to 28 feet (no hookups). Picnic tables and fire grills are provided. Drinking water and vault toilets are available. Some facilities are wheelchair-accessible. Some supplies are available at the Indian Valley Outpost nearby. Leashed pets are permitted.

Reservations, fees: Reservations are accepted at 877/444-6777 or www.recreation. gov ($10 reservation fee). Sites are $20 per night, $5 per night for each additional vehicle. Open mid-April through November, weather permitting.

Directions: From Auburn, take Highway 49 north to Nevada City and continue on Highway 49 (the road jogs left, then narrows) to Camptonville. Continue northeast for nine miles to the campground entrance. The camping area at Carlton is one mile northeast of the Highway 49 bridge at Indian Valley. The camping area at Cal-Ida is just east of the Indian Valley Outpost on the Cal-Ida Road.

Contact: Tahoe National Forest, Yuba River Ranger District, North, 530/288-3231, fax 530/288-0727; California Land Management, 530/587-9281 or 650/322-1181.

34 FIDDLE CREEK

Scenic rating: 7

on the North Yuba River in Tahoe National Forest

This camp is situated on the North Yuba River along Highway 49 in a quiet, forested area. This is a beautiful river, one of the prettiest to flow westward out of the Sierra Nevada, with deep pools and miniature waterfalls. It is popular for rafting out of Goodyears Bar, and if you can stand the cold water, there are many good swimming holes along Highway 49. It's set at 2,200 feet elevation. There are a series of campgrounds on this stretch of the Yuba River. Fiddle Creek Ridge Trail starts across the highway on Cal-Ida Road and is routed out to Indian Rock.

Campsites, facilities: There are 13 tent sites.

Picnic tables and fire rings are provided. Drinking water and vault toilets are available. Limited supplies are nearby at the Indian Valley Outpost. Some facilities are wheelchair-accessible, including a paved trail to the Yuba River. Leashed pets are permitted.

Reservations, fees: Reservations are accepted at 877/444-6777 or www.recreation.gov ($10 reservation fee). The fee is $20 per night, $5 per night for each additional vehicle. Open April to November, weather permitting.

Directions: From Auburn, take Highway 49 north to Nevada City and continue on Highway 49 (the road jogs left, then narrows) to Camptonville. Continue northeast for 9.5 miles to the campground entrance on the right.

Contact: Tahoe National Forest, Yuba River Ranger District, North, 530/288-3231, fax 530/288-0727; California Land Management, 530/587-9281 or 650/322-1181.

35 INDIAN VALLEY

Scenic rating: 7

on the North Yuba River in Tahoe National Forest

This is an easy-to-reach spot set at 2,200 feet beside the North Yuba River. Highway 49 runs adjacent to the Yuba River for miles eastward, providing easy access to the river in many areas. There are several other campgrounds in the immediate area (see the listings in this chapter for *Fiddle Creek* and *Cal-Ida,* both within a mile).

Campsites, facilities: There are 17 sites for tents or RVs up to 22 feet (no hookups). Picnic tables and fire grills are provided. Drinking water and vault toilets are available. Limited supplies are available nearby at the Indian Valley Outpost. Some facilities are wheelchair-accessible. Leashed pets are permitted.

Reservations, fees: Reservations are accepted at 877/444-6777 or www.recreation.gov ($10 reservation fee). Sites are $20 per night, $5

per night for each additional vehicle. Open year-round.

Directions: From Auburn, take Highway 49 north to Nevada City and continue on Highway 49 (the road jogs left, then narrows) to Camptonville. Drive 10 miles to the camp entrance on the right.

Contact: Tahoe National Forest, Yuba River Ranger District, North, 530/288-3231, fax 530/288-0727; California Land Management, 530/587-9281 or 650/322-1181.

36 ROCKY REST

Scenic rating: 7

on the North Yuba River in Tahoe National Forest

This is one in a series of campgrounds set at streamside on the North Yuba River. The elevation is 2,200 feet. A footbridge crosses the North Yuba River and provides an outstanding seven-mile hike.

Campsites, facilities: There are 10 dispersed camping sites for tents and RVs up to 16 feet (no hookups). Picnic tables and fire grills are provided. Drinking water and vault toilets are available. Limited supplies are nearby at the Indian Valley Outpost. Some facilities are wheelchair-accessible. Leashed pets are permitted.

Reservations, fees: Reservations are accepted at 877/444-6777 or www.recreation.gov ($10 reservation fee). Sites are $20 per night, $5 per night for each additional vehicle. Open mid-April through November, weather permitting.

Directions: From Auburn, take Highway 49 north to Nevada City and continue (the road jogs left, then narrows) to Camptonville. Continue on Highway 49 for 10 miles to the campground entrance on the right.

Contact: Tahoe National Forest, Yuba River Ranger District, North, 530/288-3231, fax 530/288-0727; California Land Management, 530/587-9281 or 650/322-1181.

CAMPING

37 RAMSHORN

Scenic rating: 7

on the North Yuba River in Tahoe National Forest

This camp is set on Ramshorn Creek, just across the road from the North Yuba River. It's one in a series of camps on this stretch of the beautiful North Yuba River. One mile east is a well-known access point for white-water rafting trips on the Yuba. The camp's elevation is 2,200 feet.

Campsites, facilities: There are 16 sites for tents or RVs up to 22 feet (no hookups). Picnic tables and fire grills are provided. Vault toilets and drinking water are available. Supplies are available in Downieville. Leashed pets are permitted.

Reservations, fees: Reservations are accepted at 877/444-6777 or www.recreation.gov ($10 reservation fee). Sites are $20 per night, $5 per night for each additional vehicle per night. Open year-round.

Directions: From Auburn, take Highway 49 north to Nevada City and continue on Highway 49 (the road jogs left, then narrows) to Camptonville. Drive 15 miles north to the campground entrance on the left.

Contact: Tahoe National Forest, Yuba River Ranger District, North, 530/288-3231, fax 530/288-0727; California Land Management, 530/587-9281 or 650/322-1181.

38 UNION FLAT

Scenic rating: 8

on the North Yuba River in Tahoe National Forest

Of all the campgrounds on the North Yuba River along Highway 49, this one has the best swimming. The camp has a nice swimming hole next to it, and the water is cold. Recre-

ational mining is also an attraction here. The elevation is 3,400 feet.

Campsites, facilities: There are 11 sites for tents or RVs up to 35 feet (no hookups). Picnic tables and fire grills are provided. Drinking water and vault toilets are available. Some facilities are wheelchair-accessible. Supplies are available in Downieville. Leashed pets are permitted.

Reservations, fees: Reservations are accepted at 877/444-6777 or www.recreation.gov ($10 reservation fee). Sites are $20 per night, $5 per night for each additional vehicle, $40 for double sites. Open May through October, weather permitting.

Directions: From Auburn, take Highway 49 north to Nevada City and continue (the road jogs left, then narrows) to Downieville. Drive six miles east to the campground entrance on the right.

Contact: Tahoe National Forest, Yuba River Ranger District, North, 530/288-3231, fax 530/288-0727; California Land Management, 530/587-9281 or 650/322-1181.

39 LOGANVILLE

Scenic rating: 8

on the North Yuba River in Tahoe National Forest

Sierra City is only two miles away, meaning you can make a quick getaway for a prepared meal or any food or drink you may need to add to your camp. Loganville is set on the North Yuba River, elevation 4,200 feet. It offers a good stretch of water in this region for trout fishing, with many pools set below miniature waterfalls.

Campsites, facilities: There are 20 sites for tents or RVs up to 22 feet (no hookups). Picnic tables and fire grills are provided. Drinking water and vault toilets are available. Supplies and a coin laundry are available in Sierra City. Leashed pets are permitted.

Reservations, fees: Reservations are accepted at 877/444-6777 or www.recreation.gov ($10 reservation fee). Sites are $20 per night, $5 per night for each additional vehicle. Open May through October, weather permitting.

Directions: From Auburn, take Highway 49 north to Nevada City and continue on Highway 49 (the road jogs left, then narrows) to Downieville. Drive 12 miles east to the campground entrance on the right (two miles west of Sierra City).

Contact: Tahoe National Forest, Yuba River Ranger District, North, 530/288-3231, fax 530/288-0727; California Land Management, 530/587-9281 or 650/322-1181.

40 WILD PLUM

Scenic rating: 8

on Haypress Creek in Tahoe National Forest

This popular Forest Service campground is set on Haypress Creek at 4,400 feet. There are several hidden waterfalls in the area, which makes this a popular camp for the people who know of them. There's a scenic hike up Haypress Trail, which goes past a waterfall to Haypress Valley. Two other nearby waterfalls are Loves Falls (on the North Yuba on Highway 49 two miles east of Sierra City) and Hackmans Falls (remote, set in a ravine one mile south of Sierra City; no road access).

Campsites, facilities: There are 44 sites for tents or RVs up to 22 feet (no hookups). Picnic tables, food lockers, and fire grills are provided. Drinking water and vault toilets are available. Supplies and a coin laundry are available in Sierra City. Leashed pets are permitted.

Reservations, fees: Reservations are accepted at 877/444-6777 or www.recreation.gov ($10 reservation fee). Sites are $20 per night, $5 per night for each additional vehicle. Open May through October, weather permitting.

Directions: From Auburn, take Highway 49 north to Nevada City and continue (the road jogs left, then narrows) past Downieville to Sierra City at Wild Plum Road. Turn right on Wild Plum Road and drive two miles to the campground entrance road on the right.

Contact: Tahoe National Forest, Yuba River Ranger District, North, 530/288-3231, fax 530/288-0727; California Land Management, 530/587-9281 or 650/322-1181.

41 COLD CREEK

Scenic rating: 8

in Tahoe National Forest

There are four small campgrounds along Highway 89 between Sierraville and Truckee, all within close range of side trips to Webber Lake, Independence Lake, and Sierra Hot Springs in Sierraville. Cold Creek is set just upstream of the confluence of Cottonwood Creek and Cold Creek, at 5,800 feet elevation.

Campsites, facilities: There are 13 sites for tents or RVs up to 22 feet (no hookups). Picnic tables and fire rings are provided. Vault toilets are available. There is no drinking water. Supplies are available in Sierraville. Leashed pets are permitted.

Reservations, fees: Reservations are accepted at 877/444-6777 or www.recreation.gov ($10 reservation fee). Sites are $12 per night, $5 per night for each additional vehicle. Open May through October.

Directions: From Truckee, drive north on Highway 89 for about 20 miles to the campground on the left side of the road. If you reach Sierraville, you have gone five miles too far.

Contact: Tahoe National Forest, Sierraville Ranger District, 530/994-3401, fax 530/994-3143; California Land Management, 530/587-9281 or 650/322-1181.

42 COTTONWOOD CREEK

Scenic rating: 7

in Tahoe National Forest

This camp sits beside Cottonwood Creek at 5,800 feet elevation. An interpretive trail starts at the upper camp and makes a short loop, and there are several nearby side-trip options, including trout fishing on the Little Truckee River to the nearby south, visiting the Sierra Hot Springs out of Sierraville to the nearby north, or venturing into the surrounding Tahoe National Forest.

Campsites, facilities: There are 46 sites for tents or RVs up to 22 feet (no hookups). Picnic tables and fire rings are provided. Drinking water and vault toilets are available. Supplies are available in Sierraville. Some facilities are wheelchair-accessible. Leashed pets are permitted.

Reservations, fees: Reservations are accepted at 877/444-6777 or www.recreation.gov ($10 reservation fee). Sites are $16 per night, $5 per night for each additional vehicle. Open mid-May through early October, weather permitting.

Directions: From Truckee, drive north on Highway 89 for about 20 miles to the campground entrance road on the right (0.5 mile past Cold Creek Camp).

Contact: Tahoe National Forest, Sierraville Ranger District, 530/994-3401, fax 530/994-3143; California Land Management, 530/587-9281 or 650/322-1181.

43 BEAR VALLEY

Scenic rating: 7

on Bear Valley Creek in Tahoe National Forest

The surrounding national forest land was largely burned by the historic Cottonwood Fire of 1994, but the camp itself was saved.

It is at 6,700 feet elevation, with a spring adjacent to the campground. The road leading southeast out of camp is routed to Sardine Peak Look-Out (8,134 feet), where there is a dramatic view of the region. There is an 18-mile loop OHV trail across the road from the campground.

Campsites, facilities: There are 10 sites for tents or RVs up to 16 feet (no hookups). Picnic tables and fire rings are provided. Vault toilets are available. There is no drinking water. Garbage must be packed out. Supplies are available in Sierraville. Leashed pets are permitted.

Reservations, fees: Reservations are not accepted. There is no fee for camping. Open May through October, weather permitting.

Directions: From Truckee, drive north on Highway 89 about 17 miles. Turn right on County Road 451 and drive northeast about six miles to the campground entrance on the right.

Contact: Tahoe National Forest, Sierraville Ranger District, 530/994-3401, fax 530/994-3143.

44 LOOKOUT

Scenic rating: 4

in Humboldt-Toiyabe National Forest

This primitive camp is set in remote country near the California/Nevada border at 6,700 feet elevation. It is a former mining site, and the highlight here is a quartz crystal mine a short distance from the campground. Stampede Lake provides a side-trip option, about 10 miles to the southwest, over the rough dirt Henness Pass Road.

Campsites, facilities: There are 18 sites for tents or RVs up to 35 feet (no hookups), and a group site for up to 16 people. Picnic tables and fire grills are provided. Vault toilets are available. There is no drinking water. Garbage must be packed out. Leashed pets are permitted.

Reservations, fees: Reservations are accepted for individual sites and are required for the group site at 775/882-2766. Sites are $6 per night and the group site is $25 per night. Open June through September.

Directions: From Truckee on I-80, drive east across the state line into Nevada to Verdi. Take the Verdi exit and drive north through town to Bridge Street and then to Old Dog Valley Road. Drive north on Old Dog Valley Road for 11 miles to the campground.

Contact: Humboldt-Toiyabe National Forest, Carson Ranger District, 775/882-2766, fax 775/884-8199.

45 LITTLE LASIER MEADOWS EQUESTRIAN

Scenic rating: 7

near Jackson Meadows Reservoir

This is the best camp in the area for those with horses. Little Lasier Meadows has open sites in the forest, adjacent to a meadow, and has a horse corral. Best of all, there is direct access to the Pacific Crest Trail. Nearby Jackson Meadows Reservoir is very pretty and provides boating, fishing, and swimming.

Campsites, facilities: There are 11 sites for tents or RVs. Drinking water and vault toilets are available. Picnic tables, fire rings, horse corrals, and tie rails are provided. Water for horses is available.

Reservations, fees: Reservations are required ($10 reservation fee) at 877/444-6777 or recreation.gov. Sites are $20, $5 each additional vehicle per night. Open year-round, weather permitting.

Directions: From Truckee, drive north 17.5 miles on Highway 89 to Forest Road 7/Fiberboard Road. Turn left and drive 15 miles to the East Meadows turnoff. Cross the metal bridge and take the first left turn. Drive approximately two miles to the campground.

Contact: Tahoe National Forest, Truckee Ranger District, 530/587-3558, fax 530/587-6914; California Land Management, 530/587-9281.

46 SILVER TIP GROUP CAMP

Scenic rating: 7

at Jackson Meadow Reservoir in Tahoe National Forest

This group camp is set on the southwest edge of Jackson Meadow Reservoir at 6,100 feet elevation, in a pretty area with pine forest, high meadows, and the trademark granite look of the Sierra Nevada. A boat ramp and swimming beach are nearby at Woodcamp. (For more information, see the *Woodcamp* listing in this chapter.)

Campsites, facilities: There are two group sites for tents or RVs up to 22 feet (no hookups) that can accommodate up to 25 people each. Picnic tables and fire rings are provided. Drinking water and vault toilets are available. Obtain supplies in Truckee or Sierraville. A boat ramp is nearby. Leashed pets are permitted.

Reservations, fees: Reservations are required at 877/444-6777 or www.recreation.gov ($10 reservation fee). The camps are $72 per night. Open June through October, weather permitting.

Directions: From Truckee, drive north on Highway 89 for 17 miles to Forest Road 7. Turn left on Forest Road 7 and drive 16 miles to Jackson Meadow Reservoir. At the lake, continue across the dam around the west shoreline and then turn left at the campground access road. The entrance is on the right just after the Woodcamp campground.

Contact: Tahoe National Forest, Sierraville Ranger District, 530/994-3401, fax 530/994-3143; California Land Management, 530/587-9281 or 650/322-1181.

47 WOODCAMP

Scenic rating: 7

at Jackson Meadow Reservoir in Tahoe
National Forest

Woodcamp and Pass Creek are the best camps for boaters at Jackson Meadow Reservoir because each is directly adjacent to a boat ramp. That is critical because fishing is far better by boat here than from shore, with a good mix of both rainbow and brown trout. The camp is set at 6,700 feet elevation along the lake's southwest shore, in a pretty spot with a swimming beach and short interpretive hiking trail nearby. All water sports are allowed. This is a beautiful lake in the Sierra Nevada, complete with pine forest and a classic granite backdrop.

Campsites, facilities: There are 20 sites for tents or RVs up to 22 feet (no hookups). Picnic tables and fire rings are provided. Drinking water, flush and vault toilets, food lockers, and firewood (fee) are available. Supplies are available in Truckee or Sierraville. A boat ramp is adjacent to the camp and a dump station is nearby. Leashed pets are permitted.

Reservations, fees: Reservations are accepted at 877/444-6777 or www.recreation.gov ($10 reservation fee). Sites are $20 per night, $5 per night for each additional vehicle. Open June through October, weather permitting.

Directions: From Truckee, drive north on Highway 89 for 17 miles to Forest Road 7. Turn left on Forest Road 7 and drive 16 miles to Jackson Meadow Reservoir. At the lake, continue across the dam around the west shoreline and then turn left at the campground access road. The entrance is on the right just before the Woodcamp boat ramp.

Contact: Tahoe National Forest, Sierraville Ranger District, 530/994-3401, fax 530/994-3143; California Land Management, 530/587-9281 or 650/322-1181.

48 FIR TOP

Scenic rating: 7

at Jackson Meadow Reservoir in Tahoe
National Forest

Jackson Meadow is a great destination for a short vacation, and that's why there are so many campgrounds available; it's not exactly a secret. This camp is set above the lake, less than a mile from a boat ramp near Woodcamp. (See the *Woodcamp* and *Pass Creek* listings in this chapter for more information.) The elevation is 6,200 feet.

Campsites, facilities: There are 14 sites for tents or RVs up to 22 feet (no hookups). Picnic tables and fire rings are provided. Drinking water, flush and vault toilets, and food lockers are available. Supplies are available in Truckee or Sierraville. Leashed pets are permitted.

Reservations, fees: Reservations are accepted at 877/444-6777 or www.recreation.gov ($10 reservation fee). Sites are $20 per night, $5 per night for each additional vehicle. Open June through November, weather permitting.

Directions: From Truckee, drive north on Highway 89 for 17.5 miles to Forest Road 7. Turn left on Forest Road 7 and drive 16 miles to Jackson Meadow Reservoir. Continue across the dam and around the lake to the west side. Turn left at the campground access road. The campground entrance is on the right across from the entrance to the Woodcamp Picnic Area.

Contact: Tahoe National Forest, Sierraville Ranger District, 530/994-3401, fax 530/994-3143; California Land Management, 530/587-9281 or 650/322-1181.

49 FINDLEY

🏃 🏊 🚣 🚤 🎣 ♿ 🚐 ⛺

Scenic rating: 7

at Jackson Meadow Reservoir in Tahoe
National Forest

Findley is set near Woodcamp Creek, 0.25
mile from where it pours into Jackson Meadow
Reservoir. Though it is not a lakeside camp,
it is quite pretty just the same, and within a
mile of the boat ramp near Woodcamp. It is set
at 6,300 feet elevation. This is one of several
camps at the lake.

Campsites, facilities: There are 14 sites for
tents or RVs up to 22 feet (no hookups). Picnic
tables and fire rings are provided. Drinking
water, flush and vault toilets, and food lockers
are available. Supplies are available in Truckee
or Sierraville. A boat ramp is nearby. Some
facilities are wheelchair-accessible. Leashed
pets are permitted.

Reservations, fees: Reservations are accepted
at 877/444-6777 or www.recreation.gov ($10
reservation fee). Sites are $20 per night, $5
per night for each additional vehicle, $40 for
double sites. Open May through October.

Directions: From Truckee, drive north on
Highway 89 for 17 miles to Forest Road 7.
Turn left on Forest Road 7 and drive 16 miles
to Jackson Meadow Reservoir. Continue across
the dam around the lake to the west side. Turn
left at the campground access road and drive
about 0.25 mile to the entrance on the left.

Contact: Tahoe National Forest, Sierraville Ranger District, 530/994-3401, fax
530/994-3143; California Land Management,
530/587-9281 or 650/322-1181.

50 JACKSON POINT BOAT-IN

🏊 🚣 🚤 🎣 5% ⛺

Scenic rating: 10

at Jackson Meadow Reservoir in Tahoe
National Forest

BEST (

This is one of the few boat-in camps available
anywhere in the high Sierra. The gorgeous
spot is situated on the end of a peninsula
that extends from the east shore of Jackson
Meadow Reservoir. Small and primitive, it's
the one place at the lake where you can gain
entry into the 5 Percent Club. From the point,
there is a spectacular view of the Sierra Buttes.
Because the lake levels are kept near full all
summer, this boat-in camp is doubly appeal-
ing. The elevation is 6,200 feet.

Campsites, facilities: There are 10 tent sites.
Picnic tables and fire rings are provided. Vault
toilets are available. No drinking water is available. Garbage must be packed out. Supplies
are available in Truckee or Sierraville. Leashed
pets are permitted.

Reservations, fees: Reservations are not accepted. There is no fee for camping. Open June
through September, weather permitting.

Directions: From Truckee, drive north on
Highway 89 for 17 miles to Forest Road 7.
Turn left on Forest Road 7 and drive 16 miles
to Jackson Meadow Reservoir. Drive to Pass
Creek and boat launch (on the left at the north
end of the lake). Launch your boat and cruise
0.5 mile south to Jackson Point and the boat-
in campsites.

Contact: Tahoe National Forest, Sierraville Ranger District, 530/994-3401, fax
530/994-3143; California Land Management,
530/587-9281 or 650/322-1181.

51 PASS CREEK
🚶 🏊 🛶 🚤 🐕 🚌 ⛺

Scenic rating: 7

at Jackson Meadow Reservoir in Tahoe
National Forest

This is the premium campground at Jackson
Meadow Reservoir, a developed site with water,
concrete boat ramp, swimming beach nearby
at Aspen Creek Picnic Area, and access to the
Pacific Crest Trail 0.5 mile to the east (you'll
pass it on the way in). This lake has the trademark look of the high Sierra, and the bonus
here is that lake levels are often kept higher
than at other reservoirs on the western slopes
of the Sierra Nevada. Trout stocks are excellent, with rainbow and brown trout planted
each summer after ice-out. The elevation is
6,100 feet.

Campsites, facilities: There are 30 sites for
tents or RVs up to 22 feet (no hookups). Picnic
tables and fire rings are provided. Drinking
water, flush and vault toilets, and food lockers are available. A dump station is nearby.
A boat ramp is nearby. Supplies are available
in Truckee or Sierraville. Leashed pets are
permitted.

Reservations, fees: Reservations are accepted
at 877/444-6777 or www.recreation.gov ($10
reservation fee). Sites are $20 per night, $5 per
night for each additional vehicle. Open May
through October, weather permitting.

Directions: From Truckee, drive north on
Highway 89 for 17 miles to Forest Road
7. Turn left on Forest Road 7 and drive 16
miles to Jackson Meadow Reservoir; the
campground is on the left at the north end
of the lake.

Contact: Tahoe National Forest, Sierraville Ranger District, 530/994-3401, fax
530/994-3143; California Land Management,
530/587-9281 or 650/322-1181.

52 EAST MEADOW
🚶 🏊 🛶 🚤 🐕 ♿ 🚌 ⛺

Scenic rating: 7

at Jackson Meadow Reservoir in Tahoe
National Forest

This camp is in a beautiful setting on the
northeast side of Jackson Meadow Reservoir,
on the edge of a sheltered cove. The Pacific
Crest Trail passes right by camp, providing
access for a day trip, though no stellar destinations are on this stretch of the PCT. The
nearest boat ramp is at Pass Creek, two miles
away. The elevation is 6,200 feet.

Campsites, facilities: There are 46 sites for
tents or RVs up to 40 feet (no hookups). Picnic
tables and fire rings are provided. Drinking
water, flush and vault toilets, food lockers, and
firewood (fee) are available. A dump station
and boat ramp are near Pass Creek. Supplies
are available in Truckee or Sierraville. Some
facilities are wheelchair-accessible. Leashed
pets are permitted.

Reservations, fees: Reservations are accepted
at 877/444-6777 or www.recreation.gov ($10
reservation fee). The fee is $20 per night, $5
per night for each additional vehicle, $40 per
night for double sites. Open May through
October, weather permitting.

Directions: From Truckee, drive north on
Highway 89 for 17 miles to Forest Road 7.
Turn left on Forest Road 7 and drive 15 miles
to the campground entrance road on the left (if
you reach Pass Creek, you have gone too far).
Turn left and drive a mile to the campground
on the right.

Contact: Tahoe National Forest, Sierraville Ranger District, 530/994-3401, fax
530/994-3143; California Land Management,
530/587-9281 or 650/322-1181.

53 ASPEN GROUP CAMP

Scenic rating: 7

at Jackson Meadow Reservoir in Tahoe National Forest

A boat ramp and easy access to adjacent Jackson Meadow Reservoir make this a premium group camp. The elevation is 6,100 feet.

Campsites, facilities: There are three group sites for tents or RVs up to 40 feet (no hookups) that can accommodate 25–50 people each. Picnic tables and fire grills are provided. Drinking water, vault toilets, food lockers, firewood (fee), and a campfire circle are available. A dump station is nearby. There is a boat ramp nearby at Pass Creek. Supplies are available in Truckee or Sierraville. Leashed pets are permitted.

Reservations, fees: Reservations are required at 877/444-6777 or www.recreation.gov ($10 reservation fee). Sites are $62–122 per night. Open mid-May through October, weather permitting.

Directions: From Truckee, drive north on Highway 89 for 17.5 miles to Forest Road 7. Turn left on Forest Road 7 and drive 16 miles (a mile past Pass Creek) to the campground entrance on the right.

Contact: Tahoe National Forest, Sierraville Ranger District, 530/994-3401, fax 530/994-3143; California Land Management, 530/587-9281 or 650/322-1181.

54 UPPER LITTLE TRUCKEE

Scenic rating: 7

on the Little Truckee River in Tahoe National Forest

This camp is set along the Little Truckee River at 6,100 feet. The Little Truckee is a pretty trout stream, with easy access not only from this campground, but also from another three miles northward along Highway 89, then from another seven miles to the west along Forest Road 7, the route to Webber Lake. It is only about a 10-minute drive from this camp to reach Stampede Lake to the east.

Campsites, facilities: There are 26 sites for tents or RVs up to 30 feet (no hookups). Picnic tables and fire rings are provided. Drinking water and vault toilets are available. Supplies are available in Sierraville. Leashed pets are permitted.

Reservations, fees: Reservations are accepted at 877/444-6777 or www.recreation.gov ($10 reservation fee). Sites are $16 per night, $5 per night for each additional vehicle. Open mid-May through October, weather permitting.

Directions: From Truckee, drive north on Highway 89 for about 11 miles to the campground on the left, a short distance beyond Lower Little Truckee Camp.

Contact: Tahoe National Forest, Sierraville Ranger District, 530/994-3401, fax 530/994-3143; California Land Management, 530/587-9281 or 650/322-1181.

55 LOWER LITTLE TRUCKEE

Scenic rating: 7

on the Little Truckee River in Tahoe National Forest

This pretty camp is set along Highway 89 and the Little Truckee River at 6,200 feet. (For more information, see the *Upper Little Truckee* listing in this chapter.)

Campsites, facilities: There are 15 sites for tents or RVs up to 20 feet (no hookups). Picnic tables and fire grills are provided. Drinking water and vault toilets are available. Supplies are available in Sierraville or Truckee. Leashed pets are permitted.

Reservations, fees: Reservations are accepted at 877/444-6777 or www.recreation.gov ($10 reservation fee). Sites are $16 per night, $5 per night for each additional vehicle. Open May through October, weather permitting.

Directions: From Truckee, drive north on Highway 89 for about 12 miles to the campground on the left. If you reach Upper Little Truckee Camp, you have gone 0.5 mile too far.

Contact: Tahoe National Forest, Sierraville Ranger District, 530/994-3401, fax 530/994-3143; California Land Management, 530/587-9281 or 650/322-1181.

56 JACKSON CREEK

Scenic rating: 7

near Bowman Lake in Tahoe National Forest

This primitive campground is at 5,600 feet elevation, adjacent to Jackson Creek, a primary feeder stream to Bowman Lake to the nearby west. There are several lakes within a five-mile radius, including Bowman Lake, Jackson Meadow Reservoir, Sawmill Lake (private), and Faucherie Lake. A trailhead is available a mile south (on the right side of the road) at the north end of Sawmill Lake. The trail is routed to a series of pretty Sierra lakes to the west of Haystack Mountain (7,391 feet).

Campsites, facilities: There are 14 primitive tent sites. Picnic tables and fire grills are provided. Vault toilets are available. No drinking water is available. Garbage must be packed out. Leashed pets are permitted.

Reservations, fees: Reservations are not accepted. There is no fee for camping. Open June through October, weather permitting.

Directions: From Sacramento, drive east on I-80 past Emigrant Gap to Highway 20. Turn west on Highway 20 and drive to Bowman Road/Forest Road 18. Turn right and drive about 16 miles to Bowman Lake (much of the road is quite rough), then continue for four miles east of the lake to the campground.

Contact: Tahoe National Forest, Yuba River Ranger District, South, 530/265-4531, fax 530/478-6109.

57 BOWMAN LAKE

Scenic rating: 8

in Tahoe National Forest

Bowman is a sapphire jewel set in Sierra granite at 5,568 feet elevation, extremely pretty and ideal for campers with car-top boats. Pine trees surround the lake, and the shoreline is sprinkled with large granite slabs. Swimming is allowed, and the boat speed limit is 10 mph. There is no boat ramp (you wouldn't want to trailer a boat on the access road anyway), but there are lots of small rainbow trout that are eager to please during the evening bite. The camp is set on the eastern end of the lake, just below where Jackson Creek pours in. The lake is flanked by Bowman Mountain (7,392 feet) and Red Hill (7,075 feet) to the south and Quartz Hill (7,025 feet) to the north.

Campsites, facilities: There are seven primitive tent sites. Vault toilets are available. No drinking water is available. Garbage must be packed out. Leashed pets are permitted.

Reservations, fees: Reservations are not accepted. There is no fee for camping. Open mid-June through October, weather permitting.

Directions: From Sacramento, drive east on I-80 past Emigrant Gap to Highway 20. Turn west on Highway 20 and drive to Bowman Road/Forest Road 18. Turn right and drive about 16 miles (much of the road is quite rough) to Bowman Lake and the campground on the right side of the road at the head of the lake.

Contact: Tahoe National Forest, Yuba River Ranger District, South, 530/265-4531, fax 530/478-6109; Big Bend Visitor Center, 530/426-3609, fax 530/426-1744.

58 FAUCHERIE LAKE GROUP CAMP

🚶 🏊 🛶 🎣 🐎 🚐 🏕

Scenic rating: 7

near Bowman Lake in Tahoe National Forest

Faucherie Lake is the kind of place that most people believe can be reached only by long, difficult hikes with a backpack. Guess again: Here it is, set in Sierra granite at 6,100 feet elevation, quiet and pristine, a classic alpine lake. It is ideal for car-top boating and has decent fishing for both rainbow and brown trout. The boating speed limit is 10 mph. This is a group camp on the lake's northern shore, a prime spot, with the outlet creek nearby. Note: Road washouts may require four-wheel drive.

Campsites, facilities: There is one group camp for tents or RVs up to 22 feet (no hookups) that can accommodate up to 25 people. Picnic tables and fire grills are provided. Vault toilets are available. No drinking water is available. Garbage must be packed out. A boat ramp is nearby. Leashed pets are permitted.

Reservations, fees: Reservations are required at 877/444-6777 or www.recreation. gov ($10 reservation fee). The camp is $55 per night. Open June through October, weather permitting.

Directions: From Sacramento, drive east on I-80 past Emigrant Gap to Highway 20. Turn west on Highway 20 and drive to Bowman Road/Forest Road 18. Turn right and drive about 16 miles (much of the road is quite rough) to Bowman Lake and continue four miles to a Y. Bear right at the Y and drive about three miles to the campground at the end of the road.

Contact: Tahoe National Forest, Yuba River Ranger District, South, 530/265-4531, fax 530/478-6109; Big Bend Visitor Center, 530/426-3609, fax 530/426-1744.

59 CANYON CREEK

🚶 🛶 🐎 🚐 🏕

Scenic rating: 6

near Faucherie Lake in Tahoe National Forest

This pretty spot is at 6,000 feet elevation in Tahoe National Forest, a mile from Sawmill Lake (which you pass on the way in) and a mile from pretty Faucherie Lake. It is set along Canyon Creek, the stream that connects those two lakes. Of the two, Faucherie provides better fishing and, because of that, there are fewer people at Sawmill. Take your pick. A trailhead is available at the north end of Sawmill Lake with a hike to several small alpine lakes, a great day or overnight backpacking trip.

Campsites, facilities: There are 20 sites for tents or RVs up to 16 feet (no hookups). Picnic tables and fire grills are provided. Vault toilets are available. No drinking water is available. Garbage must be packed out. Leashed pets are permitted.

Reservations, fees: Reservations are not accepted. There is no fee for camping. Open June through October, weather permitting.

Directions: From Sacramento, drive east on I-80 to Emigrant Gap. Take the off-ramp and head north on the short connector road to Highway 20. Turn west on Highway 20 and drive four miles to Bowman Road/Forest Road 18. Turn right and drive about 16 miles (nine of these miles are paved, but the rest is quite rough) to Bowman Lake and continue four miles to a Y. Bear right at the Y and drive about two miles to the campground on the right side of the road. (Occasionally the access route requires a four-wheel-drive vehicle.)

Contact: Tahoe National Forest, Yuba River Ranger District, South, 530/265-4531, fax 530/478-6109; Big Bend Visitor Center, 530/426-3609, fax 530/426-1744.

60 SAGEHEN CREEK

Scenic rating: 7

in Tahoe National Forest

This is a small, primitive camp set at 6,500 feet beside little Sagehen Creek, just north of a miniature mountain range called the Sagehen Hills, which top out at 7,707 feet. Sagehen Creek provides an option when the camps along Highway 89 and at Stampede, Boca, and Prosser Creek have filled. In the fall, it is popular with campers as a base camp.

Campsites, facilities: There are 10 sites for tents or RVs up to 16 feet (no hookups). Picnic tables and fire grills are provided. Vault toilets are available. No drinking water is available. Garbage must be packed out. Leashed pets are permitted.

Reservations, fees: Reservations are not accepted. There is no fee for camping. Open mid-May to mid-October, weather permitting.

Directions: From Truckee, drive 8.5 miles north on Highway 89 to Sagehen Summit Road on the left. Turn left and drive four miles to the campground.

Contact: Tahoe National Forest, Truckee Ranger District, 530/587-3558, fax 530/587-6914.

61 LOGGER

Scenic rating: 7

at Stampede Lake in Tahoe National Forest

Covering 3,400 acres and with 25 miles of shoreline, Stampede Lake is a huge lake by Sierra standards—the largest in the region after Lake Tahoe. It is set at 6,000 feet, surrounded by Sierra granite mountains and pines, and is big, and on days when the wind is down, quite beautiful. The campground is also huge, set along the lake's southern shore, a few minutes' drive from the Captain Roberts boat ramp. This camp is ideal for campers, boaters, and anglers. The lake is becoming one of the top fishing lakes in California for kokanee salmon (which can be caught only by trolling), and it also has some large Mackinaw trout and a sprinkling of planter-sized rainbow trout. All water sports are allowed. One problem at Stampede is receding water levels from midsummer through fall, a real pain, which puts the campsites some distance from the lake. Even when the lake is full, there are only a few "lakeside" campsites. However, the boat ramp has been extended to assist boaters during drawdowns.

Campsites, facilities: There are 252 sites for tents or RVs up to 32 feet (no hookups). Picnic tables and fire rings are provided. Drinking water, vault toilets, and a dump station are available. A concrete boat ramp is available one mile from camp. Some facilities are wheelchair-accessible. Leashed pets are permitted.

Reservations, fees: Reservations are accepted at 877/444-6777 or www.recreation.gov ($10 reservation fee). Sites are $20 per night, $5 per night for each additional vehicle. Open May through October.

Directions: From Truckee, drive east on I-80 for seven miles to the Boca-Hirschdale/County Road 270 exit. Take that exit and drive north on County Road 270 for about seven miles (past Boca Reservoir) to the junction with County Road S261 on the left. Turn left and drive 1.5 miles to the campground on the right.

Contact: Tahoe National Forest, Truckee Ranger District, 530/587-3558, fax 530/587-6914; California Land Management, 530/587-9281 or 650/322-1181.

62 EMIGRANT SPRINGS GROUP CAMP

Scenic rating: 7

at Stampede Lake in Tahoe National Forest

Emigrant Group Camp is set at a beautiful spot on Stampede Lake, near a point along a cove on the southeastern corner of the lake. There is a beautiful view of the lake from the point, and a boat ramp is two miles to the east. Elevation is 6,000 feet. (See the *Logger* listing in this chapter for more information.)

Campsites, facilities: There are four group sites for tents or RVs up to 32 feet (no hook-ups) that can accommodate 25–50 people each. Picnic tables and fire grills are provided. Drinking water and vault toilets are available. Bring your own firewood. A three-lane concrete boat ramp is available. Some facilities are wheelchair-accessible. Leashed pets are permitted.

Reservations, fees: Reservations are required at 877/444-6777 or www.recreation.gov ($10 reservation fee). The camp is $86–167 per night. Open May through September, weather permitting.

Directions: From Truckee, drive east on I-80 for seven miles to the Boca-Hirschdale/County Road 270 exit. Take that exit and drive north on County Road 270 for about seven miles (past Boca Reservoir) to the junction with County Road S261 on the left. Turn left and drive 1.5 miles to the campground access road on the right. Turn right and drive one mile to the camp on the left.

Contact: Tahoe National Forest, Truckee Ranger District, 530/587-3558, fax 530/587-6914; California Land Management, 530/587-9281 or 650/322-1181.

63 BOYINGTON MILL
🏃 🛶 🛖 🚐 ⛺

Scenic rating: 7

on the Little Truckee River in Tahoe National Forest

Boyington Mill is a little Forest Service camp set between Boca Reservoir to the nearby south and Stampede Lake to the nearby north, along a small inlet creek to the adjacent Little Truckee River. Though open all summer, it is most often used as an overflow camp when lakeside

campsites at Boca, Stampede, and Prosser have already filled. The elevation is 5,700 feet.

Campsites, facilities: There are 10 sites for tents or RVs up to 32 feet (no hookups). Picnic tables and fire rings are provided. Vault toilets are available. No drinking water is available. Leashed pets are permitted.

Reservations, fees: Reservations are accepted at 877/444-6777 or www.recreation.gov ($10 reservation fee). Sites are $16 per night, $5 per night for each additional vehicle. Open May through October, weather permitting.

Directions: From Truckee, drive east on I-80 for seven miles. Take the Boca-Hirschdale exit and drive north on County Road 270 for four miles (past Boca Reservoir) to the campground.

Contact: Tahoe National Forest, Truckee Ranger District, 530/587-3558, fax 530/587-6914; California Land Management, 530/587-9281 or 650/322-1181.

64 BOCA REST CAMPGROUND
🏊 🛶 🛥 🐕 🚐 ⛺

Scenic rating: 7

on Boca Reservoir in Tahoe National Forest

The Boca Dam faces I-80, so the lake is out of sight of the zillions of highway travelers who would otherwise certainly stop here. Those who do stop find that the lake is very pretty, set at 5,700 feet elevation and covering 1,000 acres with deep, blue water and 14 miles of shoreline. All water sports are allowed. This camp is on the lake's northeastern shore, not far from the inlet to the Little Truckee River. The boat ramp is some distance away.

Campsites, facilities: There are 31 sites for tents or RVs up to 22 feet (no hookups). Picnic tables and fire grills are provided. Drinking water and vault toilets are available. A hand-launch boat ramp is also available. A concrete boat ramp is three miles away on the southwest shore of Boca Reservoir. Leashed pets are permitted.

Reservations, fees: Reservations are accepted at 877/444-6777 or www.recreation.gov ($10 reservation fee). Sites are $16 per night, $5 per night for each additional vehicle. Open May through October, weather permitting.

Directions: From Truckee, drive east on I-80 for seven miles to the Boca-Hirschdale exit. Take that exit and drive north on County Road 270 for about 2.5 miles to the campground on the left side of the road.

Contact: Tahoe National Forest, Truckee Ranger District, 530/587-3558, fax 530/587-6914; California Land Management, 530/587-9281 or 650/322-1181.

65 MALAKOFF DIGGINS STATE HISTORIC PARK

🏃 🏕 🚐 ⛺

Scenic rating: 7

near Nevada City

This camp is set at 3,400 feet elevation near a small lake in the park, but the main attraction of the area is its gold-mining past. A trip here is like a walk through history. Gold-mining efforts at this site washed away entire mountains with powerful streams of water, leaving behind enormous cliffs. This practice began in the 1850s and continued for many years. Several major gold-mining operations combined hydraulic mining with giant sluice boxes. Hydraulic mining was a scourge to the land, of course, and was eventually put to an end due to litigation between mine operators and landowners downstream. Though the remains of the state's biggest hydraulic mine are now closed to public viewing, visitors can view exhibits on mining life.

The park also contains a 7,847-foot bedrock tunnel that served as a drain. Although this tunnel is not open to the public, a shorter tunnel is available for viewing. The visitors center has exhibits on life in the old mining town

of North Bloomfield. Tours of the numerous historic sites are offered during the summer.

Campsites, facilities: There are 30 sites for tents or RVs up to 24 feet (no hookups), three cabins, and one group tent site for up to 50 people. Picnic tables and fire grills are provided. Drinking water and flush toilets (except mid-November through February) are available. Leashed pets are permitted.

Reservations, fees: Reservations are accepted Memorial Day through Labor Day at 800/444-PARK (800/444-7275) or www. reserveamerica.com ($7.50 reservation fee). Sites are $11–15 per night, $6 per night for each additional vehicle, $111 per night for the group site. The cabins are $35 per night. Open year-round.

Directions: From Auburn, drive north on Highway 49 to Nevada City and continue 11 miles to the junction of Tyler Foote Crossing Road. Turn right and drive approximately 11 miles (in the process the road changes names to Cruzon Grade and Back Bone Road) to Der Bec Road. Turn right on Der Bec Road and drive one mile to North Bloomfield Road. Turn right and drive two miles to the entrance on the right. The route is well signed; the last two miles are quite steep.

Contact: California State Parks, Goldrush District, tel./fax 530/265-2740, www.parks. ca.gov.

66 SOUTH YUBA

🏃 🏊 🛶 🏕 ♿ 🚐 ⛺

Scenic rating: 7

near the Yuba River

This little-known BLM camp is set next to where little Kenebee Creek enters the Yuba River. The Yuba is about a mile away, with some great swimming holes and evening trout-fishing spots to explore. A good side trip is to nearby Malakoff Diggins State Historic Park and the town of North Bloomfield (about a 10-minute drive to the northeast on North

Bloomfield Road), which is being completely restored to its 1850s character. Twelve-mile-long South Yuba Trail begins at the state park and features outstanding spring wildflower blooms. The elevation is 2,600 feet.

Campsites, facilities: There are 16 sites for tents or RVs up to 27 feet (no hookups). Picnic tables and fire grills are provided. Drinking water and vault toilets are available. Some facilities are wheelchair-accessible. Leashed pets are permitted.

Reservations, fees: Reservations are not accepted. Sites are $5 per night. Open April through mid-October, weather permitting.

Directions: From Auburn, turn north on Highway 49, drive to Nevada City, and then continue on Highway 49 (the highway jogs left in town) a short distance to North Bloomfield Road. Turn right and drive 10 miles to the one-lane bridge at Edward's Crossing. Cross the bridge and continue 1.5 miles to the campground on the right side of the road (the road becomes quite rough). This route is not recommended for RVs or trailers.

Alternate route for RVs or vehicles with trailers: From Auburn turn north on Highway 49 to Nevada City and continue on Highway 49 (the highway jogs left in town) to Tyler Foote Crossing Road. Turn right and drive to Grizzly Hills Road (just past North Columbia). Turn right and drive two miles to North Bloomfield Road. Bear right on North Bloomfield Road and drive 0.5 mile to the campground on the left.

Contact: The Bureau of Land Management, Folsom Field Office, 916/985-4474, fax 916/985-3259.

67 GROUSE RIDGE

Scenic rating: 6

near Bowman Lake in Tahoe National Forest

Grouse Ridge is set at 7,520 feet elevation at the gateway to beautiful hiking country filled with small high Sierra lakes. The camp is primarily used as a trailhead and jump-off point, not as a destination itself. The closest hike is the 0.5-mile tromp up to Grouse Ridge Lookout, at 7,707 feet, which provides a spectacular view to the north of this area and its many small lakes. As you hike north, the trail passes Round Lake (to the left) in the first mile and Middle Lake (on the right) two miles later, with opportunities to take cutoff trails on either side of the ridge to visit numerous other lakes.

Campsites, facilities: There are nine sites for tents only. Picnic tables and fire grills are provided. Vault toilets are available. No drinking water is available. Garbage must be packed out. Leashed pets are permitted.

Reservations, fees: Reservations are not accepted. There is no fee for camping. Open June through October, weather permitting.

Directions: From Sacramento, drive east on I-80 past Emigrant Gap to Highway 20. Turn west on Highway 20 and drive to Bowman Road/Forest Road 18. Turn north on Bowman Road and drive five miles to Grouse Ridge Road. Turn right on Grouse Ridge Road and drive six miles on rough gravel to the campground.

Contact: Tahoe National Forest, Yuba River Ranger District, South, 530/265-4531, fax 530/478-6109; Big Bend Visitor Center, 530/426-3609, fax 530/426-1744.

68 LAKESIDE

Scenic rating: 7

on Prosser Creek Reservoir in Tahoe National Forest

This primitive camp is in a deep cove in the northwestern end of Prosser Creek Reservoir, near the lake's headwaters. It is a gorgeous lake, set at 5,741 feet elevation, and a 10-mph speed limit keeps the fast boats out. The adjacent shore is decent for hand-launched, car-top boats, providing the lake level is up, and a concrete boat ramp is a mile down the road. Lots of trout are stocked here every year. The trout fishing is often quite good after the ice breaks up in late spring. Sound perfect? Unfortunately for many, the Prosser OHV Park is nearby and can be noisy.

Campsites, facilities: There are 30 sites for tents or RVs up to 33 feet (no hookups). Drinking water and vault toilets are available. A boat ramp is nearby. Leashed pets are permitted.

Reservations, fees: Reservations are accepted at 877/444-6777 or www.recreation.gov ($10 reservation fee). Sites are $16 per night, $5 per night for each additional vehicle. Open June through October, weather permitting.

Directions: From Truckee, drive north on Highway 89 for three miles to the campground entrance road on the right. Turn right and drive less than a mile to the campground.

Contact: Tahoe National Forest, Truckee Ranger District, 530/587-3558, fax 530/587-6914; California Land Management, 530/587-9281 or 650/322-1181.

69 PROSSER CAMPGROUND
🏃‍♀️ 🏊 🛶 ⛵ 🎣 🚐 ⛺

Scenic rating: 9

at Prosser Reservoir

This camp is set at an elevation of 5,800 feet on the west shore peninsula of Prosser Reservoir. Though water levels can be an issue in late summer and fall, this campground is gorgeous in late spring and early summer. The landscape consists of Sierra granite sprinkled with pines, and the contrast of the emerald water, granite shore, and cobalt sky can be very special. In spring and fall, look for rainbow trout up to 18 inches. In summer, anglers have a shot a 10- to 12-inch planters. A 10-mph speed limit for boaters keeps it quiet.

Campsites, facilities: There are 29 sites for tents and small RVs, and one group site.

Drinking water and vault toilets are available. Picnic tables and fire grills are provided. A boat ramp is nearby.

Reservations, fees: Reservations are not accepted for individual sites, but are required for the group site at 877/444-6777 or recreation.gov ($10 reservation fee). Sites are $20, $113.85 for the group site, $5 each additional vehicle per night. A maximum stay of 14 days is enforced. Open late May through early September.

Directions: From Truckee, drive north on Highway 89 for four miles and turn right onto access road to Prosser Reservoir. This campground is past Lakeside Campground.

Contact: Tahoe National Forest, Truckee Ranger District, 530/587-3558, fax 530/587-6914, www.fs.fed.us.

70 BOCA SPRINGS CAMPGROUND AND GROUP CAMP
🏃‍♀️ 🏊 🛶 ⛵ 🎣 ♿ 🚐 ⛺

Scenic rating: 7

in Tahoe National Forest

Boca Springs is located just past the north end of Boca Lake, near the Little Truckee River and a short way beyond Lakeside Campground. Boca is known for good trolling for trout and large kokanee salmon. A Forest Road provides access to a good stretch of the Little Truckee River, which can also provide good fishing for small trout. The elevation is 5,800 feet.

Campsites, facilities: There are seven tent sites, eight sites for tents or RVs, and one group site. Some sites are pull-through. Drinking water and vault toilets are available. Picnic tables and fire grills are provided. Horses are permitted in the campground, and a watering trough is provided. Some facilities are wheelchair accessible.

Reservations, fees: Reservations are accepted ($10 reservation fee) at 877/444-6777 or recreation.gov. Sites are $16, $48.40 for the group site, $5 each additional vehicle fee. A maximum stay of 14 days is enforced. Open mid-May through September.

Directions: From Truckee, drive north on Highway 89 for four miles and turn right onto access road to Prosser Reservoir. This campground is past Lakeside Campground.

Contact: Tahoe National Forest, Truckee Ranger District, 530/587-3558, fax 530/587-6914.

71 BOCA
🏊 ⛵ 🎣 🐕 🚐 ⛰

Scenic rating: 7

on Boca Reservoir in Tahoe National Forest

Boca Reservoir is known as a "big fish factory," with some huge but rare brown trout and rainbow trout sprinkled among a growing fishery for kokanee salmon. The lake is set at 5,700 feet amid a few sparse pines. While the surrounding landscape is not in the drop-dead beautiful class, the lake can still seem a Sierra gem on a windless dawn out on a boat. It is within a few miles of I-80. The camp is the best choice for anglers/boaters, with a launch ramp set just down from the campground.

Campsites, facilities: There are 20 sites for tents or RVs up to 16 feet (no hookups). Picnic tables and fire grills are provided. Vault toilets are available. No drinking water is available. A concrete boat ramp is north of the campground on Boca Reservoir. Truckee is the nearest place for telephones and supplies. Leashed pets are permitted.

Reservations, fees: Reservations are accepted at 877/444-6777 or www.recreation.gov ($10 reservation fee). Sites are $16 per night, $5 per night for each additional vehicle. Open May through October, weather permitting.

Directions: From I-80 in Truckee, take the exit for Highway 89-North. At the stoplight, turn left onto Highway 89-North and drive approximately one mile to Prosser Dam Road.

Turn right and drive 4.5 miles to Prosser-Boca Road. Turn right and drive approximately four miles to the camp on the left.

Contact: Tahoe National Forest, Truckee Ranger District, 530/587-3558, fax 530/587-6914; California Land Management, 530/587-9281 or 650/322-1181.

72 SCOTTS FLAT LAKE RECREATION AREA
🏊 ⛵ 🎣 🐕 🚴 ♿ 🚐 ⛰

Scenic rating: 8

near Grass Valley

Scotts Flat Lake (at 3,100 feet elevation) is shaped like a large teardrop and is one of the prettier lakes in the Sierra foothills, with 7.5 miles of shoreline circled by forest. Rules prohibiting personal watercraft keep the place sane. The camp is set on the lake's north shore, largely protected from spring winds and within short range of the marina and one of the lake's two boat launches. Trout fishing is good here in the spring and early summer. When the lake heats up, waterskiing and powerboating become more popular. Sailing and sailboarding are also good during afternoon winds.

Campsites, facilities: There are 187 sites for tents or RVs up to 35 feet (no hookups). Picnic tables and fire pits are provided. Restrooms with flush toilets and coin showers, coin laundry, and a dump station are provided. A general store, bait and tackle, boat rentals, boat ramp, and a playground are also available. Groups can be accommodated. Some facilities are wheelchair-accessible. Leashed pets are permitted.

Reservations, fees: Reservations are recommended in the summer at 530/265-5302. Sites are $19–30 per night, $6.25 per night for each additional vehicle, $3 per pet per night, $6 boat launch fee. Maximum stay 14 days. Some credit cards accepted. Open year-round, weather permitting.

Directions: From Auburn, drive north on

Highway 49 to Nevada City and the junction with Highway 20. Continue straight onto Highway 20 and drive five miles (east) to Scotts Flat Road. Turn right and drive four miles to the camp entrance road on the right (on the north shore of the lake).

Contact: Scotts Flat Lake Recreation Area, 530/265-5302 or 530/265-8861, fax 530/265-3777, www.scottsflatlake.net.

73 WHITE CLOUD
🚶 🚴 🐴 ♿ 🚐 ⛺

Scenic rating: 5

in Tahoe National Forest

This camp is set along historic Pioneer Trail, which has turned into one of the top mountain-bike routes in the Sierra Nevada, easy and fast. The trail traces the route of the first wagon road opened by emigrants and gold seekers in 1850. It is best suited for mountain biking, with a lot of bikers taking the one-way downhill ride (with an extra car for a shuttle ride) from Bear Valley to Lone Grave. The Omega Overlook is the highlight, with dramatic views of granite cliffs and the Yuba River. The elevation is 4,200 feet.

Campsites, facilities: There are 46 sites for tents or RVs of any length (no hookups). Picnic tables and fire grills are provided. Drinking water, flush toilets, and vault toilets are available. Some facilities are wheelchair-accessible. Leashed pets are permitted.

Reservations, fees: Reservations are accepted at 877/444-6777 or www.recreation.gov ($10 reservation fee). Sites are $22 per night, $5 per night for each additional vehicle. Open May through October, weather permitting.

Directions: From Sacramento, drive east on I-80 to Emigrant Gap. Take the off-ramp and then head north on the short connector road to Highway 20. Turn west on Highway 20 and drive about 15 miles to the campground entrance on the left.

Contact: Tahoe National Forest, Yuba River Ranger District, South, 530/265-4531, fax 530/478-6109; Big Bend Visitor's Center, 530/426-3609, fax 530/426-1744.

74 SKILLMAN FAMILY, EQUESTRIAN, AND GROUP CAMP
🚶 🚴 🐴 🚐 ⛺

Scenic rating: 5

in Tahoe National Forest

Skillman Group Camp is set at 4,400 feet, on a loop access road just off Highway 20, and historic Pioneer Trail runs right through it. (See the *White Cloud* listing in this chapter for more information.)

Campsites, facilities: There are 16 sites for tents or RVs up to 25 feet (no hookups). This campground can also be used as a group camp for tents or RVs up to 25 feet and can accommodate up to 75 people. Picnic tables and fire grills are provided. Vault toilets and drinking water are available. Horse corrals, tie rails, troughs, and stock water are available. Leashed pets are permitted.

Reservations, fees: Reservations are accepted at 877/444-6777 or www.recreation.gov ($10 reservation fee). Sites are $22 per night, double sites are $44 per night, and the group camp is $110–330 per night. Open May through October, weather permitting.

Directions: From Sacramento, drive east on I-80 past Emigrant Gap to Highway 20. Turn west on Highway 20 and drive 12 miles to the campground entrance on the left.

Contact: Tahoe National Forest, Yuba River Ranger District, South, 530/265-4531, fax 530/478-6109; Sierra Recreation Managers, 209/295-4512; Big Bend Visitor Center, 530/426-3609, fax 530/426-1744.

75 LAKE SPAULDING

🏊 🛶 🚐 🏕 ♿ 🚌 ⛺

Scenic rating: 8

near Emigrant Gap

Lake Spaulding is set at 5,000 feet elevation in the Sierra Nevada, complete with huge boulders and a sprinkling of conifers. Its clear, pure, very cold water has startling effects on swimmers. The 772-acre lake is extremely pretty, with the Sierra granite backdrop looking as if it has been cut, chiseled, and smoothed. Just one problem: There's not much of a lake view from the campground, although there are a few sites with filtered views. In fact, the lake is about a quarter mile from the campground. The drive here is nearly a straight shot up I-80, so there will be plenty of company at the campground. All water sports are allowed, except personal watercraft. Fishing for kokanee salmon and rainbow trout is often good, as well as fishing for trout at the nearby South Fork Yuba River. There are many other lakes set in the mountain country to the immediate north that can make for excellent side trips, including Bowman, Weaver, and Faucherie Lakes.

Campsites, facilities: There are 25 sites (13 are walk-in) for tents or RVs up to 30 feet (no hookups) and an overflow area. Picnic tables and fire grills are provided. Drinking water, vault toilets, and picnic areas are available. A boat ramp is nearby. Supplies are available in Nevada City. Some facilities are wheelchair-accessible. Leashed pets are permitted.

Reservations, fees: Reservations are not accepted. Sites are $16 per night, $3 per night for each additional vehicle, $1 per pet per night, $7 per day for boat launching. Open mid-May through September, weather permitting.

Directions: From Sacramento, drive east on I-80 past Emigrant Gap to Highway 20. Drive west on Highway 20 for 2.3 miles to Lake Spaulding Road. Turn right on Lake Spaulding Road and drive 0.5 mile to the campground.

Contact: PG&E Land Projects, 916/386-5164; Big Bend Visitor Center, 530/426-3609, fax 530/426-1744, www.pge.com/recreation.

76 INDIAN SPRINGS

🚶 🏊 🛶 🏕 ♿ 🚌 ⛺

Scenic rating: 8

near the Yuba River in Tahoe National Forest

The camp is easy to reach from I-80 yet is in a beautiful setting at 5,600 feet along the South Fork Yuba River. This is a gorgeous stream, running deep blue-green and pure through a granite setting, complete with giant boulders and beautiful pools. Trout fishing is fair. There is a small beach nearby where you can go swimming, though the water is cold. There are also several lakes in the vicinity.

Campsites, facilities: There are 35 sites for tents or RVs up to 26 feet (no hookups). Picnic tables and fire grills are provided. Drinking water and vault toilets are available. A grocery store and propane gas are nearby. Some facilities are wheelchair-accessible. Leashed pets are permitted.

Reservations, fees: Reservations are accepted at 877/444-6777 or www.recreation.gov ($10 reservation fee). Sites are $22 per night, $5 per night for each additional vehicle. Open June through September, weather permitting.

Directions: From Sacramento, drive east on I-80 to Yuba Gap and continue for about three miles to the Eagle Lakes exit. Head north on Eagle Lakes Road for a mile to the campground on the left side of the road.

Contact: Tahoe National Forest, Yuba River Ranger District, South, 530/265-4531, fax 530/478-6109; Big Bend Visitor Center, 530/426-3609, fax 530/426-1744.

CAMPING

77 WOODCHUCK

Scenic rating: 8

on Rattlesnake Creek in Tahoe National Forest

This small camp is only a few miles from I-80, but it is quite obscure and little known to most travelers. It is set on Rattlesnake Creek at 6,300 feet in Tahoe National Forest, at the threshold of some great backcountry and four-wheel-drive roads that lead to many beautiful lakes. To explore, a map of Tahoe National Forest is a must.

Campsites, facilities: There are eight sites for tents. Picnic tables and fire grills are provided. Vault toilets are available. No drinking water is available. Garbage must be packed out. A grocery store and propane gas are available nearby. Leashed pets are permitted.

Reservations, fees: Reservations are not accepted. There is no fee for camping. Open June through October, weather permitting.

Directions: From Sacramento, drive east on I-80 to Yuba Gap and continue for about four miles to the Cisco Grove exit north. Take that exit, turn left on the frontage road, and drive a short distance to the stop sign and Rattlesnake Road/frontage road. Turn left on the frontage road/Rattlesnake Road and drive a short distance. Turn right and continue on Rattlesnake Road (gravel, steep, and curvy; trailers not recommended) and drive four miles to the campground on the right.

Contact: Tahoe National Forest, Yuba River Ranger District, South, 530/265-4531, fax 530/478-6109; Big Bend Visitor's Center, 530/426-3609, fax 530/426-1744.

78 LODGEPOLE

Scenic rating: 8

on Lake Valley Reservoir in Tahoe National Forest

Lake Valley Reservoir is set at 5,786 feet elevation and covers 300 acres. It is gorgeous when full, its shoreline sprinkled with conifers and boulders. The lake provides decent results for anglers, who have the best luck while trolling. A 15-mph speed limit prohibits waterskiing and personal watercraft, and that keeps the place quiet and peaceful. The camp is about a quarter mile from the lake's southwest shore and two miles from the boat ramp on the north shore. A trailhead from camp leads south up Monumental Ridge and to Monumental Creek (three miles, one-way) on the northwestern flank of Quartz Mountain (6,931 feet).

Campsites, facilities: There are 35 sites for tents or RVs up to 30 feet (no hookups). Picnic tables and fire grills are provided. Drinking water and vault toilets are available. A boat ramp is available nearby. Supplies can be obtained off I-80. Some facilities are wheelchair-accessible. Leashed pets are permitted.

Reservations, fees: Reservations are not accepted. Sites are $18 per night, $3 per night for each additional vehicle, $1 per pet per night. Open late May through September, weather permitting.

Directions: From I-80, take the Yuba Gap exit and drive south for 0.4 mile to Lake Valley Road. Turn right on Lake Valley Road and drive for 1.2 miles until the road forks. Bear right and continue for 1.5 miles to the campground entrance road to the right on another fork.

Contact: PG&E Land Projects, 916/386-5164, www.pge.com/recreation.

79 HAMPSHIRE ROCKS
🚶‍♂️ 🏊 🎣 🐕 ♿ 🚐 ⛺

Scenic rating: 8

on the Yuba River in Tahoe National Forest

This camp sits along the South Fork of the Yuba River at 5,800 feet elevation, with easy access off I-80 and a nearby Forest Service information center. Fishing for trout is fair. There are some swimming holes, but the water is often very cold. Nearby lakes that can provide side trips include Sterling and Fordyce Lakes (drive-to) to the north, and the Loch Leven Lakes (hike-to) to the south.

Campsites, facilities: There are 31 sites for tents or RVs up to 22 feet (no hookups) and four walk-in tent sites. Picnic tables and fire grills are provided. Drinking water and vault toilets are available. A convenience store, restaurant, and propane gas are available nearby. Some facilities are wheelchair-accessible. Leashed pets are permitted.

Reservations, fees: Reservations are accepted at 877/444-6777 or www.recreation.gov ($10 reservation fee). Sites are $22 per night, $5 per night for each additional vehicle. Open June through September, weather permitting.

Directions: From Sacramento, drive east on I-80 to Cisco Grove and continue for a mile to the Big Bend exit. Take that exit (remaining just south of the highway), then turn left on the frontage road and drive east for two miles to the campground on the right.

Contact: Tahoe National Forest, Yuba River Ranger District, South, 530/265-4531, fax 530/478-6109; Big Bend Visitor Center, 530/426-3609, fax 530/426-1744.

80 KIDD LAKE GROUP CAMP
🏊 🎣 🚐 🐕 ⛺

Scenic rating: 7

west of Truckee

Kidd Lake is one of four lakes bunched in a series along the access road just south of I-80.

It is set in the northern Sierra's high country, at 6,750 feet, and gets loaded with snow every winter. In late spring and early summer, always call ahead for conditions on the access road. The fishing is frustrating, consisting of a lot of tiny brook trout. Only car-top boats are permitted on Kidd Lake, with a primitive area available for launching. The camp is set just northeast of the lake, within walking distance of the shore. It features 10 small group sites that can accommodate 100 people when reserved together.

Campsites, facilities: There are 10 group tent sites for up to 10 people each. Picnic tables and fire grills are provided. Drinking water and vault toilets are available. Supplies are available in Truckee. Leashed pets are permitted.

Reservations, fees: Reservations are required at 916/386-5164 and must be reserved in increments of at least two sites. Groups sites are $40–125 per night, $1 per pet per night. Open June through mid-September, weather permitting.

Directions: From Sacramento, drive east on I-80 toward Truckee. Take the Norden/Soda Springs exit, drive a short distance, turn south on Soda Springs Road, and drive 0.8 mile to Pahatsi Road. Turn right and drive two miles. When the road forks, bear right and drive a mile to the campground entrance road on the left.

Contact: PG&E Land Projects, 916/386-5164, www.pge.com/recreation.

81 DONNER MEMORIAL STATE PARK
🚶‍♂️ 🚴 🏊 🎣 🚣 🐕 ♿ 🚐 ⛺

Scenic rating: 9

on Donner Lake

The remarkable beauty of Donner Lake often evokes a deep, heartfelt response. Nearly everybody passing by from nearby I-80 has looked down and seen it. The lake is big, three miles long and 0.75 mile wide, gemlike blue, and set near the Sierra crest at 5,900 feet. The area is well developed, with a number of cabins and access roads, and this state park is the feature destination. Along the southeastern end of the lake, it is extremely pretty, but the campsites are set in forest, not along the lake. Fishing is good here (typically only in the early morning), trolling for kokanee salmon or rainbow trout, with big Mackinaw and brown trout providing wild cards. The park features more than three miles of frontage of Donner Creek and Donner Lake, with 2.5 miles of hiking trails. Donner Lake itself has 7.5 miles of shoreline. The lake is open to all water sports, but there is no boat launch at the park; a public ramp is available in the northwest corner of the lake. Campers get free admission to Emigrant Trail Museum.

Campsites, facilities: There are 150 sites for tents or RVs up to 28 feet (no hookups) and trailers up to 24 feet, and two hike-in/bike-in sites. Picnic tables and fire pits are provided. Drinking water, coin showers, vault toilets, picnic area, and interpretive trail are available. Supplies are available about one mile away in Truckee. Some facilities are wheelchair-accessible. Leashed pets are permitted.

Reservations, fees: Reservations are accepted at 800/444-PARK (800/444-7275) or www.reserveamerica.com ($7.50 reservation fee). Sites are $20–25 per night, $6 per night for each additional vehicle, $3 per person per night for hike-in/bike-in sites. Open late May to mid-September, weather permitting.

Directions: From Auburn, drive east on I-80 just past Donner Lake to the Donner State Park exit. Take that exit and turn south (right) on Donner Pass Road and drive 0.5 mile to the park entrance on the left at the southeast end of the lake.

Contact: Donner Memorial State Park, 530/582-7892 or 530/582-7894. For boat-launching info, call 530/582-7720, www.parks.ca.gov.

82 COACHLAND RV PARK

Scenic rating: 6

in Truckee

Truckee is the gateway to recreation at North Tahoe. Within minutes are Donner Lake, Prosser Creek Reservoir, Boca Reservoir, Stampede Lake, the Truckee River, and ski resorts. Squaw Valley is a short distance to the south off Highway 89, and Northstar is just off Highway 267. The park is set in a wooded area near I-80, providing easy access. The downtown Truckee area (with restaurants) is a half mile away. This is one of the few parks in the area that is open year-round. The elevation is 6,000 feet. One problem: Only 25 of the 131 sites are available for overnighters, with the rest taken by long-term rentals.

Campsites, facilities: There are 131 pull-through sites with full hookups (30 amps, 13 sites provide 50 amps) for trailers or RVs up to 40 feet. No tents. Picnic tables are provided. Restrooms with showers, coin laundry, cable TV, modem access, Wi-Fi, playground, horseshoes, athletic field, tetherball, clubhouse, and propane are available. Some facilities are wheelchair-accessible. Leashed pets are permitted.

Reservations, fees: Reservations are recommended. Sites are $41 per night, $1.50–3 per person per night for more than two people, $2 per night for each additional vehicle. Monthly rates available. Some credit cards accepted. Open year-round.

Directions: From eastbound I-80 in Truckee, take the 188A exit to Donner Pass Road. Turn north on Donner Pass Road and drive one block to Pioneer Trail. Turn left and drive a short distance to the park at 10100 Pioneer Trail on the left side of the road.

From westbound I-80 in Truckee, take the 188 exit to Highway 89. Turn right on Highway 89 and drive north one block to Donner Pass Road. Turn left and drive one block to Pioneer Trail. Turn right and continue to the park.

Contact: Coachland RV Park, 530/587-3071, fax 530/587-6976, www.coachlandrvpark.com.

83 MARTIS CREEK LAKE

Scenic rating: 7

near Truckee

If only this lake weren't so often windy in the afternoon, it would be heaven to fly fishers in float tubes. To some it's heaven anyway, with Lahontan cutthroat trout growing to 25 inches here. This is a special catch-and-release fishery where anglers are permitted to use only artificial lures with single, barbless hooks. The setting is somewhat sparse and open—a small lake, 70 acres, on the eastern edge of the Martis Valley. No motors are permitted at the lake, making it ideal (when the wind is down) for float tubes or prams. Sailing, sailboarding, and swimming are permitted. There is no boat launch, but small boats can be hand-launched. The lake level can fluctuate daily, which, along with the wind, can be frustrating for those who show up expecting automatic perfection; that just isn't the way it is out there. At times, the lake level can even be very low. The elevation is 5,800 feet.

Campsites, facilities: There are 25 sites for tents or RVs up to 30 feet (no hookups). Some sites are pull-through. Picnic tables and fire grills are provided. Drinking water, vault toilets, tent pads, and pay phones are available. Some facilities are wheelchair-accessible. Supplies are available six minutes away in Truckee. Leashed pets are permitted.

Reservations, fees: Reservations accepted for the wheelchair-accessible sites only at 530/587-8113. Sites are $16 per night. Open late May through mid-October, weather permitting.

Directions: From Truckee, drive south on Highway 267 for about three miles (past the airport) to the lake entrance road on the left.

Turn left and drive another 2.5 miles to the campground at the end of the road.

Contact: U.S. Army Corps of Engineers, Sacramento District, 530/587-8113, fax 530/587-8623.

84 NORTH FORK

Scenic rating: 7

on the North Fork of the American River in Tahoe National Forest

This is gold-mining country, and this camp is set along the Little North Fork of the North Fork American River at 4,400 feet in elevation, where you might still find a few magic gold flecks. Unfortunately, they will probably be fool's gold, not the real stuff. This feeder stream is small and pretty, and the camp is fairly remote and overlooked by most. It is set on the edge of a network of backcountry Forest Service roads. To explore them, a map of Tahoe National Forest is a must.

Campsites, facilities: There are 17 sites for tents or RVs up to 16 feet (no hookups). Picnic tables and fire grills are provided. Drinking water and vault toilets are available. Supplies are available at Emigrant Gap, Cisco Grove, and Soda Springs. Leashed pets are permitted.

Reservations, fees: Reservations are accepted at 877/444-6777 or www.recreation.gov ($10 reservation fee). Sites are $18 per night, $5 per night for each additional vehicle. Open June through October, weather permitting.

Directions: From Sacramento, drive east on I-80 to the Emigrant Gap exit. Take that exit and drive south a short distance to Texas Hill Road/Forest Road 19. Turn right and drive about seven miles to the camp on the right.

Contact: Tahoe National Forest, Yuba River Ranger District, South, 530/265-4531, fax 530/478-6109; Big Bend Visitor Center, 530/426-3609, fax 530/426-1744.

85 TUNNEL MILL GROUP CAMP

Scenic rating: 7

on the North Fork of the American River in
Tahoe National Forest

This is a good spot for a Boy or Girl Scout
camp-out. It's a rustic, quiet group camp set
all by itself along the (take a deep breath) East
Fork of the North Fork of the North Fork of
the American River (whew). (See the *North
Fork* listing in this chapter for more recreation
information.) The elevation is 4,400 feet.

Campsites, facilities: There are two group
sites for tents or RVs up to 40 feet (no hookups) that can accommodate up to 30 people
each. Picnic tables and fire grills are provided. Vault toilets are available. No drinking
water is available. Supplies are available at the
Nyack exit near Emigrant Gap. Leashed pets
are permitted.

Reservations, fees: Reservations are required at
877/444-6777 or www.recreation.gov ($10 res-
ervation fee). The camp is $99 per night. Open
June through October, weather permitting.

Directions: From Sacramento, drive east on
I-80 to the Emigrant Gap exit. Drive south
for a short distance to Texas Hill Road/For-
est Road 19. Turn right and drive about nine
miles to the campground on the right side
of the road.

Contact: Tahoe National Forest, Yuba River
Ranger District, South, 530/265-4531, fax
530/478-6109; Big Bend Visitor Center,
530/426-3609, fax 530/426-1744.

86 GRANITE FLAT

Scenic rating: 6

on the Truckee River in Tahoe National Forest

This camp is set along the Truckee River at
5,800 feet elevation. The area is known for a
ton of traffic on adjacent Highway 89, as well
as decent trout fishing and, in the spring and
early summer, rafting. It is about a 15-minute
drive to Squaw Valley or Lake Tahoe. A bike
route is also available along the Truckee River
out of Tahoe City.

Campsites, facilities: There are 68 sites for
tents or RVs up to 40 feet (no hookups) and
seven walk-in tent sites. Picnic tables and fire
grills are provided. Drinking water and vault
toilets are available. Some facilities are wheelchair-accessible. Leashed pets are permitted.

Reservations, fees: Reservations are accepted
at 877/444-6777 or www.recreation.gov ($10
reservation fee). Sites are $18 per night, $5 per
night for each additional vehicle. Open May
through October, weather permitting.

Directions: From Truckee, drive south on
Highway 89 for 1.5 miles to the campground
entrance on the left.

Contact: Tahoe National Forest, Truckee Ranger District, 530/587-3558, fax
530/587-6914; California Land Management,
530/587-9281 or 650/322-1181.

87 GOOSE MEADOWS

Scenic rating: 6

on the Truckee River in Tahoe National Forest

There are three campgrounds set along the
Truckee River off Highway 89 between Truckee and Tahoe City. Goose Meadows provides
good fishing access with decent prospects,
despite the high number of vehicles roaring
past on the adjacent highway. This stretch of
river is also popular for rafting. The elevation
is 5,800 feet.

Campsites, facilities: There are 24 sites for
tents or RVs up to 30 feet (no hookups). Picnic
tables and fire grills are provided. Drinking
water and vault toilets are available. Supplies
are available in Truckee and Tahoe City. Some
facilities are wheelchair-accessible. Leashed
pets are permitted.

Reservations, fees: Reservations are accepted at 877/444-6777 or www.recreation.gov ($10 reservation fee). Sites are $16 per night, $5 per night for each additional vehicle. Open May through October, weather permitting.

Directions: From Truckee, drive south on Highway 89 for four miles to the campground entrance on the left (river) side of the highway.

Contact: Tahoe National Forest, Truckee Ranger District, 530/587-3558, fax 530/587-6914; California Land Management, 530/587-9281 or 650/322-1181.

88 SILVER CREEK

Scenic rating: 8

on the Truckee River in Tahoe National Forest

This pretty campground is set near where Silver Creek enters the Truckee River. The trout fishing is often good in this area. This is one of three campgrounds along Highway 89 and the Truckee River, between Truckee and Tahoe City. The elevation is 6,000 feet.

Campsites, facilities: There are 21 sites for tents or RVs up to 40 feet (no hookups) and seven walk-in tent sites. Picnic tables and fire grills are provided. Drinking water and vault toilets are available. Supplies are available in Truckee and Tahoe City. Some facilities are wheelchair-accessible. Leashed pets are permitted.

Reservations, fees: Reservations are accepted at 877/444-6777 or www.recreation.gov ($10 reservation fee). Sites are $16 per night, $5 per night for each additional vehicle. Open June through September, weather permitting.

Directions: From Truckee, drive south on Highway 89 for six miles to the campground entrance on the river side of the highway.

Contact: Tahoe National Forest, Truckee Ranger District, 530/587-3558, fax 530/587-6914; California Land Management, 530/587-9281 or 650/322-1181.

89 ORCHARD SPRINGS RESORT

Scenic rating: 7

on Rollins Lake

Orchard Springs Resort is set on the shore of Rollins Lake among pine, oak, and cedar trees in the Sierra Nevada foothills. The summer heat makes the lake excellent for waterskiing, boating, and swimming. Spring and fall are great for trout and bass fishing.

Campsites, facilities: There are 90 tent sites and 16 sites with full hookups (30 amps) for tents or RVs up to 40 feet. Two sites are pull-through. Four camping cabins are also available. Picnic tables, fire rings, and barbecues are provided. Drinking water, restrooms with flush toilets and showers, launch ramp, boat rentals, slips, bait and tackle, swimming beach, group picnic area, and a convenience store are available. Some facilities are wheelchair-accessible. Leashed pets are permitted.

Reservations, fees: Reservations are accepted. Sites are $29–39 per night, $6.25 per night for each additional vehicle unless towed, $5.75 per boat per night, $3 per pet per night. Some credit cards accepted. Open year-round.

Directions: From Auburn, drive northeast on I-80 for about 20 miles to the Colfax/Grass Valley exit. Take that exit and loop back over the freeway to the stop sign. Turn right and drive a short distance to Highway 174. Turn right and drive north on Highway 174 (a winding, two-lane road) for 3.7 miles (bear left at Giovanni's Restaurant) to Orchard Springs Road. Turn right on Orchard Springs Road and drive 0.5 mile to the road's end. Turn right at the gatehouse and continue to the campground.

Contact: Orchard Springs Resort, 530/346-2212, www.osresort.net.

90 PENINSULA CAMPING AND BOATING RESORT

🚴 🏊 🎣 🛶 🐴 🚐 ⛺

Scenic rating: 8

on Rollins Lake

Peninsula Campground is set on a point that extends into Rollins Lake, flanked on each side by two sprawling lake arms. The resort has 280 acres and 1.5 miles of lake frontage. A bonus is that you can boat directly from some of the lakefront sites. If you like boating, waterskiing, or swimming, you'll definitely like this place in the summer. All water sports are allowed. This is a family-oriented campground with lots of youngsters on summer vacation. Fishing is available for rainbow and brown trout, small- and largemouth bass, perch, crappie, and catfish.

Campsites, facilities: There are 78 sites for tents or RVs up to 40 feet (no hookups), and three group sites for 16–40 people. Three cabins are also available. Picnic tables and fire pits are provided. Restrooms with flush toilets and showers, drinking water, Wi-Fi, dump station, boat rentals (fishing boats, patio boats, canoes, and kayaks), boat ramp, limited fishing licenses, fish-cleaning station, swimming beach, horseshoes, volleyball, and a convenience store are available. Marine gas is available on the lake. Leashed pets are permitted, but call for current status.

Reservations, fees: Reservations are accepted by phone or website. Sites are $26–32 per night, $10 per night for each additional vehicle, $65–160 per night for a group site, $3 per pet per night. Maximum 14-day stay. Some credit cards accepted. Open mid-April through September.

Directions: From Auburn, drive northeast on I-80 for about 20 miles to the Colfax/Grass Valley exit. Take that exit and loop back over the freeway to the stop sign. Turn right and drive a short distance to Highway 174. Turn right and drive north on Highway 174 (a winding, two-lane road) for eight miles to You Bet Road. Turn right and drive 4.3 miles (turning right again to stay on You Bet Road), and continue another 3.1 miles to the campground entrance at the end of the road.

Contact: Peninsula Camping and Boating Resort, 530/477-9413 or 866/4MY-CAMP (866/469-2267), www.penresort.com.

91 GIANT GAP

🏃 🏊 🎣 🛶 🐴 ♿ 🚐 ⛺

Scenic rating: 7

on Sugar Pine Reservoir in Tahoe National Forest

This is a lakeside spot along the western shore of Sugar Pine Reservoir at 4,000 feet elevation in Tahoe National Forest. There is a ramp on the south shore for boaters. Note that a 10-mph speed limit is the law, making this lake ideal for anglers in search of quiet water. Other recreation notes: There's a little less than a mile of paved trail, which goes through the day-use area. Big Reservoir (also known as Morning Star Lake), five miles to the east, is the only other lake in the region and also has a campground. The trout and bass fishing at Sugar Pine is fair—not usually great, not usually bad. Swimming is allowed; kayaking and canoeing are also popular.

Campsites, facilities: There are 30 sites for tents or RVs of any length (no hookups). Picnic tables and fire grills are provided. Drinking water and vault toilets are available. Some facilities are wheelchair-accessible. A dump station and boat ramp are on the south shore. Supplies can be obtained in Foresthill. Leashed pets are permitted.

Reservations, fees: Reservations are accepted at 877/444-6777 or www.recreation.gov ($10 reservation fee). Sites are $18 per night, $36 per night for a double site. Open May to mid-October, weather permitting.

Directions: From Sacramento, drive east on I-80 to the north end of Auburn and the Foresthill Road exit. Take that exit and drive east for 20 miles to Foresthill. Drive through Foresthill (road changes to Foresthill Divide Road) and continue for eight miles to Sugar Pine Road. Turn left and drive five miles to a fork. Turn right and drive one mile to the campground.

Contact: Tahoe National Forest, American River Ranger District, Foresthill Ranger Station, 530/367-2224, fax 530/367-2992.

92 SHIRTTAIL CREEK
🚶🏊🚣🎣🐎🦽🚐🏕

Scenic rating: 7

on Sugar Pine Reservoir in Tahoe National Forest

This camp is set near the little creek that feeds into the north end of Sugar Pine Reservoir. The boat ramp is all the way around the south side of the lake, near Forbes Creek Group Camp. (For recreation information, see the *Giant Gap* listing in this chapter.)

Campsites, facilities: There are 30 sites for tents or RVs of any length (no hookups, double and triple sites are available). Picnic tables and fire grills are provided. Drinking water and vault toilets are available. Some facilities are wheelchair-accessible. A dump station and boat ramp are on the south shore. Supplies can be obtained in Foresthill. Leashed pets are permitted.

Reservations, fees: Reservations are accepted at 877/444-6777 or www.recreation.gov ($10 reservation fee). Sites are $18 for single sites, $36 for double sites, $54 for triple site, per night. Open May through mid-October, weather permitting.

Directions: From Sacramento, drive east on I-80 to the north end of Auburn and the Foresthill Road exit. Take that exit and drive east for 20 miles to Foresthill. Drive through Foresthill (road changes to Foresthill Divide Road) and continue for eight miles to Sugar Pine Road. Turn left and drive five miles to the campground access road. Turn right (signed) and drive to the campground.

Contact: Tahoe National Forest, American River Ranger District, Foresthill Ranger Station, 530/367-2224, fax 530/367-2992.

93 BIG RESERVOIR/ MORNING STAR LAKE
🚣🛶🏊🎣🐎🏕🦽🚐🏕

Scenic rating: 7

on Big Reservoir in Tahoe National Forest

Here's a quiet lake where only electric boat motors are allowed; no gas motors are permitted. That makes it ideal for canoeists, rowboaters, and tube floaters who don't like the idea of having to dodge water-skiers. The lake is stocked with rainbow trout; free fishing permits are required and can be obtained at the lake. Big Reservoir (also known as Morning Star Lake) is quite pretty with a nice beach and some lakefront campsites. The elevation is 4,000 feet.

Campsites, facilities: There are 100 sites for tents or RVs up to 40 feet (no hookups). Picnic tables and fire grills are provided. Drinking water, vault toilets, free showers, dump station, and firewood (fee) are available. There is a small store near the campground and supplies are also available in Foresthill. Some facilities are wheelchair-accessible. Leashed pets are permitted.

Reservations, fees: Reservations are accepted at 530/367-2129. Sites are $23–35 per night. Fishing fees are charged. Open May through October, weather permitting.

Directions: From Sacramento, drive east on I-80 to the north end of Auburn and the Foresthill Road exit. Take that exit and drive east for 20 miles to Foresthill. Drive through Foresthill (road changes to Foresthill Divide Road) and continue for eight miles to Sugar Pine Road. Turn left and drive about three miles to Forest Road 24 (signed Big Reservoir). Continue straight onto Forest Road 24 and drive about three miles to the campground entrance road on the right.

Contact: Tahoe National Forest, American River Ranger District, Foresthill Ranger Station, 530/367-2224, fax 530/367-2992; concessionaire: DeAnza Placer Gold Mining Company, 530/367-2129.

94 FORBES CREEK GROUP CAMP

🚶 🏊 🛶 ➡ 🚤 🦌 ♿ 🚐 ⛺

Scenic rating: 7

on Sugar Pine Reservoir in Tahoe National Forest

The boat launch is nearby, but note: A 10-mph speed limit is the law. That makes for quiet water, perfect for anglers, canoeists, and other small boats. A paved trail circles the 160-acre lake. (For more information see the *Giant Gap* listing in this chapter.)

Campsites, facilities: There are two group campsites, Madrone and Rocky Ridge, for tents or RVs up to 45 feet (no hookups) that can accommodate up to 50 people each. Picnic tables and fire grills are provided. Drinking water and vault toilets are available. Some facilities are wheelchair-accessible. A campfire circle, central parking area, dump station, and a boat ramp are available nearby. Supplies can be obtained in Foresthill. Leashed pets are permitted.

Reservations, fees: Reservations are accepted at 877/444-6777 or www.recreation.gov ($10 reservation fee). Sites are $120 per night. Open May through mid-October, weather permitting.

Directions: From Sacramento, drive east on I-80 to the north end of Auburn and the Foresthill Road exit. Take that exit and drive east for 20 miles to Foresthill. Drive through Foresthill (road changes to Forest-hill Divide Road) and continue for eight miles to Sugar Pine Road/Forest Road 10. Turn left and drive five miles to the fork in the road (still Sugar Pine Road/Forest Road 10). Bear left and drive approximately 4.5 miles to the boat ramp (still

Sugar Pine Road/Forest Road 10). Turn right, head up the hill, and drive approximately seven miles to the camp.

Contact: Tahoe National Forest, American River Ranger District, Foresthill Ranger Station, 530/367-2224, fax 530/367-2992.

95 BEAR RIVER CAMPGROUND

🚶 🏊 🛶 🦌 🚐 ⛺

Scenic rating: 7

near Colfax on Bear River

This RV park is set in the Sierra foothills at 1,800 feet, near Bear River, and features riverfront campsites. The park covers 200 acres, offers five miles of hiking trails, and is set right on the Placer and Nevada County lines. It fills up on weekends and is popular with both locals and out-of-towners. In the spring, when everything is green, it can be a gorgeous landscape. Fishing is OK for rainbow and brown trout, smallmouth bass, and bluegill. Noncommercial gold panning is permitted, and some rafting is popular on the river. A 14-day maximum stay is enforced.

Campsites, facilities: There are 25 sites for tents or small RVs up to 40 feet (no hookups), and two group sites for tents or RVs up to 35 feet for 50–100 people. Picnic tables and fire rings are provided. Pit toilets are available. There is no drinking water. Supplies are available within five miles in Colfax or Bowman. Leashed pets are permitted.

Reservations, fees: Reservations are accepted only for the group sites at 530/886-4901 ($5 reservation fee). Sites are $10 per night, $2 per night for each additional vehicle, $1 per pet per night, and $40–75 per night for group sites. A certificate of insurance is required for group sites. Open March through November.

Directions: From Sacramento, drive east on I-80 east of Auburn to West Weimar Crossroads exit. Take that exit on to Weimar Cross Road and drive north for 1.5 miles to Placer

Hills Road. Turn right and drive 2.5 miles to Plum Tree Road. Turn left and drive one mile to the campground on the left. The access road is steep and narrow.

Contact: Bear River Campground, Placer County Facilities Services, 530/886-4901, www.placer.ca.gov.

96 ROBINSON FLAT
🏕 🐕 ♿ 🚐 ⛺

Scenic rating: 5

near French Meadows Reservoir in Tahoe National Forest

This camp is set at 6,800 feet elevation in remote Tahoe National Forest, on the eastern flank of Duncan Peak (7,116 feet), with a two-mile drive south to Duncan Peak Lookout (7,182 feet). A trail out of camp follows along a small stream, a fork to Duncan Creek, in Little Robinsons Valley. French Meadows Reservoir is 15 miles southeast. An equestrian camp with seven sites is also available.

Campsites, facilities: There are seven sites for tents or RVs up to 25 feet, plus an equestrian camp with seven sites for tents or RVs up to 45 feet. No hookups. Picnic tables and fire grills are provided. Drinking water and vault toilets are available. Garbage must be packed out. Supplies are available in Foresthill. Some facilities are wheelchair-accessible. Leashed pets are permitted.

Reservations, fees: Reservations are not accepted. There is no fee for camping. Open mid-May through October, weather permitting.

Directions: From Sacramento, drive east on I-80 to the north end of Auburn and the Foresthill Road exit. Take that exit and drive east to Foresthill (the road name changes to Foresthill Divide Road) and continue northeast (the road is narrow and curvy) for 27 miles to the junction with County Road 43. The campground is at the junction.

Contact: Tahoe National Forest, American River Ranger District, Foresthill Ranger Station, 530/367-2224, fax 530/367-2992.

97 POPPY HIKE-IN/BOAT-IN
🏕 🏞 🏊 🛶 🎣 🐕 5% ⛺

Scenic rating: 10

on French Meadows Reservoir in Tahoe National Forest

This camp is on the north side of French Meadows Reservoir, about midway along the lake's shore. It can be reached only by boat or on foot, supplying a great degree of privacy compared to the other camps on this lake. A trail that is routed along the north shore of the reservoir runs right through the camp, providing two different trailhead access points, as well as a good side-trip hike. The lake is quite big, covering nearly 2,000 acres when full, at 5,300 feet elevation on a dammed-up section of the Middle Fork American River. It is stocked with rainbow trout but also has prime habitat for brown trout, and big ones are sometimes caught by surprise.

Campsites, facilities: There are 12 tent sites, accessible by boat or by a mile-long foot trail from McGuire boat ramp. Picnic tables and fire grills are provided. Vault toilets are available. No drinking water is available. Garbage must be packed out. Supplies are available in Foresthill. Leashed pets are permitted.

Reservations, fees: Reservations are not accepted. There is no fee for camping. Open May through October, weather permitting.

Directions: From Sacramento, drive east on I-80 to the north end of Auburn and the Foresthill Road exit. Take that exit and drive east to Foresthill and Mosquito Ridge Road (Forest Road 96). Turn right (east) and drive 40 miles (curvy) to French Meadows Reservoir Dam and to a junction. Turn left (still Mosquito Ridge Road) and continue for three miles to the lake and campground.

Contact: Tahoe National Forest, American River Ranger District, Foresthill Ranger Station, 530/367-2224, fax 530/367-2992.

98 LEWIS

Scenic rating: 7

on French Meadows Reservoir in Tahoe National Forest

This camp is not right at lakeside but is just across the road from French Meadows Reservoir. It is still quite pretty, set along a feeder creek near the lake's northwest shore. A boat ramp is available only 0.5 mile to the south, and the adjacent McGuire boat ramp area has a trailhead that is routed along the lake's northern shoreline. This lake is big (2,000 acres) and pretty, created by a dam on the Middle Fork American River, with good fishing for rainbow trout.

Campsites, facilities: There are 40 sites for tents or RVs up to 45 feet (no hookups). Picnic tables and fire grills are provided. Drinking water and vault toilets are available. A concrete boat ramp is nearby. Supplies are available in Foresthill. Some facilities are wheelchair-accessible. Leashed pets are permitted.

Reservations, fees: Reservations are accepted at 877/444-6777 or www.recreation.gov ($10 reservation fee). Sites are $18 per night, $6 per night for each additional vehicle. Open mid-May through early September.

Directions: From Sacramento, drive east on I-80 to the north end of Auburn and the Foresthill Road exit. Take that exit and drive east to Foresthill and Mosquito Ridge Road (Forest Road 96). Turn right (east) and drive 40 miles (curvy) to Anderson Dam and to a junction. Turn left (still Mosquito Ridge Road) and then continue along the southern shoreline of French Meadows Reservoir for five miles to a fork at the head of the lake.

Bear left at the fork and drive 0.5 mile to the camp on the right side of the road.

Contact: Tahoe National Forest, American River Ranger District, Foresthill Ranger Station, 530/367-2224, fax 530/367-2992.

99 AHART

Scenic rating: 7

near French Meadows Reservoir in Tahoe National Forest

This camp is a mile north of French Meadows Reservoir near where the Middle Fork of the American River enters the lake. It is on the Middle Fork and is primarily used for campers who would rather camp near this river than French Meadows Reservoir. Note: This is bear country in the summer.

Campsites, facilities: There are 12 sites for tents or RVs up to 40 feet (no hookups). Picnic tables and fire grills are provided. Vault toilets are available. No drinking water is available. Supplies are available in Foresthill. Some facilities are wheelchair-accessible. Leashed pets are permitted.

Reservations, fees: Reservations are not accepted. Sites are $16 per night, $6 per night for each additional vehicle. Open late May through October, weather permitting.

Directions: From Sacramento, drive east on I-80 to the north end of Auburn and the Foresthill Road exit. Take that exit and drive east to Foresthill and Mosquito Ridge Road (Forest Road 96). Turn right (east) and drive 40 miles (curvy) to Anderson Dam and to a junction. Turn left (still Mosquito Ridge Road) and then continue along the southern shoreline of French Meadows Reservoir for seven miles.

Contact: Tahoe National Forest, American River Ranger District, Foresthill Ranger Station, 530/367-2224, fax 530/367-2992.

100 GATES GROUP CAMP

🏃 🏊 ⚓ 🏕 🚐 ⛰

Scenic rating: 7

on the North Fork of the American River in
Tahoe National Forest

This group camp is well secluded along the
North Fork American River, just upstream
from where it pours into French Meadows Reservoir. (For recreation options, see the *French
Meadows, Lewis,* and *Coyote Group Camp* listings in this chapter.)

Campsites, facilities: There are three group
sites for tents or RVs of any length (no hookups) that can accommodate 25–75 people
each. Picnic tables and fire grills are provided. Drinking water, vault toilets, central
parking, and a campfire circle are available.
Obtain supplies in Foresthill. Leashed pets
are permitted.

Reservations, fees: Reservations are required
at 877/444-6777 or www.recreation.gov ($10
reservation fee). Sites are $75–135 per night.
Open mid-May through October, weather
permitting.

Directions: From Sacramento, drive east on
I-80 to the north end of Auburn and the Foresthill Road exit. Take that exit and drive east
to Foresthill and Mosquito Ridge Road (Forest Road 96). Turn right (east) and drive 40
miles (curvy) to Anderson Dam and to a junction. Turn left (still Mosquito Ridge Road)
and continue along the southern shoreline of
French Meadows Reservoir for five miles to
a fork at the head of the lake. Bear left at the
fork (Forest Road 68) and drive a mile to the
camp at the end of the road.

Contact: Tahoe National Forest, American
River Ranger District, Foresthill Ranger Station, 530/367-2224, fax 530/367-2992.

101 TALBOT

🏃 ⚓ 🏕 ⛰

Scenic rating: 7

on the Middle Fork of the American River in
Tahoe National Forest

Talbot camp is set at 5,600 feet elevation along
the Middle Fork of the American River, primarily used as a trailhead camp for backpackers heading into the Granite Chief Wilderness.
The trail is routed along the Middle Fork
American River, turning south into Picayune
Valley, flanked by Needle Peak (8,971 feet),
Granite Chief (9,886 feet), and Squaw Peak
to the east, then beyond to connect with the
Pacific Crest Trail. The nearby trailhead has
stock trailer parking. Hitching rails are available at the trailhead.

Campsites, facilities: There are five tent sites.
Picnic tables and fire grills are provided. Vault
toilets are available. No drinking water is available. Garbage must be packed out. Supplies are
available in Foresthill. The camp is within a
state game refuge and no firearms are permitted. Leashed pets are permitted.

Reservations, fees: Reservations are not accepted. There is no fee for camping. Open
June through October, weather permitting.

Directions: From Sacramento, drive east on
I-80 to the north end of Auburn and the Foresthill Road exit. Take that exit and drive east
to Foresthill and Mosquito Ridge Road (Forest
Road 96). Turn right (east) and drive 40 miles
(curvy) to Anderson Dam and to a junction.
Turn left (still Mosquito Ridge Road) and
then continue along the southern shoreline
of French Meadows Reservoir for four miles
(road turns into dirt) and continue four more
miles to the campground.

Contact: Tahoe National Forest, American
River Ranger District, Foresthill Ranger Station, 530/367-2224, fax 530/367-2992.

102 COYOTE GROUP CAMP

🚶 🏞 🛶 🚤 🐴 🚐 ⛺

Scenic rating: 6

on French Meadows Reservoir in Tahoe
National Forest

This group camp is set right at the head of
French Meadows Reservoir, at 5,300 feet
elevation. A boat ramp is two miles to the
south, just past Lewis on the lake's north
shore. (For recreation options, see the *Poppy
Hike-In/Boat-In* and *French Meadows* listings
in this chapter.)

Campsites, facilities: There are three group
sites for tents or RVs of any length (no hookups) that can accommodate 25–50 people
each. Picnic tables and fire grills are provided.
Drinking water and vault toilets are available.
A campfire circle and central parking area are
also available. Supplies are available in Foresthill. Leashed pets are permitted.

Reservations, fees: Reservations are required
at 877/444-6777 or www.recreation.gov ($10
reservation fee). Sites are $75–110 per night.
Open mid-May through October.

Directions: From Sacramento, drive east on
I-80 to the north end of Auburn and the Foresthill Road exit. Take that exit and drive east
to Foresthill and Mosquito Ridge Road (Forest
Road 96). Turn right (east) and drive 40 miles
(curvy) to Anderson Dam and to a junction.
Turn left (still Mosquito Ridge Road) and
then continue along the southern shoreline
of French Meadows Reservoir for five miles
to a fork at the head of the lake. Bear left at
the fork and drive 0.5 mile to the camp on the
left side of the road.

Contact: Tahoe National Forest, American
River Ranger District, Foresthill Ranger Station, 530/367-2224, fax 530/367-2992.

103 FRENCH MEADOWS

🚶 🏞 🛶 🚤 🐴 ♿ 🚐 ⛺

Scenic rating: 7

on French Meadows Reservoir in Tahoe
National Forest

The nearby boat launch makes this the choice
for boating campers. The camp is on French
Meadows Reservoir at 5,300 feet elevation.
It is set on the lake's southern shore, with the
boat ramp about a mile to the south (you'll
see the entrance road on the way in). This is a
big lake set in remote Tahoe National Forest
in the North Fork American River Canyon
with good trout fishing. All water sports are allowed. The lake level often drops in late summer, and then a lot of stumps and boulders
start poking through the lake surface. This
creates navigational hazards for boaters and
water skiers, but it also makes it easier for the
anglers to know where to find the fish. If the
fish don't bite here, boaters should make the
nearby side trip to pretty Hell Hole Reservoir
to the south.

Campsites, facilities: There are 75 sites for
tents or RVs up to 45 feet (no hookups). Picnic
tables and fire grills are provided. Drinking
water and vault toilets are available. Some facilities are wheelchair-accessible. A concrete
boat ramp is nearby. Supplies are available in
Foresthill. Leashed pets are permitted.

Reservations, fees: Reservations are accepted
at 877/444-6777 or www.recreation.gov ($10
reservation fee). Sites are $18 per night, $6 per
night for each additional vehicle. Open late
May through October, weather permitting.

Directions: From Sacramento, drive east on
I-80 to the north end of Auburn and the Foresthill Road exit. Take that exit and drive east
to Foresthill and Mosquito Ridge Road (Forest
Road 96). Turn right (east) and drive 40 miles
(curvy) to Anderson Dam and to a junction.
Turn left (still Mosquito Ridge Road) and
then continue along the southern shoreline
of French Meadows Reservoir for four miles
to the campground.

Contact: Tahoe National Forest, American River Ranger District, Foresthill Ranger Station, 530/367-2224, fax 530/367-2992.

104 BIG MEADOWS

🧍‍♂️🌊⛵🛶🏠♿🚐⛰️

Scenic rating: 7

near Hell Hole Reservoir in Eldorado National Forest

This camp sits on a meadow near the ridge above Hell Hole Reservoir, which is about two miles away. (For more information, see the *Hell Hole* listing in this chapter.)

Campsites, facilities: There are 54 sites for tents or RVs of any length (no hookups). Picnic tables are provided. Drinking water and flush and vault toilets are available. A boat ramp is nearby. Some facilities are wheelchair accessible. Leashed pets are permitted.

Reservations, fees: Reservations are not accepted. Sites are $10 per night, $5 per night for each additional vehicle. Open late May through early November, weather permitting.

Directions: From Sacramento, drive east on I-80 to the north end of Auburn. Take the Elm Avenue exit and turn left at the first stoplight onto Elm Avenue. Drive 0.1 mile, turn left on High Street, and continue through the signal where High Street merges with Highway 49. Continue on Highway 49 for about 3.5 miles, turn right over the bridge, and drive about 2.5 miles into the town of Cool. Turn left on Georgetown Road/Highway 193 and drive about 14 miles into Georgetown. At the four-way stop turn left on Main Street (which becomes Wentworth Springs/Forest Road 1) and drive about 25 miles. Turn left on Forest Road 2 and drive 21 miles to the campground on the left.

Contact: Eldorado National Forest, Georgetown Ranger District, 530/333-4312, fax 530/333-5522.

105 MIDDLE MEADOWS GROUP CAMP

🏠🚐⛰️

Scenic rating: 7

on Long Canyon Creek in Eldorado National Forest

This group camp is within range of several adventures. To the nearby east is Hell Hole Reservoir (you'll need a boat here to do it right), and to the nearby north is French Meadows Reservoir (you'll drive past the dam on the way in). Unfortunately, there isn't a heck of a lot to do at this camp other than watch the water flow by on adjacent Long Canyon Creek.

Campsites, facilities: There are two group sites for tents or RVs up to 16 feet (no hookups), including one that can accommodate 25–50 people. Picnic tables and fire grills are provided. Drinking water and flush and vault toilets are available. Supplies can be obtained in Foresthill. Leashed pets are permitted.

Reservations, fees: Reservations are accepted at 877/444-6777 or www.recreation.gov ($10 reservation fee). Sites are $25–50 per night. Open mid-May through mid-September, weather permitting.

Directions: From Sacramento, drive east on I-80 to the north end of Auburn. Take the Elm Avenue exit and turn left at the first stoplight onto Elm Avenue. Drive 0.1 mile, turn left on High Street, and continue through the signal where High Street merges with Highway 49. Travel on Highway 49 for about 3.5 miles, turn right over the bridge, and drive about 2.5 miles into the town of Cool. Turn left on Georgetown Road/Highway 193 and drive about 14 miles into Georgetown. At the four-way stop turn left on Main Street (which becomes Wentworth Springs/Forest Road 1) and drive about 25 miles. Turn left on Forest Road 2 and drive 19 miles to the campground on the right.

Contact: Eldorado National Forest, Georgetown Ranger District, 530/333-4312, fax 530/333-5522.

106 HELL HOLE

Scenic rating: 8

near Hell Hole Reservoir in Eldorado National Forest

Hell Hole is a mountain temple with sapphire-blue water. For the most part, there is limited bank access because of its granite-sculpted shore, and that's why there are no lakeside campsites. This is the closest drive-to camp at Hell Hole Reservoir, about a mile away with a boat launch nearby. All water sports are allowed. Be sure to bring a boat and then enjoy the scenery while you troll for kokanee salmon, brown trout, Mackinaw trout, and a sprinkling of rainbow trout. This is a unique fishery compared to the put-and-take rainbow trout at so many other lakes. The lake has 15 miles of shoreline, and the elevation is 4,700 feet; the camp elevation is 5,200 feet. Note that afternoon winds can make the water choppy.

Campsites, facilities: There are 10 sites for tents only. Picnic tables and fire rings are provided. Drinking water and vault toilets are available. Supplies can be obtained in Georgetown. A boat launch is available nearby at the reservoir. Leashed pets are permitted.

Reservations, fees: Reservations are not accepted. Sites are $10 per night, $5 per night for each additional vehicle. Open late May through early November, weather permitting.

Directions: From Sacramento, drive east on I-80 to the north end of Auburn. Take the Elm Avenue exit and turn left at the first stoplight onto Elm Avenue. Drive 0.1 mile, turn left on High Street, and continue through the signal where High Street merges with Highway 49. Continue on Highway 49 for about 3.5 miles, turn right over the bridge, and drive about 2.5 miles into the town of Cool. Turn left on Georgetown Road/Highway 193 and drive about 14 miles into Georgetown. At the four-way stop turn left on Main Street (which becomes Wentworth Springs/Forest Road 1) and drive about 25 miles. Turn left on Forest Road 2 and drive about 22 miles to the campground on the left.

Contact: Eldorado National Forest, Georgetown Ranger District, 530/333-4312, fax 530/333-5522.

107 UPPER HELL HOLE WALK-IN/BOAT-IN

Scenic rating: 10

on Hell Hole Reservoir in Eldorado National Forest

When the lake is full, this is a beautiful spot, set on the southern shore at the upper end of Hell Hole Reservoir in remote national forest seen by relatively few people. Getting here requires a boat-in or 3.5-mile walk on a trail routed along the southern edge of the lake overlooking Hell Hole. The trail's short rises and falls feel longer than 3.5 miles and can tire you out on a hot day—bring plenty of water. When the lake level is high, an access road on the opposite side of the lake leads to a put-in for kayaks and canoes that can shorten the trip. You'll arrive at this little trail camp, ready to explore onward the next day into the Granite Chief Wilderness, or just do nothing except enjoy adjacent Buck Meadow, the lake's headwaters, and the paradise you have discovered. Note that bears frequent this area, so store your food properly and avoid scented products.

Campsites, facilities: There are 15 tent sites, accessible by trail or boat only. Picnic tables and fire grills are provided. Vault toilets are available. No drinking water is available, so bring a water filter. Garbage must be packed out. A boat launch is at the reservoir and the camp can be reached by boat, but low water levels during August and September can make passage difficult or impossible; call for current status. Supplies can be obtained in Georgetown. Leashed pets are permitted.

Reservations, fees: Reservations are not accepted. There is no fee for camping. Campfire permits are required from the Forest Service. Open May to early September, weather permitting.

Directions: From Sacramento, drive east on I-80 to the north end of Auburn. Take the Elm Avenue exit and turn left at the first stoplight onto Elm Avenue. Drive 0.1 mile, turn left on High Street, and continue through the signal where High Street merges with Highway 49. Continue on Highway 49 for about 3.5 miles, turn right over the bridge, and drive about 2.5 miles into the town of Cool. Turn left on Georgetown Road/Highway 193 and drive about 14 miles into Georgetown. At the four-way stop turn left on Main Street (which becomes Wentworth Springs/Forest Road 1) and drive about 25 miles. Turn left on Forest Road 2 and drive about 23 miles (a mile past the Hell Hole Campground access road) to the parking area at the boat ramp. From the trailhead, hike 3.5 miles to the camp.

Contact: Eldorado National Forest, Georgetown Ranger District, 530/333-4312, fax 530/333-5522.

108 SANDY BEACH CAMPGROUND

🏊 ⛴ 🎣 🐕 🚐 ⛺

Scenic rating: 8

on Lake Tahoe

Sandy Beach Campground is set at 6,200 feet elevation near the northwest shore of Lake Tahoe. A nearby boat ramp provides access to one of the better fishing areas of the lake for Mackinaw trout. A public beach is across the road. But the water in Tahoe is always cold, and though a lot of people will get suntans on beaches next to the lake, swimmers need to be members of the Polar Bear Club. A short drive to the east will take you past the town of Kings Beach and into Nevada, where there are some small casinos near the shore of Crystal Bay. Note that some sites fill up for the summer season.

Campsites, facilities: There are 27 sites with full or partial hookups (30 amps) for tents or RVs up to 40 feet. Some sites are pull-through. Picnic tables, barbecues, and fire rings are provided. Drinking water, restrooms with showers and flush toilets, and a dump station are available. A boat ramp is half a block away. A grocery store and propane gas are available nearby. Leashed pets are permitted.

Reservations, fees: Reservations are recommended. Sites are $20–25 per night for up to six people with two vehicles, two-dog limit. For weeklong stays, seventh night is free. Some credit cards accepted. Open May through October.

Directions: From Truckee, drive south on Highway 267 to Highway 28. Turn right and drive one mile to the park on the right side of the road (entrance well signed).

Contact: Sandy Beach Campground, 530/546-7682.

109 LAKE FOREST CAMPGROUND

🏊 ⛴ 🎣 🐕 ♿ 🚐 ⛺

Scenic rating: 8

on Lake Tahoe

The north shore of Lake Tahoe provides beautiful lookouts and excellent boating access. The latter is a highlight of this camp, with a boat ramp nearby. From here it is a short cruise to Dollar Point and around the corner north to Carnelian Bay, one of the better stretches of water for trout fishing. The elevation is 6,200 feet. There is a 10-day camping limit.

Campsites, facilities: There are 20 sites for tents or RVs up to 20 feet (no hookups). Picnic tables and fire grills are provided. Drinking water and vault toilets are available. Some facilities are wheelchair-accessible. A grocery store, coin laundry, and propane gas are available within four miles. Leashed pets are permitted.

Reservations, fees: Reservations are not accepted. Sites are $15 per night. Open May through October, weather permitting.

Directions: From Truckee, drive south on Highway 89 through Tahoe City to Highway 28. Bear north on Highway 28 and drive four miles to the campground entrance road (Lake Forest Road) on the right.

Contact: Tahoe City Public Utility District, Parks and Recreation, 530/583-3796, ext. 10, fax 530/583-8452.

110 TAHOE STATE RECREATION AREA

Scenic rating: 9

on Lake Tahoe

This is a popular summer-only campground at the north shore of Lake Tahoe. The Tahoe State Recreation Area covers a large area just west of Highway 28 near Tahoe City. There are opportunities for hiking and horseback riding nearby (though not right at the park). It is also near shopping, restaurants, and, unfortunately, traffic jams in Tahoe City. A boat ramp is two miles to the northwest at nearby Lake Forest, and bike rentals are available in Tahoe City for rides along Highway 89 near the shore of the lake. For a more secluded site nearby at Tahoe, get reservations instead for Sugar Pine Point State Park, 11 miles south on Highway 89.

Campsites, facilities: There are 25 sites for tents or RVs up to 27 feet (no hookups) and trailers up to 24 feet. Picnic tables, food lockers, barbecues, and fire pits are provided. Drinking water, vault toilets, and coin showers are available. Firewood, other supplies, and a coin laundry are available within walking distance. Leashed pets are permitted.

Reservations, fees: Reservations are accepted at 800/444-PARK (800/444-7275) or www.

reserveamerica.com ($7.50 reservation fee). Sites are $20–25 per night, $6 per night for each additional vehicle. Open May through October, weather permitting.

Directions: From Truckee, drive south on Highway 89 through Tahoe City. Turn north on Highway 28 and drive 0.9 mile to the campground entrance on the right side of the road.

Contact: Tahoe State Recreation Area, 530/583-3074; Sierra District, 530/525-7232, www.parks.ca.gov.

111 WILLIAM KENT

Scenic rating: 8

near Lake Tahoe in the Lake Tahoe Basin

William Kent camp is a little pocket of peace set near the busy traffic of Highway 89 on the western shore corridor. It is on the west side of the highway, meaning visitors have to cross the highway to get lakeside access. The elevation is 6,300 feet, and the camp is wooded with primarily lodgepole pines. The drive here is awesome or ominous, depending on how you look at it, with the view of incredible Lake Tahoe to the east, the third-deepest blue lake in North America and the 10th-deepest lake in the world. But you often have a lot of time to look at it, since traffic rarely moves quickly.

Campsites, facilities: There are 55 tent sites and 36 sites for RVs up to 40 feet (no hookups). Picnic tables, food lockers, and fire grills are provided. Drinking water, flush toilets, and a dump station are available. A grocery store, coin laundry, and propane gas are available nearby. Some facilities are wheelchair-accessible. Leashed pets are permitted.

Reservations, fees: Reservations are accepted at 877/444-6777 or www.recreation.gov ($10 reservation fee). Sites are $20 per night, $5 per night for each additional vehicle. Open late May through mid-October, weather permitting.

Directions: From Truckee, drive south on Highway 89 to Tahoe City. Turn south on Highway 89 and drive three miles to the campground entrance on the right side of the road.

Contact: Lake Tahoe Basin Management Unit, 530/543-2600, fax 530/543-2693; Taylor Creek Visitor Center, 530/543-2674; California Land Management, 530/583-3642.

112 KASPIAN

🏃 🏊 🛶 🎣 🚐 ⛺

Scenic rating: 7

on Lake Tahoe

As gorgeous and as huge as Lake Tahoe is, there are relatively few camps or even restaurants with lakeside settings. This is one of the few. Kaspian is set along the west shore of the lake at 6,235 feet elevation, near the little town of Tahoe Pines. A Forest Service road (03) is available adjacent to the camp on the west side of Highway 89, routed west into national forest (becoming quite rough) to a trailhead. From there you can hike up to Barker Peak (8,166 feet) for incredible views of Lake Tahoe, as well as access to the Pacific Crest Trail.

Campsites, facilities: There are nine walk-in sites for tents only. RVs up to 20 feet may use the parking lot on a space-available basis. Picnic tables and fire grills are provided. Drinking water, food lockers, and flush toilets are available. A grocery store, coin laundry, and propane gas are nearby. Leashed pets are permitted.

Reservations, fees: Reservations are accepted at 877/444-6777 or www.recreation.gov ($10 reservation fee). Sites are $15 per night, $5 per night for each additional vehicle. Open May through September, weather permitting.

Directions: From Truckee, drive south on Highway 89 to Tahoe City. Turn south on Highway 89 and drive four miles to the campground (signed) on the west side of the road. The tent sites require a walk-in of 50–100 feet.

Contact: Lake Tahoe Basin Management Unit,

113 SUGAR PINE POINT STATE PARK

🏃 🏊 🛶 ❄ 🎣 👤 ♿ 🚐 ⛺

Scenic rating: 10

on Lake Tahoe

This is one of three beautiful and popular state parks on the west shore of Lake Tahoe. It is just north of Meeks Bay on General Creek, with almost two miles of lake frontage available, though the campground is on the opposite side of Highway 89. General Creek, a feeder stream to Lake Tahoe, is one of the clearest streams imaginable. A pretty trail is routed seven miles along the creek up to Lost Lake, just outside the northern boundary of the Desolation Wilderness. This stream also provides trout fishing from mid-July to mid-September. This park contains one of the finest remaining natural areas at Lake Tahoe. The park features dense forests of pine, fir, aspen, and juniper, covering more than 2,000 acres of beautiful landscape. There are many hiking trails, a swimming beach, and, in winter, 20 kilometers of cross-country skiing trails and a heated restroom. There is also evidence of occupation by Washoe Indians, with bedrock mortars, or grinding rocks, near the Ehrman Mansion. The elevation is 6,200 feet.

Campsites, facilities: There are 175 sites for tents or RVs up to 32 feet and trailers up to 26 feet (no hookups). There are also 10 group sites for up to 40 people each. Picnic tables and fire rings are provided. Drinking water, restrooms with flush toilets and coin showers (except in winter), dump station, a day-use area, and nature center with bird display are available. A grocery store, coin laundry, and propane gas are available nearby. Some facilities are wheelchair-accessible. Leashed pets are permitted.

Reservations, fees: Reservations are accepted at 800/444-PARK (800/444-7275) or www. reserveamerica.com ($7.50 reservation fee). Sites are $20–25 per night, $6 per night for each additional vehicle, $111 per night for a group site. Open year-round.

Directions: From Truckee, drive south on Highway 89 through Tahoe City. Continue south on Highway 89 and drive 9.3 miles to the campground (signed) on the right (west) side of the road.

Contact: Sugar Pine Point State Park, 530/525-7982; Sierra District, 530/525-7232, www.parks.ca.gov.

114 MEEKS BAY

Scenic rating: 9

on Lake Tahoe

Meeks Bay is a beautiful spot along the western shore of Lake Tahoe. A bicycle trail is available nearby and is routed along the lake's shore, but it requires occasionally crossing busy Highway 89.

Campsites, facilities: There are 40 sites for tents or RVs up to 20 feet (no hookups). Picnic tables, food lockers, and fire grills are provided. Drinking water and flush toilets are available. Coin laundry and groceries are available nearby. Leashed pets are permitted.

Reservations, fees: Reservations are accepted at 877/444-6777 or www.recreation.gov ($10 reservation fee). Sites are $20 per night, $5 per night for each additional vehicle. Open mid-May through mid-October, weather permitting.

Directions: In South Lake Tahoe at the junction of Highway 89 and U.S. 50, turn north on Highway 89 and drive 17 miles to the campground (signed) on the east side of Highway 89.

Contact: Lake Tahoe Basin Management Unit, 530/543-2600, fax 530/543-2693; Taylor Creek Visitor Center, 530/543-2674;

California Land Management, 530/587-9281 or 650/322-1181.

115 MEEKS BAY RESORT AND MARINA

Scenic rating: 7

on Lake Tahoe

Prime access for boating makes this a camp of choice for the boater/camper at Lake Tahoe. This campground is extremely popular and often booked well ahead of time for July and August. A boat launch is on the premises, and access to Rubicon Bay and beyond to breathtaking Emerald Bay is possible, a six-mile trip one-way for boats. The resort is adjacent to a 20-mile paved bike trail, with a swimming beach also nearby. A 14-day stay limit is enforced.

Campsites, facilities: There are 22 sites with full hookups (50 amps) for RVs up to 60 feet, and 12 sites for tents. Some sites are pull-through. Lodge rooms, cabins, and a house are also available. Picnic tables and fire grills are provided. Restrooms with showers and flush toilets, snack bar, gift shop, and a camp store are available. A boat ramp, boat rentals (kayaks, canoes, and paddle boats), and boat slips are also available. No pets are allowed.

Reservations, fees: Reservations are accepted at 877/326-3357. RV sites are $45 per night, tent sites are $25 per night, $60 per night for boat slips, $25 to launch boats. Some credit cards accepted. Open May through September.

Directions: In South Lake Tahoe at the junction of Highway 89 and U.S. 50, turn north on Highway 89 and drive 17 miles to the campground on the right at 7941 Emerald Bay Road.

Contact: Meeks Bay Resort and Marina, 530/525-6946 or 988/326-3357, www.meeksbayresort.com.

116 AIRPORT FLAT

🏃 🏊 🛶 ⛵ 🎣 🐴 ♿ �foodRV ⛺

Scenic rating: 6

near Loon Lake in Eldorado National Forest

Loon Lake is a gorgeous mountain lake in the Crystal Basin. Airport Flat provides an overflow area when the camps at Loon Lake (see listing in this chapter) are full. Trout fishing is good and Loon Lake, along with Ice House Reservoir, is a favorite spot whether for a weekend or a week. Smaller Gerle Creek Reservoir and Union Valley Reservoir are also in the area. The elevation is 5,300 feet.

Campsites, facilities: There are 16 sites for tents or RVs. Vault toilets, picnic tables, fire rings, and bear-proof boxes are provided. No drinking water is available. Garbage must be packed out. All sites are wheelchair-accessible. Leashed pets are allowed.

Reservations, fees: Reservations are not accepted. There is no camping fee. Open Memorial Day weekend to mid-October.

Directions: From Placerville, drive east on U.S. 50 for 23 miles to Riverton and the junction with Ice House Road/Forest Road 3. Turn north and drive 27 miles (past Union Valley Reservoir) to a fork with Forest Road 30. Turn left toward Gerle Creek Reservoir and the campground is about three miles from the fork, on the right.

Contact: Eldorado National Forest, Pacific Ranger District, 530/644-2349, fax 530-647-5405, www.fs.fed.us.

117 PONDEROSA COVE

🏃 🏊 🛶 �foodRV 🎣 �foodRV ⛺

Scenic rating: 9

at Stumpy Meadows Reservoir

Ponderosa Cove is located just east of the dam at Stumpy Meadows Reservoir, a pretty spot with lake views and good trout fishing in the spring and early summer. This is a beautiful lake, surrounded by forest, with clear water and good fishing. A 5-mph speed limit keeps the place quiet and calm. The elevation is 4,400 feet.

Campsites, facilities: There are 18 sites for tents and small RVs. Fire rings are provided. Drinking water and vault toilets are available. A boat launch and a dump station are nearby.

Reservations, fees: Reservations are not accepted. Sites are $12 per night.

Directions: From Sacramento, drive east on I-80 to the north end of Auburn. Take the Elm Avenue exit and at the first signal turn left onto Elm Avenue. Drive 0.1 mile, turn left on High Street, and continue through the signal where High Street merges with Highway 49. Drive on Highway 49 for about 3.5 miles, turn right over the bridge and drive about 2.5 miles into the town of Cool. Turn left on Georgetown Road/Hwy 193 and drive about 14 miles into Georgetown. At the four-way stop, turn left on Main Street (which becomes Wentworth Springs/Forest Road 1) and drive about 16 miles.

Contact: Eldorado National Forest, Georgetown Ranger District, 530/333-4312, fax 530/333-5522.

118 STUMPY MEADOWS

🏃 🏊 🛶 �foodRV 🎣 🐴 �foodRV ⛺

Scenic rating: 7

on Stumpy Meadows Lake in Eldorado National Forest

This is the camp of choice for visitors to Stumpy Meadows Lake. The first things visitors notice are the huge ponderosa pine trees, noted for their distinctive, mosaic-like bark. The lake is set at 4,400 feet elevation in Eldorado National Forest and covers 320 acres with water that is cold and clear. The lake has both rainbow and brown trout, and in the fall provides good fishing for big browns (they move up into the head of the lake, near where Pilot Creek enters).

Campsites, facilities: There are 40 sites for tents or RVs of any length (no hookups). Two of the sites are double units. Picnic tables and fire grills are provided. Drinking water and vault toilets are available. A boat ramp is nearby. Leashed pets are permitted.

Reservations, fees: Reservations are accepted at 877/444-6777 or www.recreation.gov ($10 reservation fee). Sites are $17 per night, $34 per night for double-unit sites, $5 per night for each additional vehicle. Boat launching is $8 per day. Open May through mid-October, weather permitting.

Directions: From Sacramento on I-80, drive east to the north end of Auburn. Turn left on Elm Avenue and drive about 0.1 mile. Turn left on High Street and drive through the signal that marks the continuation of High Street as Highway 49. Drive 3.5 miles on Highway 49, turn right over the bridge, and drive 2.5 miles into the town of Cool. Turn left on Georgetown Road/Highway 193 and drive 14 miles into Georgetown. At the four-way stop, turn left on Main Street, which becomes Georgetown–Wentworth Springs Road/Forest Road 1. Drive about 18 miles to Stumpy Meadows Lake. Continue about a mile and turn right into Stumpy Meadows campground.

Contact: Eldorado National Forest, Georgetown Ranger District, 530/333-4312, fax 530/333-5522.

119 BLACK OAK GROUP CAMP

Scenic rating: 7

near Stumpy Meadows Lake in Eldorado National Forest

This group camp is set directly adjacent to Stumpy Meadows Campground. (See the *Stumpy Meadows* listing in this chapter for more information.) The boat ramp for the lake is just south of the Mark Edson Dam, near the picnic area. The elevation is 4,400 feet.

Campsites, facilities: There are three group sites for tents and one group site for RVs of any length (no hookups) that can accommodate 25–75 people each. Picnic tables and fire grills are provided. Drinking water and vault toilets are available. A boat ramp is nearby. Leashed pets are permitted.

Reservations, fees: Reservations are accepted at 877/444-6777 or www.recreation.gov ($10 reservation fee). Sites are $50–100 per night. Boat launching is $8 per day. Open mid-May through mid-September, weather permitting.

Directions: From Sacramento on I-80, drive east to the north end of Auburn. Turn left on Elm Avenue and drive about 0.1 mile. Turn left on High Street and drive through the signal that marks the continuation of High Street as Highway 49. Drive 3.5 miles on Highway 49, turn right over the bridge, and drive 2.5 miles into the town of Cool. Turn left on Georgetown Road/Highway 193 and drive 14 miles into Georgetown. At the four-way stop, turn left on Main Street, which becomes Georgetown–Wentworth Springs Road/Forest Road 1. Drive about 18 miles to Stumpy Meadows Lake, and then continue for two miles to the north shore of the lake and the campground entrance road on the right.

Contact: Eldorado National Forest, Georgetown Ranger District, 530/333-4312, fax 530/333-5522.

120 GERLE CREEK

Scenic rating: 7

on Gerle Creek Reservoir in Eldorado National Forest

This is a small, pretty, but limited spot set along the northern shore of little Gerle Creek Reservoir at 5,231 feet elevation. The lake is ideal for canoes or other small boats because no motors are permitted and no boat ramp is available. That makes for quiet water. It is set in the Gerle Creek Canyon, which feeds into the South Fork Rubicon River. No trout plants are made at this lake, and fishing can be correspondingly poor. A wild brown trout population lives here, though. A network of Forest Service roads to the north can provide great exploring. A map of Eldorado National Forest is a must.

Campsites, facilities: There are 50 sites for tents or RVs up to 40 feet (no hookups). Picnic tables and fire grills are provided. Drinking water and vault toilets are available. Wheelchair-accessible trails and fishing pier are available nearby. Leashed pets are permitted.

Reservations, fees: Reservations are accepted at 877/444-6777 or www.recreation.gov ($10 reservation fee). Sites are $20 per night, $6 per night for each additional vehicle. Open mid-May through mid-October, weather permitting.

Directions: From Placerville, drive east on U.S. 50 for 23 miles to Riverton and the junction with Ice House Road/Forest Road 3. Turn north and drive 27 miles (past Union Valley Reservoir) to a fork with Forest Road 30. Turn left, drive two miles, bear left on the campground entrance road, and drive a mile to the campground.

Contact: Eldorado National Forest, Pacific Ranger District, 530/644-2349, fax 530/647-5405.

121 SOUTH FORK GROUP CAMP
🏞🛶🎣🏕

Scenic rating: 8

on the South Fork of the Rubicon River in Eldorado National Forest

This primitive national forest camp sits alongside the South Fork Rubicon River, just over a mile downstream from the outlet at Gerle Creek Reservoir. Trout fishing is fair, the water tastes extremely sweet (always pump filter with a water purifier), and there are several side trips available. These include Loon Lake (eight miles to the northeast), Gerle Creek Reservoir (to the nearby north), and Union Valley Reservoir (to the nearby south). The elevation is 5,200 feet.

Campsites, facilities: There is a group camp for tents only that can accommodate up to 125 people. Picnic tables and fire grills are provided. Vault toilets are available. No drinking water is available. Garbage must be packed out. Leashed pets are permitted.

Reservations, fees: Reservations are required at 877/444-6777 or www.recreation.gov ($10 reservation fee). The camp is $100 per night. Open late May through early September.

Directions: From Placerville, drive east on U.S. 50 for 23 miles to Riverton and the junction with Ice House Road/Forest Road 3. Turn north and drive about 23 miles to the junction with Forest Road 13N28 (3.5 miles past Union Valley Reservoir). Bear left on Forest Road 13N28 and drive two miles to the campground entrance on the right.

Contact: Eldorado National Forest, Pacific Ranger District, 530/644-2349, fax 530/647-5405.

122 RED FIR GROUP CAMP
🏊🛶🎣🐕♿🏕

Scenic rating: 6

on Loon Lake in Eldorado National Forest

This is a pretty, wooded camp, ideal for medium-sized groups. It is across the road from the 600-acre lake, offering a secluded, quiet spot. Lake access is a short hike away. All water sports are allowed on Loon Lake. (See the *Loon Lake* and *Northshore* listings in this chapter for more information.) The elevation is 6,500 feet.

Campsites, facilities: This tents-only group site can accommodate up to 25 people. Drinking water, vault toilets, fire rings, and grills are available. Some facilities are wheelchair-accessible. Leashed pets are permitted.

Reservations, fees: Reservations are required

at 877/444-6777 or www.recreation.gov ($10 reservation fee). The camp is $40 per night. Open mid-June through mid-October, weather permitting.

Directions: From Placerville, drive east on U.S. 50 for 23 miles to Riverton and the junction with Ice House Road/Forest Road 3. Turn left and drive 34 miles to a fork at the foot of Loon Lake. Turn left and drive three miles to the campground (just beyond the Loon Lake Northshore camp).

Contact: Eldorado National Forest, Pacific Ranger District, 530/644-2349, fax 530/644-5405.

123 WENTWORTH SPRINGS FOUR-WHEEL DRIVE
🏃🚣🛶🏕️⛺

Scenic rating: 7

near Loon Lake in Eldorado National Forest

There is one reason people come here: to set up a base camp for an OHV adventure, whether they are the owners of four-wheel drives, all-terrain vehicles, or dirt bikes. A network of roads leads from this camp, passable only by these vehicles; these roads would flat-out destroy your average car. The camp is set deep in Eldorado National Forest, at 6,200 feet elevation. While the north end of Loon Lake is a mile to the east, the road there is extremely rough (perfect, right?). The road is gated along the lake, preventing access to this camp for those who drive directly to Loon Lake.

Campsites, facilities: There are eight sites for tents only. Picnic tables and fire grills are provided. Vault toilets are available. No drinking water is available. Garbage must be packed out. Leashed pets are permitted.

Reservations, fees: Reservations are not accepted. There is no fee for camping. Open June through October, weather permitting.

Directions: From Placerville, drive east on U.S. 50 for 23 miles to Riverton and the junction with Ice House Road/Forest Road 3. Turn left and drive 30 miles to the junction with Forest Road 30. Bear left and drive 3.5 miles to Forest Road 33. Turn right and drive seven miles to the campground on the left side of the road. (The access road is suitable for four-wheel-drive vehicles and off-highway motorcycles only.)

Contact: Eldorado National Forest, Pacific Ranger District, 530/644-2349, fax 530/644-5405.

124 NORTHSHORE
🏃🚶🏊🚣🛶🐕♿🚐⛺

Scenic rating: 9

on Loon Lake in Eldorado National Forest

The waterfront sites are in an extremely pretty setting on the northwestern shore of Loon Lake. There are few facilities, though, and no boat ramp; the boat ramp is near the Loon Lake campground and picnic area at the south end of the lake. (For more information, see the *Loon Lake* and *Pleasant Hike-In/Boat-In* listings.)

Campsites, facilities: There are 15 sites for tents or RVs up to 35 feet (no hookups). Picnic tables and fire grills are provided. Vault toilets are available. There is no drinking water. Some facilities are wheelchair-accessible. Leashed pets are permitted.

Reservations, fees: Reservations are not accepted. Sites are $10 per night, $6 per night for each additional vehicle. Open June through September, weather permitting.

Directions: From Placerville, drive east on U.S. 50 for 23 miles to Riverton and the junction with Ice House Road/Forest Road 3. Turn left and drive 34 miles to a fork at the foot of Loon Lake. Turn left and drive three miles to the campground.

Contact: Eldorado National Forest, Pacific Ranger District, 530/644-2349, fax 530/644-5405.

125 LOON LAKE

🚶 🏊 🛶 ⛵ 🐎 ♿ 🚐 ⛺

Scenic rating: 9

in Eldorado National Forest

Loon Lake is set near the Sierra crest at 6,400 feet, covering 600 acres with depths up to 130 feet. This is the lake's primary campground, and it is easy to see why, with a picnic area, beach (includes a small unit for changing clothes), and boat ramp adjacent to the camp. The lake provides good trout fishing, and the lake is stocked on a regular basis once the access road is clear of snow. Afternoon winds drive anglers off the lake but are cheered by sailboarders. An excellent trail is also available here, with the hike routed along the lake's eastern shore to Pleasant Hike-In/Boat-In, where there's a trailhead for the Desolation Wilderness.

Campsites, facilities: There are 53 sites for tents or RVs up to 40 feet, nine equestrian sites, and one group equestrian site for tents or RVs up to 40 feet that can accommodate up to 25 people. No hookups. Picnic tables and fire grills are provided. Drinking water and vault toilets are available. Tie lines are available for horses. A boat ramp and swimming beach are nearby. A dump station is two miles away. Some facilities are wheelchair-accessible. Leashed pets are permitted.

Reservations, fees: Reservations are accepted at 877/444-6777 or www.recreation.gov ($10 reservation fee). Sites are $20 per night, $40 per night for a double site, $6 per night for each additional vehicle. Open June through mid-October, weather permitting.

Directions: From Placerville, drive east on U.S. 50 for 23 miles to Riverton and the junction with Ice House Road/Forest Road 3. Turn left and drive 34 miles to a fork at the foot of Loon Lake. Turn right and drive one mile to the Loon Lake Picnic Area or boat ramp.

Contact: Eldorado National Forest, Pacific Ranger District, 530/644-2349, fax 530/644-5405.

126 PLEASANT HIKE-IN/ BOAT-IN

🚶 🏊 🛶 ⛵ 🐎 ⛺

Scenic rating: 9

on Loon Lake in Eldorado National Forest

This premium Sierra camp, hike-in or boat-in only, is set on the remote northeast shore of Loon Lake at 6,378 feet elevation. In many ways this makes for a perfect short vacation. A trail is routed east from the camp for four miles past Buck Island Lake (6,436 feet) and Rockbound Lake (6,529 feet), set just inside the northern border of the Desolation Wilderness. When the trail is clear of snow, this makes for a fantastic day hike; a wilderness permit is required if staying overnight inside the wilderness boundary.

Campsites, facilities: There are 10 boat-in or hike-in tent sites. Picnic tables and fire rings are provided. No drinking water or toilets are available. Garbage must be packed out. The camp is accessible by boat or trail only. Leashed pets are permitted.

Reservations, fees: Reservations are not accepted. There is no fee for camping. Open mid-June to mid-October, weather permitting.

Directions: From Placerville, drive east on U.S. 50 for 23 miles to Riverton and the junction with Ice House Road/Forest Road 3. Turn left and drive 34 miles to a fork at the foot of Loon Lake. Turn right and drive a mile to the Loon Lake Picnic Area or boat ramp. Either hike or boat 2.5 miles to the campground on the northeast shore of the lake.

Contact: Eldorado National Forest, Pacific Ranger District, 530/644-2349, fax 530/644-5405.

127 BIG SILVER GROUP CAMP

🚶 🚵 🏊 ⛴ 🛶 🐴 ♿ 🚐 ⛺

Scenic rating: 7

on Big Silver Creek in Eldorado National Forest

This camp was built along the Union Valley bike trail, less than a mile from Union Valley Reservoir. The paved bike trail stretches for miles both north and south of the campground and is wheelchair-accessible. It's a classic Sierra forest setting, with plenty of ponderosa pine on the north side of Big Silver Creek.

Campsites, facilities: There is one group site for tents or RVs up to 50 feet (no hookups) that can accommodate up to 50 people. Picnic tables and fire grills are provided. Vault toilets are available. No drinking water is available. There is also a group kitchen area with pedestal grills. Some facilities are wheelchair-accessible. Leashed pets are permitted.

Reservations, fees: Reservations are required at 877/444-6777 or www.recreation.gov ($10 reservation fee). The camp is $50 per night. Open late May through mid-October, weather permitting.

Directions: From Placerville, drive east on U.S. 50 for 23 miles to Riverton and the junction with Ice House Road/Forest Road 3. Turn left (north) and drive about 16 miles to the campground.

Contact: Eldorado National Forest, Pacific Ranger District, 530/644-2349, fax 530/647-5405.

128 WEST POINT

🚶 🏊 ⛴ 🛶 🏊 ♿ 🚐 ⛺

Scenic rating: 9

at Union Valley Reservoir in Eldorado National Forest

West Point is a pretty, primitive campground on the northwest shore of little Union Valley Reservoir. This is a pretty spot in the Crystal Basin that sometimes gets overlooked in the shadow of Loon Lake and Ice House Reservoir. But the camping, low-speed boating, and trout fishing can be excellent. Some surprise giant mackinaw trout and brown trout can provide a fish of a lifetime when the lake first opens in late spring. The elevation is 4,875 feet.

Campsites, facilities: There are eight sites for tents or RVs. Vault toilet and a boat launch are available. Fire rings are provided, but there are no grills or picnic tables. Drinking water is not available. Some sites are wheelchair-accessible.

Reservations, fees: Reservations are not accepted. There is no camping fee.

Directions: From Placerville, drive east on Highway 50 for 23 miles to Riverton and the junction with Ice House Road/Forest Road 3. Turn north on Ice House Road, and drive 7 miles to Peavine Ridge Road. Turn left on Peavine Ridge Road and drive east for 3 miles to Bryant Springs Road. Turn right on Bryant Springs Road and drive north 5 miles to just past West Point Boat Ramp on the right.

Contact: Eldorado National Forest, Pacific Ranger District, 530/644-2349, fax 530/647-5405, www.fs.fed.us.

129 WOLF CREEK AND WOLF CREEK GROUP

🚶 🏊 🛶 ⛴ 🐴 ♿ 🚐 ⛺

Scenic rating: 9

on Union Valley Reservoir in Eldorado National Forest

Wolf Creek Camp is on the north shore of Union Valley Reservoir. Listen up? Notice that it's quieter? Yep. That's because there are not as many water-skiers in the vicinity. Why? The nearest boat ramp is three miles away. The view of the Crystal Range from the campground is drop-dead gorgeous. The elevation is 4,900 feet.

Campsites, facilities: There are 42 sites for tents or RVs up to 40 feet, and three group sites for tents or RVs up to 40 feet that can accommodate up to 50 people each. No hook-ups. Picnic tables and fire grills are provided. Drinking water and vault toilets are available. Some facilities are wheelchair-accessible. A boat ramp is three miles away at the camp-ground at Yellowjacket. Leashed pets are permitted.

Reservations, fees: Reservations are accepted for individual sites and required for group sites at 877/444-6777 or www.recreation.gov ($10 reservation fee). Sites are $20 per night for a single site, $40 per night for a double site, $5 per night for each additional vehicle. Group sites are $100–150 per night. Open mid-May through mid-September, weather permitting.

Directions: From Placerville, drive east on U.S. 50 for 23 miles to Riverton and the junction with Ice House Road/Forest Road 3. Turn left (north) and drive 19 miles to Forest Road 12N78/Union Valley Road (at the head of Union Valley Reservoir). Turn left (west) and drive two miles to the campground.

Contact: Eldorado National Forest, Pa-cific Ranger District, 530/644-2349, fax 530/647-5405.

130 CAMINO COVE

Scenic rating: 10

on Union Valley Reservoir in Eldorado National Forest

Camino Cove Camp is the nicest spot at Union Valley Reservoir, a slam dunk. It is set at the north end of the lake on a peninsula, absolutely beautiful, a tree-covered landscape and yet with sweeping views of the Crystal Basin. The nearest boat ramp is 1.5 miles to the west at West Point. If this camp is full, there is a small camp at West Point, with just eight sites. The elevation is 4,900 feet.

Campsites, facilities: There are 32 sites for tents or RVs up to 30 feet (no hookups). Fire rings are provided. Vault toilets are available. No

drinking water is available. Garbage must be packed out. A swimming beach is nearby and a boat ramp is 1.5 miles away at the campground at West Point. Some facilities are wheelchair-accessible. Leashed pets are permitted.

Reservations, fees: Reservations are not ac-cepted. There is no fee for camping. Open early May through October, weather permitting.

Directions: From Placerville, drive east on U.S. 50 for 23 miles to Riverton and the junction with Ice House Road/Forest Road 3. Turn north on Ice House Road and drive seven miles to Peavine Ridge Road. Turn left and drive three miles to Bryant Springs Road. Turn right and drive five miles north past the West Point boat ramp, and continue 1.5 miles east to the campground entrance on the right.

Contact: Eldorado National Forest, Pa-cific Ranger District, 530/644-2349, fax 530/647-5405.

131 YELLOWJACKET

Scenic rating: 8

on Union Valley Reservoir in Eldorado National Forest

The camp is set at 4,900 feet elevation on the north shore of gorgeous Union Valley Res-ervoir. A boat launch adjacent to the camp makes this an ideal destination for trout-angling campers with boats. Union Valley Reservoir, a popular weekend destination for campers from the Central Valley, is stocked with brook trout and rainbow trout by the Department of Fish and Game.

Campsites, facilities: There are 40 sites for tents or RVs up to 30 feet (no hookups). Picnic tables and fire rings are provided. Drinking water and vault toilets are available. A boat ramp and dump station are nearby. Leashed pets are permitted.

Reservations, fees: Reservations are accepted at 877/444-6777 or www.recreation.gov ($10 reservation fee). Sites are $20 per night, $6 per night for each additional vehicle. Open mid-May through mid-September, weather permitting.

Directions: From Placerville, drive east on U.S. 50 for 23 miles to Riverton and the junction with Ice House Road/Forest Road 3. Turn left (north) and drive 19 miles to Forest Road 12N78/Union Valley Road (at the head of Union Valley Reservoir). Turn left (west) and drive one mile to Forest Road 12N33. Turn left (south) and drive 0.5 mile to the campground.

Contact: Eldorado National Forest, Pacific Ranger District, 530/644-2349, fax 530/647-5405.

132 WENCH CREEK AND WENCH CREEK GROUP

Scenic rating: 7

on Union Valley Reservoir in Eldorado National Forest

Wench Creek is on the northeast shore of Union Valley Reservoir. (For more information, see the *Jones Fork* and *Peninsula Recreation Area* listings in this chapter.) The elevation is 4,900 feet.

Campsites, facilities: There are 100 sites for tents or RVs up to 25 feet (no hookups), and two group tent sites for up to 50 people each. Picnic tables and fire grills are provided. Drinking water and vault toilets are available. A boat ramp is three miles away at the Yellowjacket campground. Leashed pets are permitted.

Reservations, fees: Reservations are not accepted for individual sites, but are accepted for group sites at 877/444-6777 or www.recreation.gov ($10 reservation fee). Sites are $20 per night, $6 per night for each additional vehicle. The group sites are $120 per night. Open mid-May through September.

Directions: From Placerville, drive east on U.S. 50 for 23 miles to Riverton and the junction with Ice House Road/Forest Road 3. Turn left and drive 15 miles to the campground

entrance road (four miles past the turnoff for Sunset Camp). Turn left and drive a mile to the campground at the end of the road.

Contact: Eldorado National Forest, Pacific Ranger District, 530/644-2349, fax 530/647-5405.

133 AZALEA COVE HIKE-IN/BOAT-IN

Scenic rating: 7

on Union Valley Reservoir in Eldorado National Forest

Union Valley Reservoir, at 4,900 feet elevation, has 4.5 miles of bike trail on its shores, in addition to boating and fishing activities. The distance to the campsite is less than a half-mile by trail and approximately one mile by boat. (For additional information, see the *Wench Creek* and *Peninsula Recreation Area* listings in this chapter.)

Campsites, facilities: There are 10 sites for tents only. Picnic tables and fire rings are provided. Vault toilets are available. No drinking water is available. Garbage must be packed out. Some facilities are wheelchair-accessible. Leashed pets are permitted.

Reservations, fees: Reservations are not accepted. There is no fee for camping. Open mid-June through mid-October, weather permitting.

Directions: From Placerville, drive east on U.S. 50 for 23 miles to Riverton and the junction with Ice House Road/Forest Road 3. Turn left (north) and drive about 16 miles to the Big Silver Group Campground parking lot. Park and then hike or cycle approximately 0.5 mile to Azalea Cove Campground. To reach Azalea Cove Campground by boat, continue for three miles on Ice House Road to Forest Road 12N78. Turn left (west) and drive one mile to Forest Road 12N33. Turn left (south) and drive 0.5 mile to Yellowjacket Campground. Park and boat approximately one mile to Azalea Cove Campground.

Contact: Eldorado National Forest, Pacific Ranger District, 530/644-2349, fax 530/647-5405.

134 PENINSULA RECREATION AREA

Scenic rating: 8

on Union Valley Reservoir in Eldorado National Forest

The two campgrounds here, Sunset and Fashoda, are the prettiest of all the camps at Union Valley Reservoir, set at the eastern tip of the peninsula that juts into the lake at the mouth of Jones Fork. A nearby boat ramp (you'll see it on the left on the way in) is a big plus, along with a picnic area and beach. All water sports are allowed. The lake has decent trout fishing, with brook trout, brown trout, rainbow trout, Mackinaw, kokanee salmon, and smallmouth bass. The place is gorgeous, set at 4,900 feet elevation in the Sierra Nevada.

Campsites, facilities: There are 131 sites for tents or RVs up to 50 feet (no hookups) at Sunset Camp and 30 walk-in tent sites at Fashoda Camp. Picnic tables, fire rings, and fire grills are provided. Drinking water, coin showers (at Fashoda), vault toilets, boat ramp, and a dump station are available. Some facilities are wheelchair-accessible. Leashed pets are permitted.

Reservations, fees: Reservations are accepted at 877/444-6777 or www.recreation.gov ($10 reservation fee). Sites are $20 per night, $40 per night for a double site, $6 per night for each additional vehicle. Open late May through late September, weather permitting.

Directions: From Placerville, drive east on U.S. 50 for 23 miles to Riverton and the junction with Ice House Road/Forest Road 3. Turn left and drive 14 miles to the campground entrance road (a mile past the turnoff for Jones Fork Camp). Turn left and drive 1.5 miles to the campground at the end of the road.

Contact: Eldorado National Forest, Pacific Ranger District, 530/644-2349, fax 530/647-5405.

135 LONE ROCK

Scenic rating: 9

near Union Valley Reservoir in Eldorado National Forest

This is a hike-in, bike-in, or boat-in spot at Union Valley Reservoir. It is little known, but once you claim it, it will always be on your list. Lake views and quiet tent sites in a primitive do-it-yourself setting makes this a winner for those who know of it. The elevation is 4,800 feet.

Campsites, facilities: There are five sites for tents only that can only be accessed by bike, trail, or boat. Vault toilets are available. Picnic tables, fire rings, and a bike rack are provided. There is no drinking water.

Reservations, fees: Reservations are not accepted. There is no camping fee.

Directions: From Placerville, drive east on Highway 50 for 23 miles to Riverton and the junction with Ice House Road/Forest Road 3. If hiking or biking, turn left and drive 14 miles to the Jones Fork campground entrance and begin there. For boat-in camping, drive 14 miles to the Sunset Camp entrance to launch from there.

Contact: Eldorado National Forest, Pacific Ranger District, 530/644-2349, fax 530-647-5405, www.fs.fed.us.

136 JONES FORK

Scenic rating: 7

on Union Valley Reservoir in Eldorado National Forest

The Crystal Basin Recreation Area is the most popular backcountry region for campers from the Sacramento area, and Union

Valley Reservoir is the centerpiece. The area gets its name from the prominent granite Sierra ridge, which looks like crystal when it is covered with frozen snow. This is a big lake, set at 4,900 feet elevation, with numerous lakeside campgrounds and three boat ramps providing access. This is the first camp you will arrive at, set at the mouth of the Jones Fork Cove.

Campsites, facilities: There are 10 sites for tents or RVs up to 25 feet (no hookups). Picnic tables and fire rings are provided. Vault toilets are available. No drinking water is available. Leashed pets are permitted.

Reservations, fees: Reservations are not accepted. Sites are $10 per night, $5 per night for each additional vehicle. Open June through October.

Directions: From Placerville, drive east on U.S. 50 for 23 miles to Riverton and the junction with Ice House Road/Forest Road 3. Turn left and drive 14 miles to the campground entrance road on the left (at the south end of Union Valley Reservoir). Turn left and drive 0.5 mile to the campground.

Contact: Eldorado National Forest, Pacific Ranger District, 530/644-2349, fax 530/647-5405.

137 SILVER CREEK GROUP

Scenic rating: 5

near Ice House Reservoir in Eldorado National Forest

Silver Creek is a pretty spot at 5,200 feet elevation. Ice House is only two miles north, and Union Valley Reservoir is four miles north. Either bring your own drinking water or bring a water filtration pump for stream water. Note: RVs and trailers are not allowed.

Campsites, facilities: There is one group tent site that can accommodate up to 40 people. Picnic tables and fire rings are provided. Vault

toilets are available. No drinking water is available. Leashed pets are permitted.

Reservations, fees: Reservations are required at 877/444-6777 or www.recreation.gov ($10 reservation fee). The site is $100 per night. Open June through October, weather permitting.

Directions: From Placerville, drive east on U.S. 50 for 23 miles to Riverton and the junction with Ice House Road/Forest Road 3. Turn left and drive about nine miles to the campground entrance road on the left (if you reach the junction with Forest Road 3, you have gone 0.25 mile too far). Turn left and drive 0.25 mile to the campground.

Contact: Eldorado National Forest, Pacific Ranger District, 530/644-2349, fax 530/647-5405.

138 ICE HOUSE UPPER AND LOWER

Scenic rating: 8

on Ice House Reservoir in Eldorado National Forest

Along with Loon Lake and Union Valley Reservoir, Ice House Reservoir is a feature destination in the Crystal Basin Recreation Area. Ice House gets most of the anglers and Union Valley gets most of the campers. All water sports are allowed at Ice House, though. The camp is set on the lake's northwestern shore, at 5,500 feet elevation, just up from the dam and adjacent to the lake's boat ramp. The lake, created by a dam on South Fork Silver Creek, covers 650 acres with the deepest spot about 130 feet deep. It is stocked with rainbow trout, brook trout, and brown trout. A 2.5-mile bike trail connects Ice House to Northwind and Strawberry Point campgrounds.

Campsites, facilities: There are 83 sites for tents or RVs up to 30 feet (no hookups). Picnic tables and fire grills are provided. Drinking water, vault toilets, boat ramp, and a dump station are available. Some facilities are wheelchair-accessible. Leashed pets are permitted.

Reservations, fees: Reservations are accepted at 877/444-6777 or www.recreation.gov ($10 reservation fee). Sites are $20 per night, $40 per night for a double site, $6 per night for each additional vehicle. Open late May through mid-October, weather permitting.

Directions: From Placerville, drive east on U.S. 50 for 23 miles to Riverton and the junction with Ice House Road/Forest Road 3. Turn left (north) and drive 11 miles to Forest Road 32/Ice House/Wrights Tie Road. Turn right (east) and drive 1.5 miles to the campground access road on the right.

Contact: Eldorado National Forest, Pacific Ranger District, 530/644-2349, fax 530/647-5405.

139 NORTHWIND

Scenic rating: 7

on Ice House Reservoir in Eldorado National Forest

This camp sits on the north shore of Ice House Reservoir. It is slightly above the reservoir, offering prime views. A 2.5-mile bike trail connects Northwind with Ice House and Strawberry Point campgrounds. (See the *Ice House* listing for more information.)

Campsites, facilities: There are nine sites for tents or RVs up to 40 feet (no hookups). Picnic tables and fire grills are provided. Vault toilets are available. No drinking water is available. Some facilities are wheelchair-accessible. Leashed pets are permitted.

Reservations, fees: Reservations are not accepted. Sites are $10 per night, $5 per night for each additional vehicle. Open May through mid-October, weather permitting.

Directions: From Placerville, drive east on U.S. 50 for 23 miles to Riverton and the junction with Ice House Road/Forest Road 3.

Turn left (north) and drive 11 miles to Forest Road 32/Ice House/Wrights Tie Road. Turn right (east) and drive three miles (two miles past the boat ramp) to the campground access road on the right.

Contact: Eldorado National Forest, Pacific Ranger District, 530/644-2349, fax 530/647-5405.

140 STRAWBERRY POINT

Scenic rating: 7

on Ice House Reservoir in Eldorado National Forest

This camp is set on the north shore of Ice House Reservoir, at 5,400 feet elevation. A 2.5-mile bike trail connects Strawberry Point with Northwind and Ice House campgrounds. (For more information, see the *Ice House* listing in this chapter.)

Campsites, facilities: There are 10 sites for tents or RVs up to 40 feet (no hookups). Picnic tables and fire grills are provided. Vault toilets are available. No drinking water is available. Some facilities are wheelchair-accessible. Leashed pets are permitted.

Reservations, fees: Reservations are not accepted. Sites are $10 per night, $5 per night for each additional vehicle. Open May through December, weather permitting.

Directions: From Placerville, drive east on U.S. 50 for 23 miles to Riverton and the junction with Ice House Road/Forest Road 3. Turn left (north) and drive 11 miles to Forest Road 32/Ice House/Wrights Tie Road. Turn right (east) and drive three miles (three miles past the boat ramp) to the campground access road on the road.

Contact: Eldorado National Forest, Pacific Ranger District, 530/644-2349, fax 530/647-5405.

CAMPING

141 WRIGHTS LAKE AND EQUESTRIAN

🏃 🏊 🛶 ⚓ 🏇 ♿ 🚐 ⛺

Scenic rating: 9

in Eldorado National Forest

This high mountain lake (7,000 feet) has shoreline picnicking and good fishing and hiking. There is no boat ramp, and the rules do not permit motors, so it is ideal for canoes, rafts, prams, and people who like quiet. Swimming is allowed. Fishing is fair for both rainbow trout and brown trout. It is a classic alpine lake, though small (65 acres), with a trailhead for the Desolation Wilderness at its north end. From here it is only a three-mile hike to the beautiful Twin Lakes and Island Lake, set on the western flank of Mount Price (9,975 feet).

Campsites, facilities: There are 67 sites for tents or RVs up to 50 feet (no hookups) and 15 sites at the equestrian camp. Picnic tables and fire grills are provided. Drinking water and vault toilets are available. Some facilities are wheelchair-accessible, including a boat dock. Leashed pets are permitted.

Reservations, fees: Reservations are accepted and are required for some sites in July and August at 877/444-6777 or www.recreation.gov ($10 reservation fee). Sites are $20 per night, $40 per night for a double site, $5 per night for each additional vehicle. Open late June through mid-October, weather permitting.

Directions: From Placerville, drive east on U.S. 50 for 23 miles to Riverton and the junction with Ice House Road/Forest Road 3. Turn left (north) and drive 11 miles to Forest Road 32/Ice House/Wrights Tie Road. Turn right (east) and drive nine miles to Forest Road 4/Wrights Lake Road. Turn left (north) and drive two miles to the campground on the right side of the road.

Contact: Eldorado National Forest, Pacific Ranger District, 530/644-2349, fax 530/644-5405.

142 D. L. BLISS STATE PARK

🏃 🚲 🏊 ⚓ 🏇 ♿ 🚐 ⛺

Scenic rating: 10

on Lake Tahoe

BEST ☾

D. L. Bliss State Park is set on one of Lake Tahoe's most beautiful stretches of shoreline, from Emerald Point at the mouth of Emerald Bay northward to Rubicon Point, spanning about three miles. The camp is at the north end of the park, the sites nestled amid pine trees, with 80 percent of the campsites within 0.5–1 mile of the beach. The park is named for a pioneering lumberman, railroad owner, and banker of the region, whose family donated this 744-acre parcel to California in 1929. There are two great easy hiking trails. Rubicon Trail is one of Tahoe's most popular easy hikes, a meandering path just above the southwest shore of Lake Tahoe, wandering through pine, cedar, and fir, with breaks for fantastic panoramas of the lake, as well as spots where you can see nearly 100 feet into the lake. Don't be surprised if you are joined by a chipmunk circus, many begging, sitting upright, hoping for their nut for the day. While this trail is beautiful and solitary at dawn, by noon it can be crowded with hikers and chipmunks alike. Another trail, a great hike for youngsters, is Balancing Rock Trail, just a 0.5-mile romp, where after about 40 yards you arrive at this 130-ton, oblong granite boulder that is set on a tiny perch, and the whole thing seems to defy gravity. Some day it has to fall, right? Not yet. Rubicon Trail runs all the way past Emerald Point to Emerald Bay.

Campsites, facilities: There are 165 sites for tents or RVs up to 18 feet (no hookups) and trailers up to 15 feet, one hike-in/bike-in site, and a group site for up to 50 people. Picnic tables, fire grills, and food lockers are provided. Restrooms with coin showers and flush toilets are available. All water must sometimes be pump-filtered or boiled before use, depending on current water conditions. Some facilities are wheelchair-accessible. Leashed pets are permitted at campsites only.

Reservations, fees: Reservations are accepted at 800/444-PARK (800/444-7275) or www. reserveamerica.com ($7.50 reservation fee). Sites are $20–35 per night, $6 per night for each additional vehicle, $111 per night for group site, $6 per night for hike-in/bike-in site. Open late May through late September, weather permitting.

Directions: In South Lake Tahoe at the junction of Highway 89 and U.S. 50, turn north on Highway 89 and drive 10.5 miles to the state park turnoff on the right side of the road. Turn right (east) and drive to the park entrance. (If arriving from the north, drive from Tahoe City south on Highway 89 for 17 miles to the park entrance road.)

Contact: D. L. Bliss State Park, 530/525-7277; Sierra District, 530/525-7232, www.parks. ca.gov.

143 EMERALD BAY STATE PARK AND BOAT-IN

🚶 🚴 🏊 ⛵ 🛶 🎣 🐕 🚐 ⛺

Scenic rating: 10

on Lake Tahoe

BEST (

Emerald Bay is a place of rare and divine beauty, one of the most striking and popular state parks on the planet. With its deep cobalt-blue waters, awesome surrounding ridgelines, glimpses of Lake Tahoe out the mouth of the bay, and even a little island, there may be no place more perfect to run a boat or kayak.

There are boat-in camps on the northern side of Emerald Bay, set in pine forest with water views. Even when Tahoe is packed, there are times when you can paddle right up and find a site—though reservations at one of the 22 boat-in sites makes for a sure thing, of course. Drive-in campsites are available near Eagle Point at the mouth of Emerald Bay. Sites are also accessible via the Rubicon Trail from D. L. Bliss State Park.

Emerald Bay is a designated underwater park featuring Fanette Island, Tahoe's only island, and Vikingsholm, one of the greatest examples of Scandinavian architecture in North America. Vikingsholm is located along the shore about a mile's hike from the campground and tours are very popular. The park also has several short hiking trails.

Campsites, facilities: There are 100 sites for tents or RVs up to 21 feet (no hookups) and trailers up to 18 feet and 22 boat-in sites. Picnic tables and fire grills are provided. Drinking water and restrooms with flush toilets and coin showers are available. At boat-in sites, drinking water and vault toilets are available. Leashed pets are permitted in the campground and on asphalt, but not on trails.

Reservations, fees: Reservations are accepted at 800/444-PARK (800/444-7275) or www. reserveamerica.com ($7.50 reservation fee). Sites are $20–25 per night, $6 per night for each additional vehicle, $11–15 per night for boat-in sites. Open early June through mid-September, weather permitting.

Directions: In South Lake Tahoe at the junction of Highway 89 and U.S. 50, turn north on Highway 89 and drive 6.5 miles to the state park entrance turnoff on the right side of the road.

Contact: Emerald Bay State Park, 530/541-3030, or D. L. Bliss State Park, 530/525-7277, www.parks.ca.gov.

144 HISTORIC CAMP RICHARDSON RESORT

🚴 🏊 ⛵ 🚐 🎿 🚶 ♿ 🚐 ⛺

Scenic rating: 7

on Lake Tahoe

BEST (

Camp Richardson Resort is within minutes of boating, biking, gambling, and, in the winter, skiing and snowboarding. It's a take-your-pick deal. With cabins, restaurant, and live music (often nightly in summer) also on the property, this is a place that offers one big package. The campsites are set in the woods, not on the lake itself. From here you can gain access to an excellent bike route that runs for three miles, then loops around by the lake for another three miles, most of it flat and easy, all of it beautiful. Expect company. The elevation is 6,300 feet.

Campsites, facilities: There are 223 sites for tents, and 112 sites with full or partial hookups (30 amps) for RVs up to 35 feet, including two pull-through sites. Cabins, duplex units, inn rooms, and hotel rooms are also available. Picnic tables and fire pits are provided. Restrooms with showers and flush toilets, drinking water, dump station, group facilities, and playground are available. A full-service marina, boat ramp, boat rentals, swimming beach, bike rentals, general store, restaurant, ice cream parlor, and propane gas are nearby. Some facilities are wheelchair-accessible.

Reservations, fees: Reservations are accepted at 800/544-1801. Sites are $30–38 per night, $5 per night for each additional vehicle. Some credit cards accepted. Open June through October, with lodging available year-round.

Directions: In South Lake Tahoe at the junction of Highway 89 and U.S. 50, turn north on Highway 89 and drive 2.5 miles to the resort on the right side of the road.

Contact: Historic Camp Richardson Resort, 530/541-1801, www.camprichardson.com.

145 CAMP SHELLY

Scenic rating: 7

near Lake Tahoe in the Lake Tahoe Basin

This campground is set near South Lake Tahoe within close range of an outstanding bicycle trail. The camp is set in the woods, with campfire programs available on Saturday night in summer. Nearby to the west is the drive to Inspiration Point and the incredible lookout of Emerald Bay, as well as the parking area for the short hike to Eagle Falls. Nearby

to the east are Fallen Leaf Lake and the south shore of Lake Tahoe.

Campsites, facilities: There are 26 sites for tents or RVs up to 24 feet long and 10.5 feet high (no hookups). Picnic tables and fire grills are provided. Drinking water, restrooms with free showers and flush toilets, horseshoes, ping-pong, volleyball, and basketball are available. Some facilities are wheelchair-accessible. Groceries, propane, and a boat ramp are available nearby at Camp Richardson. Leashed pets are permitted.

Reservations, fees: Reservations can be made in person, 9 A.M.–4 P.M. Monday–Friday, at the Robert Livermore Community Center, 4444 East Avenue, Livermore, CA 94550. Reservations can also be made by mail, fax, or at the campground office, which is intermittently staffed during the season. A reservation form can be downloaded from the website. Sites are $30 per night, ($25 for Livermore residents), $5 per night for each additional vehicle. Open mid-June through Labor Day weekend.

Directions: In South Lake Tahoe at the junction of U.S. 50 and Highway 89, turn north on Highway 89, drive 2.5 miles to Camp Richardson, and then continue for 1.3 miles to the sign for Mount Tallac. Turn left at the sign for Mount Tallac Trailhead/Camp Shelly and drive to the campground on the right.

Contact: Camp Shelly, 530/541-6985; Livermore Area Recreation and Park District, 925/373-5700 or 925/960-2400, fax 925/960-2457, www.larpd.dst.ca.us.

146 FALLEN LEAF CAMPGROUND

Scenic rating: 7

in the Lake Tahoe Basin

This is a large camp near the north shore of Fallen Leaf Lake, set at 6,337 feet elevation. The lake is big (three miles long), quite deep (430 feet at its deepest point), and almost as blue as nearby Lake Tahoe. A concessionaire operates the campground. There are a variety of recreational opportunities, including boat rentals at the marina and horseback-riding at Camp Richardson Resort. Fishing is best in the fall for kokanee salmon. Because Fallen Leaf Lake is circled by forest—much of it private property—you will need a boat to fish or explore the lake. A visitors center is north of the Fallen Leaf Lake turnoff on Highway 89.

Campsites, facilities: There are 75 sites for tents and 130 sites for tents or RVs up to 40 feet (no hookups). Picnic tables, food lockers, and fire grills are provided. Drinking water, vault toilets, and coin showers are available. A boat ramp, coin laundry, and supplies are nearby. Some facilities are wheelchair-accessible. Leashed pets are permitted.

Reservations, fees: Reservations are accepted at 877/444-6777 or www.recreation.gov ($10 reservation fee). Sites are $25 per night, $5 per night for each additional vehicle. Open mid-May through mid-October, weather permitting.

Directions: In South Lake Tahoe at the junction of U.S. 50 and Highway 89, turn north on Highway 89 and drive two miles to the Fallen Leaf Lake turnoff. Turn left and drive 1.5 miles to the campground.

Contact: Lake Tahoe Basin Management Unit, 530/543-2600, fax 530/543-2693; Taylor Creek Visitor Center, 530/543-2674; California Land Management, 530/587-9281 or 650/322-1181; Fallen Leaf Lake Marina, 530/544-0787.

147 TAHOE VALLEY CAMPGROUND

Scenic rating: 5

near Lake Tahoe

This is a massive, privately operated park near South Lake Tahoe. The nearby attractions include five golf courses, horseback riding,

casinos, and, of course, "The Lake." Note that about half of the sites are filled with seasonal renters.

Campsites, facilities: There are 305 sites with full or partial hookups (30 and 50 amps) for RVs of any length, 77 sites for tents, and two group sites. Some RV sites are pull-through. Picnic tables and fire grills are provided. Restrooms with showers, cable TV, Wi-Fi, modem access, dump station, coin laundry, seasonal heated swimming pool, playground, tennis courts, grocery store, RV supplies, propane gas, ice, firewood, and recreation room are available. Some facilities are wheelchair-accessible. Leashed pets are permitted.

Reservations, fees: Reservations are recommended. Sites are $36–54 per night. Monthly rates available. Credit cards accepted. Open year-round.

Directions: Entering South Lake Tahoe on U.S. 50, drive east on U.S. 50 to Meyers. Continue on U.S. 50 about five miles beyond Meyers to the signed entrance on the right. Turn right on C Street and drive 1.5 blocks to the campground.

Contact: Tahoe Valley Campground, 530/541-2222, fax 530/541-1825, www.rvonthego.com.

148 CAMPGROUND BY THE LAKE

Scenic rating: 5

near Lake Tahoe

This city-operated campground provides an option at South Lake Tahoe. It is set at 6,200 feet elevation, across the road from the lake, with pine trees and views of the lake.

Campsites, facilities: There are 175 sites for tents or RVs up to 40 feet, and one group site for up to 30 people. Some sites have partial hookups (30 and 50 amps) and/or are pull-through. One cabin is also available. Picnic tables, barbecues, and fire grills are provided.

Drinking water, restrooms with flush toilets and showers, dump station, playground, and boat ramp (check current status) are available. An indoor ice-skating rink and a public indoor heated pool are nearby (fee for access). Some facilities are wheelchair-accessible. Supplies and a coin laundry are nearby. Leashed pets are permitted.

Reservations, fees: Reservations are accepted at 530/542-6096 ($3.50 reservation fee). Sites are $23–31 per night, $4 per night for each additional vehicle, $152.50 per night for the group site, $1 per pet per night. Weekly rates available. Some credit cards accepted. Open April through October, with a 14-day maximum stay.

Directions: If entering South Lake Tahoe on U.S. 50, drive east on U.S. 50 to Rufus Allen Boulevard. Turn right and drive 0.25 mile to the campground on the right side of the road.

Contact: Campground by the Lake, 530/542-6096; City of South Lake Tahoe, Parks and Recreation Department, 530/542-6055, www.recreationintahoe.com.

149 KOA SOUTH LAKE TAHOE

Scenic rating: 5

near Lake Tahoe

Like so many KOA camps, this one is on the outskirts of a major destination area, in this case, South Lake Tahoe. It is within close range of gambling, fishing, hiking, and bike rentals. The camp is set at 6,300 feet elevation.

Campsites, facilities: There are 40 sites with full hookups (30 amps) for RVs up to 36 feet, and 16 sites with no hookups for tents and RVs. Some sites are pull-through. A lodge is also available. Picnic tables and fire grills are provided. Restrooms with showers, cable TV, Wi-Fi, dump station, recreation room,

seasonal heated swimming pool, playground, coin laundry, convenience store, RV supplies, horseshoes, firewood, ice, and propane gas are available. Leashed pets are permitted.

Reservations, fees: Reservations are recommended at 800/562-3477. Sites are $36–66 per night, $5 per person per night for more than two people, $5 per night for each additional vehicle, $10–25 per boat per night, $5 per pet per night. Weekly and monthly rates available. Holiday rates are higher. Some credit cards accepted. Open April through mid-October.

Directions: From Sacramento, take U.S. 50 and drive east over the Sierra Nevada past Echo Summit to Meyers. As you enter Meyers, it will be the first campground on the right. Turn right and enter the campground.

Contact: KOA South Lake Tahoe, 530/577-3693, www.laketahoekoa.com.

150 SAND FLAT-AMERICAN RIVER

Scenic rating: 7

on the South Fork of the American River in Eldorado National Forest

This first-come, first-served campground often gets filled up by U.S. 50 travelers. And why not? You get easy access, a well-signed exit, and a nice setting on the South Fork of the American River. The elevation is 3,900 feet. The river is very pretty here, but fishing is often poor. In winter, the snow level usually starts just a few miles uphill.

Campsites, facilities: There are 29 sites for tents or RVs of any length (no hookups) and six walk-in tent sites. Picnic tables and fire grills are provided. Drinking water and vault toilets are available. Groceries, restaurant, and gas are nearby. Some facilities are wheelchair-accessible. Leashed pets are permitted.

Reservations, fees: Reservations are not accepted. Sites are $16 per night, $32 per night for a double site, $6 per night for each additional vehicle. Open May through late October, weather permitting.

Directions: From Sacramento, drive east on U.S. 50 to Placerville and then continue 28 miles to the campground on the right. (If you reach the Kyburz store, you have driven about one mile too far.)

Contact: Eldorado National Forest, Placerville Ranger District, 530/644-2324, fax 530/647-5315.

151 CHINA FLAT

Scenic rating: 7

on the Silver Fork of the American River in Eldorado National Forest

China Flat sits across the road from the Silver Fork American River, with a nearby access road that is routed along the river for a mile. This provides access for fishing, swimming, gold panning, and exploring. The elevation is 4,800 feet. The camp feels far off the beaten path, even though it is only five minutes from that parade of traffic on U.S. 50.

Campsites, facilities: There are 18 sites for tents or RVs of any length (no hookups). Picnic tables and fire grills are provided. Drinking water and vault toilets are available. Some facilities are wheelchair-accessible. Leashed pets are permitted.

Reservations, fees: Reservations are not accepted. Sites are $16 per night, $32 per night for double sites, $6 per night for each additional vehicle. Open May through October, weather permitting.

Directions: From Sacramento, drive east on U.S. 50 to Kyburz and Silver Fork Road. Turn right and drive three miles to the campground on the right side of the road.

Contact: Eldorado National Forest, Placerville Ranger District, 530/644-2324, fax 530/647-5315.

152 CAPPS CROSSING GROUP CAMP

Scenic rating: 7

on the North Fork of the Cosumnes River in Eldorado National Forest

This camp is set out in the middle of nowhere along the North Fork of the Cosumnes River. It's a primitive spot that doesn't get much use. This camp is in the western reaches of a vast number of backcountry Forest Service roads. A map of Eldorado National Forest is a must to explore them. The elevation is 5,200 feet.

Campsites, facilities: There is one group tent site for up to 40 people. Picnic tables and fire grills are provided. Drinking water and vault toilets are available. Leashed pets are permitted.

Reservations, fees: Reservations are required at 877/444-6777 or www.recreation.gov ($10 reservation fee). The camp is $75 per night. Open mid-May through mid-September, weather permitting.

Directions: From Sacramento, drive east on U.S. 50 to Placerville and continue for 12 miles to the Sly Park Road exit. Turn right and drive about six miles to the Mormon Emigrant Trail/Forest Road 5. Turn left on Mormon Emigrant Trail and drive about 13 miles to North-South Road/Forest Road 6. Turn right (south) on North-South Road and drive about six miles to the campground on the left side of the road.

Contact: Eldorado National Forest, Placerville Ranger District, 530/644-2324, fax 530/647-5315.

153 SILVER FORK

🚶 🏊 🚣 🐕 🏕 ♿ 🚐 ⛺

Scenic rating: 7

on the Silver Fork of the American River in Eldorado National Forest

The tons of vacationers driving U.S. 50 along the South Fork American River always get frustrated when they try to fish or camp, because there are precious few opportunities for either. But, just 20 minutes off the highway, you can find both at Silver Fork Camp. The access road provides many fishing opportunities and the stream is stocked with rainbow trout by the state. The camp is set right along the river, at 5,500 feet elevation, in Eldorado National Forest.

Campsites, facilities: There are 35 sites for tents or RVs of any length (no hookups) and four double sites. Picnic tables and fire grills are provided. Drinking water and vault toilets are available. Some of the facilities are wheelchair-accessible. Leashed pets are permitted.

Reservations, fees: Reservations are not accepted. Sites are $16 per night, $32 per night for double sites, $6 per night for each additional vehicle. Open May through October, weather permitting.

Directions: From Sacramento, drive east on U.S. 50 to Kyburz and Silver Fork Road. Turn right and drive eight miles to the campground on the right side of the road.

Contact: Eldorado National Forest, Placerville Ranger District, 530/644-2324, fax 530/647-5315.

154 KIRKWOOD LAKE

🚶 🏊 🚣 🚐 🏕 ⛺

Scenic rating: 8

in Eldorado National Forest

Little Kirkwood Lake is in a beautiful Sierra setting, with good shoreline access, fishing for small rainbow trout, and quiet water. Despite that, it is often overlooked in favor of nearby Silver Lake and Caples Lake along Highway 88. No boat motors are allowed, but swimming is permitted. Nearby Kirkwood Ski Resort stays open all summer and offers excellent opportunities for horseback riding, hiking, and meals. The elevation is 7,600 feet. Note: No trailers. The access road is too narrow.

Campsites, facilities: There are 12 sites for tents only. Picnic tables and fire grills are provided. Drinking water, vault toilets, and food lockers are available. Leashed pets are permitted.

Reservations, fees: Reservations are not accepted. Sites are $20 per night, $5 per night for each additional vehicle. Open June through mid-October, weather permitting.

Directions: From Jackson, drive east on Highway 88 for 60 miles (four miles past Silver Lake) to the campground entrance road on the left (if you reach the sign for Kirkwood Ski Resort, you have gone 0.5 mile too far). Turn left and drive 0.25 mile (road not suitable for trailers or large RVs) to the campground on the left.

Contact: Eldorado National Forest, Amador Ranger District, 209/295-4251, fax 209/295-5998.

155 CAPLES LAKE

🚶 🏊 🚣 🚤 🏕 🐕 ♿ 🚐 ⛺

Scenic rating: 8

in Eldorado National Forest

Caples Lake, in the high country at 7,800 feet, is a pretty lake right along Highway 88. It covers 600 acres, has a 5-mph speed limit, and provides good trout fishing and excellent hiking terrain. Swimming is allowed. The camp is set across the highway (a little two-laner) from the lake, with the Caples Lake Resort and boat rentals nearby. There is a parking area at the west end of the lake, and from here you can begin a great 3.5-mile hike to Emigrant Lake, in the Mokelumne Wilderness on the western flank of Mount Round Top (10,310 feet).

Campsites, facilities: There are 30 sites for tents or RVs up to 35 feet (no hookups), and six walk-in tent sites (requiring a 200-foot walk). Picnic tables and fire grills are provided. Drinking water and vault toilets are available. Groceries, propane gas, boat ramp, and boat rentals are nearby. Some facilities are wheelchair-accessible. Leashed pets are permitted.

Reservations, fees: Reservations are not accepted. Sites are $20 per night, $5 per night for each additional vehicle, $40 per night for a double site. Open June through mid-October, weather permitting.

Directions: From Jackson, drive east on Highway 88 for 63 miles (one mile past the entrance road to Kirkwood Ski Area) to the camp entrance road on the left.

Contact: Eldorado National Forest, Amador Ranger District, 209/295-4251, fax 209/295-5998; Caples Lake Resort, 209/258-8888.

156 WOODS LAKE

🚶 🏊 ⛵ 🎣 🐕 ♿ ⛺

Scenic rating: 9

in Eldorado National Forest

Woods Lake is only two miles from Highway 88, yet it can provide campers the feeling of visiting a far-off land. It is a small but beautiful lake in the granite backdrop of the high Sierra, set at 8,200 feet elevation near Carson Pass. Boats with motors are not permitted, making it ideal for canoes and rowboats. Trout fishing is fair. A great trailhead is available here, a three-mile loop hike to little Round Top Lake and Winnemucca Lake (twice the size of Woods Lake) and back. They are set on the northern flank of Mount Round Top (10,310 feet).

Campsites, facilities: There are 25 tent sites. Picnic tables and fire rings are provided. Drinking water and vault toilets are available. Groceries and propane gas are available within

five miles. Some facilities are wheelchair-accessible. Leashed pets are permitted.

Reservations, fees: Reservations are not accepted. Sites are $20 per night, $5 per night for each additional vehicle, $40 per night for double site. Open late June through October, weather permitting.

Directions: From Jackson, drive east on Highway 88 to Caples Lake and continue for a mile to the Woods Lake turnoff on the right (two miles west of Carson Pass). Turn south and drive a mile to the campground on the right (trailers and RVs are not recommended).

Contact: Eldorado National Forest, Amador Ranger District, 209/295-4251, fax 209/295-5998.

157 SILVER LAKE WEST

🚶 🏊 ⛵ 🛥 🐕 🚐 ⛺

Scenic rating: 9

on Silver Lake in Eldorado National Forest

The Highway 88 corridor provides access to three excellent lakes: Lower Bear River Reservoir, Silver Lake, and Caples Lake. Silver Lake is difficult to pass by, with cabin rentals, pretty campsites, decent trout fishing, and excellent hiking. The lake is set at 7,200 feet elevation in a classic granite cirque just below the Sierra ridge. This camp is on the west side of Highway 88, across the road from the lake. A great hike starts at the trailhead on the east side of the lake, a two-mile tromp to little Hidden Lake, one of several nice hikes in the area. In addition, horseback-riding is available nearby at Plasse's Resort. Note that bears frequent this campground, so store food properly and avoid scented products.

Campsites, facilities: There are 35 sites for tents or RVs up to 30 feet (no hookups). Picnic tables, food lockers, and fire pits are provided. Vault toilets and drinking water are available. A boat ramp and boat rentals are nearby. Leashed pets are permitted. There is a maximum of six people and two pets per site.

CAMPING

Reservations, fees: Reservations are not accepted. Sites are $20–24 per night, $6 per night for each additional vehicle, $2 per pet per night. Open Memorial Day Weekend through October, weather permitting.

Directions: From Jackson, drive east on Highway 88 for 50 miles (to the north end of Silver Lake) to the campground entrance road on the left.

Contact: Eldorado Irrigation District, 530/644-1960, fax 530/647-5155.

158 SILVER LAKE EAST

Scenic rating: 7

in Eldorado National Forest

Silver Lake is an easy-to-reach alpine lake set at 7,200 feet, providing a beautiful setting, good trout fishing, and hiking. This camp is on the northeast side of the lake, with a boat ramp nearby. (See the *Silver Lake West* listing in this chapter for more information.)

Campsites, facilities: There are 62 sites for tents or RVs up to 40 feet (no hookups). Picnic tables and fire grills are provided. Drinking water and vault toilets are available. A grocery store, boat rentals, boat ramp, and propane gas are nearby. Leashed pets are permitted.

Reservations, fees: Reservations are accepted at 877/444-6777 or www.recreation.gov ($10 reservation fee). Sites are $22 per night, $5 per night for each additional vehicle, $44 per night for a double site. Open June through mid-October, weather permitting.

Directions: From Jackson, drive east on Highway 88 for 50 miles (to the north end of Silver Lake) to the campground entrance road on the right.

Contact: Eldorado National Forest, Amador Ranger District, 209/295-4251, fax 209/295-5998; Silver Lake Resort, 209/258-8598.

159 BEAR RIVER GROUP CAMP

Scenic rating: 6

on Bear River Reservoir in Eldorado National Forest

This is a group camp set near Bear River Reservoir, a pretty lake that provides powerboating and trout fishing. (See the listing in this chapter for *South Shore,* which is just a mile from this camp.)

Campsites, facilities: There are four tent-only group sites that can accommodate 25–50 people each. Picnic tables and fire grills are provided. Drinking water, vault toilets, coin showers, food lockers, and wash racks are available. A grocery store, boat ramp, boat rentals, and propane gas are available nearby. Leashed pets are permitted.

Reservations, fees: Reservations are required at 877/444-6777 or www.recreation.gov ($10 reservation fee). The sites are $75–150 per night. Open mid-June through mid-September, weather permitting.

Directions: From Stockton, drive east on Highway 88 for about 80 miles to the lake entrance on the right side of the road (well signed). Turn right and drive five miles (past the dam) to the campground entrance on the left side of the road.

Contact: Eldorado National Forest, Amador Ranger District, 209/295-4251, fax 209/295-5998.

160 BEAR RIVER LAKE RESORT

Scenic rating: 8

on Bear River Reservoir

Bear River Lake Resort is a complete vacation service lodge, with everything you could ask for. A lot of people have been asking in recent years, making this a popular spot that often requires a reservation. The resort also sponsors fishing derbies in the summer and sweetens the pot considerably by stocking exceptionally large rainbow trout. Other fish species include brown trout and Mackinaw trout. The resort is set at 6,000 feet. The lake freezes over in the winter. (See the *South Shore* listing in this chapter for more information about Bear River Reservoir.)

Campsites, facilities: There are 152 sites with partial hookups (15 amps) for tents or RVs up to 35 feet, a group site for up to 60 people, and six rental trailers. Picnic tables and fire pits are provided. Restrooms with flush toilets and coin showers, drinking water, dump station, boat ramp, boat rentals, berthing, bait and tackle, fishing licenses, video arcade, playground, firewood, ice, propane gas, coin laundry, pay phone, restaurant and cocktail lounge, and grocery store are available. ATVs are permitted, but no motorcycles are allowed. Some facilities are wheelchair-accessible. Leashed pets are permitted at campsites, but not in lodging units.

Reservations, fees: Reservations are recommended. Sites are $33 per night, $5 per night for each additional vehicle with a maximum of two vehicles, $255 per night for the group site, $5 one-time pet fee. Some credit cards accepted. Open April through October.

Directions: From Stockton, drive east on Highway 88 for about 80 miles to the lake entrance on the right side of the road, 42 miles east of Jackson. Turn right and drive 2.5 miles to a junction (if you pass the dam, you have gone 0.25 mile too far). Turn left and drive 0.5 mile to the campground entrance on the right side of the road.

Contact: Bear River Lake Resort, 209/295-4868, www.bearrivercampground.com.

161 SUGAR PINE POINT

Scenic rating: 7

near Bear River Reservoir in Eldorado National Forest

This camp is similar in nature to Pardoes Point (see listing in this chapter), with one exception: It is located directly across the lake, on the other shoreline, that is, from Pardoes.

Campsites, facilities: There are eight sites for tents only, including two double sites. Picnic tables and fire rings are provided. Pit toilets are available. Drinking water is not available. Leashed pets permitted.

Reservations, fees: Reservations are not accepted. Sites are $18, $5 each additional vehicle per night. Open from May to mid-November.

Directions: From Stockton, drive east on Highway 88 for about 80 miles to Bear River Road. Turn right and drive 2.5 miles south on Bear River Road to Forest Road 8N20. Turn right on Forest Road 8N20 and drive three miles to the campground.

Contact: Eldorado National Forest, Amador Ranger District, 209/295-4251, fax 209/295-5998, www.fs.fed.us.

162 PARDOES POINT

Scenic rating: 7

in Eldorado National Forest

There are several camps at Bear River Reservoir—Bear River Resort is the most popular because you can see the lake, it has a boat ramp, and you can get supplies. Pardoes Point is located near the lower end of the reservoir. It's not a true "lakeside" camp, though you can get glimpses of the lake from some sites. Bear River Reservoir often provides good fishing. The elevation is 6,000 feet and ice-outs occur earlier than at Silver Lake and Caples Lake farther up Highway 88.

Campsites, facilities: There are 10 tent sites. Picnic tables and fire rings are provided. Drinking water and pit toilets are available. Leashed pets permitted.

Reservations, fees: Reservations are not accepted. Sites are $20, $5 per each additional vehicle per night. Open from May to mid-November.

Directions: From Stockton, drive east on Highway 88 for about 80 miles to Bear River Road. Turn right and drive south on Bear River Road for four miles to the campground.

Contact: Eldorado National Forest, Amador Ranger District, 209/295-4251, fax 209/295-5998, www.fs.fed.us.

163 SOUTH SHORE

Scenic rating: 7

on Bear River Reservoir in Eldorado National Forest

Bear River Reservoir is set at 5,900 feet, which means it becomes ice-free earlier in the spring than its uphill neighbors to the east, Silver Lake and Caples Lake. It is a good-sized lake—725 acres—and cold and deep, too. All water sports are allowed. It gets double-barreled trout stocks, receiving fish from the state and from the operator of the lake's marina and lodge. This campground is on the lake's southern shore, just east of the dam. Explorers can drive south for five miles to Salt Springs Reservoir, which has a trailhead and parking area on the north side of the dam for a great day hike along the lake.

Campsites, facilities: There are 22 sites for tents or RVs up to 35 feet (no hookups). Picnic tables and fire grills are provided. Drinking water and vault toilets are available. A boat ramp, grocery store, boat rentals, and propane gas are available at nearby Bear River Lake Resort. Some facilities are wheelchair-accessible. Leashed pets are permitted.

Reservations, fees: Reservations are accepted at 877/444-6777 or www.recreation.gov ($10 reservation fee). Sites are $20 per night, $40 per night for double site. Open mid-May through mid-October, weather permitting.

Directions: From Stockton, drive east on Highway 88 for about 80 miles to the lake entrance on the right side of the road (well signed). Turn right and drive four miles (past the dam) to the campground entrance on the right side of the road.

Contact: Eldorado National Forest, Amador Ranger District, 209/295-4251, fax 209/295-5998.

164 WHITE AZALEA

Scenic rating: 7

on the Mokelumne River in Eldorado National Forest

Out here in the remote Mokelumne River Canyon are three primitive camps set on the Mokelumne's North Fork. White Azalea, at 3,500 feet elevation, is the closest of the three to Salt Springs Reservoir, the prime recreation destination. It's about a three-mile drive to the dam and an adjacent parking area for a wilderness trailhead for the Mokelumne Wilderness. This trail makes a great day hike, routed for four miles along the north shore of Salt Springs Reservoir to Blue Hole at the head of the lake.

Campsites, facilities: There are six tent sites. Portable toilets are provided. No drinking water is available. Garbage must be packed out. Leashed pets are permitted.

Reservations, fees: Reservations are not accepted. There is no fee for camping. Open year-round, weather permitting.

Directions: From Jackson, drive east on Highway 88 to Pioneer and then continue for 18 miles to Ellis Road/Forest Road 92 (78 miles from Jackson), at a signed turnoff for Lumberyard Campground. Turn right on Ellis Road and drive 12 miles to Salt Springs Road (Forest

Road 9). Turn left, cross the Bear River, and continue for three miles to the campground on the right. The road is steep, narrow, and curvy in spots, not good for RVs or trailers.
Contact: Eldorado National Forest, Amador Ranger District, 209/295-4251, fax 209/295-5998.

165 MOORE CREEK

Scenic rating: 7

on the Mokelumne River in Eldorado National Forest

This camp is set at 3,200 feet elevation on little Moore Creek, a feeder stream to the nearby North Fork Mokelumne River. It's one of three primitive camps within two miles. (See the *White Azalea* listing for more information.)
Campsites, facilities: There are eight tent sites. Picnic tables are provided. Portable toilets are available. No drinking water is available. Garbage must be packed out. Leashed pets are permitted.
Reservations, fees: Reservations are not accepted. There is no fee for camping. Open year-round, weather permitting.
Directions: From Jackson, drive east on Highway 88 to Pioneer and then continue for 18 miles to Ellis Road/Forest Road 92 (78 miles from Jackson), at a signed turnoff for Lumberyard Campground. Turn right on Ellis Road and drive 12 miles to Salt Springs Road (Forest Road 9). Turn right and drive 2.5 miles, cross the bridge over the Mokelumne River, and turn right on the campground entrance road. Drive 0.25 mile to the campground on the right. The road is steep, narrow, and winding in spots—not good for RVs or trailers.
Contact: Eldorado National Forest, Amador Ranger District, 209/295-4251, fax 209/295-5998.

166 MOKELUMNE

Scenic rating: 7

on the Mokelumne River in Eldorado National Forest

This primitive spot is set beside the Mokelumne River at 3,200 feet elevation, one of three primitive camps in the immediate area. (See the *White Azalea* listing in this chapter for more information.) There are some good swimming holes nearby. Fishing is fair, with the trout on the small side.
Campsites, facilities: There are 13 sites for tents only. Vault toilets are provided. No drinking water is available. Garbage must be packed out (it is occasionally serviced in summer). Leashed pets are permitted.
Reservations, fees: Reservations are not accepted. There is no fee for camping. Open year-round, weather permitting.
Directions: From Jackson, drive east on Highway 88 to Pioneer and then continue for 18 miles to Ellis Road/Forest Road 92 (78 miles from Jackson), at a signed turnoff for Lumberyard Campground. Turn right on Ellis Road and drive 12 miles to Salt Springs Road (Forest Road 9). Turn right and drive 2.5 miles to the campground on the left side of the road (at the Mokelumne River).
Contact: Eldorado National Forest, Amador Ranger District, 209/295-4251, fax 209/295-5998.

167 WA KA LUU HEP YOO

Scenic rating: 8

on the Stanislaus River in Stanislaus National Forest

This is a riverside Forest Service campground that provides good trout fishing on the Stanislaus River and a put-in for white-water rafting. The highlight for most is the fishing here—one of the best spots on the Stanislaus, stocked by Fish and Game, and good for rainbow, brook, and brown trout. It is four miles downstream of Dorrington and was first opened in 1999 as part of the Sourgrass Recreation Complex. There are cultural sites and preserved artifacts, such as grinding rocks. It is a pretty streamside spot, with ponderosa pine and black oak providing good screening. A wheelchair-accessible trail is available along the stream. The camp is set at an elevation of 3,900 feet, but it feels higher. By the way, I was told that the name of the campground means "wild river."

Campsites, facilities: There are 49 sites for tents or RVs up to 50 feet (no hookups) and four walk-in tent sites. Picnic tables and fire grills are provided. Drinking water and restrooms with flush and vault toilets are available. Some facilities are wheelchair-accessible. Leashed pets are permitted.

Reservations, fees: Reservations are not accepted. Sites are $16 per night. Free campfire permits are required. Open Memorial Day weekend through October, weather permitting.

Directions: From Angels Camp, drive east on Highway 4, past Arnold to Dorrington and Boards Crossing Road. Turn right and drive four miles to the campground on the left (just before the bridge that crosses the Stanislaus River).

Contact: Stanislaus National Forest, Calaveras Ranger District, 209/795-1381, fax 209/795-6849.

168 BIG MEADOW AND BIG MEADOW GROUP CAMP
🏠 🚐 ⛰️

Scenic rating: 5

in Stanislaus National Forest

Big Meadow is set at 6,460 feet elevation on the western slopes of the Sierra Nevada. There are a number of recreation attractions nearby, the most prominent being the North

Fork Stanislaus River two miles to the south in a national forest (see the *Sand Flat Four-Wheel Drive* listing in this chapter), with access available from a four-wheel-drive road just east of camp, or on Spicer Reservoir Road (see the *Stanislaus River* listing in this chapter). Lake Alpine, a pretty lake popular for trout fishing, is nine miles east on Highway 4. Three mountain reservoirs—Spicer, Utica, and Union—are all within a 15-minute drive. Big Meadow is also a good base camp for hunting.

Campsites, facilities: There are 68 sites for tents or RVs up to 27 feet (no hookups), and one group tent site (requires a walk in of 100 feet) that can accommodate up to 25 people. Picnic tables and fire grills are provided. Drinking water and vault toilets are available. Groceries, coin laundry, and propane gas are within five miles. Leashed pets are permitted.

Reservations, fees: Reservations are accepted for individual sites and required for the group camp at 877/444-6777 or www.recreation.gov ($10 reservation fee). Sites are $17 per night, $45 per night for the group camp. Open June through October, weather permitting.

Directions: From Angels Camp on Highway 49, turn east on Highway 4 and drive about 30 miles (three miles past Ganns Meadows) to the campground on the right.

Contact: Stanislaus National Forest, Calaveras Ranger District, 209/795-1381, fax 209/795-6849.

169 SAND FLAT FOUR-WHEEL DRIVE
🏃 🛶 🏠 5% ⛰️

Scenic rating: 7

on the Stanislaus River in Stanislaus National Forest

This one is for four-wheel-drive cowboys who want to carve out a piece of the Sierra Nevada wildlands for themselves. It is set at 5,900 feet elevation on the North Fork Stanislaus River, where there is decent fishing for small trout, with the fish often holding right where white water runs into pools. You won't get bugged by anyone at this tiny, primitive camp, named for the extensive sandy flat on the south side of the river. The access road is steep and often rough. Trailers are not allowed.

Campsites, facilities: There are 10 sites for tents only. Picnic tables and fire rings are provided. Vault toilets are available. No drinking water is available. Garbage must be packed out. Leashed pets are permitted.

Reservations, fees: Reservations are not accepted. There is no fee for camping. Free campfire permits are required. Open June through October, weather permitting.

Directions: From Angels Camp on Highway 49, turn east on Highway 4, drive about 25 miles (0.5 mile past Big Meadows) to a dirt/gravel road on the right. Turn right and drive two miles on a steep, unimproved road (four-wheel drive required).

Contact: Stanislaus National Forest, Calaveras Ranger District, 209/795-1381, fax 209/795-6849.

170 STANISLAUS RIVER

Scenic rating: 8

in Stanislaus National Forest

As you might figure from its name, this camp provides excellent access to the adjacent North Fork Stanislaus River. The elevation is 6,200 feet, with timbered sites and the river just south of camp.

Campsites, facilities: There are 25 sites for tents or RVs up to 35 feet (no hookups). Fire grills and picnic tables are provided. Drinking water and vault toilets are available. Supplies are available in Bear Valley. Leashed pets are permitted.

Reservations, fees: Reservations are not accepted. Sites are $8 per night. Open June through October, weather permitting.

Directions: From Angels Camp on Highway 49, turn east on Highway 4 and drive about 44 miles to Spicer Reservoir Road. Turn right and drive four miles to the campground on the right side of the road.

Contact: Stanislaus National Forest, Calaveras Ranger District, 209/795-1381, fax 209/795-6849.

171 GOLDEN PINES RV RESORT AND CAMPGROUND

Scenic rating: 6

near Arnold

This is a privately operated park set at 5,800 feet elevation on the slopes of the Sierra Nevada. The resort is surrounded by 400 acres of forest and has a self-guided nature trail. Nearby destinations include Stanislaus National Forest, the North Stanislaus River, and Calaveras Big Trees State Park (two miles away). The latter features 150 giant sequoias, along with the biggest stump you can imagine, and two easy hikes, one routed through the North Grove, another through the South Grove. The Bear Valley/Mount Reba ski resort is nearby. Note that about half the sites here are long-term vacation leases.

Campsites, facilities: There are 33 sites with full or partial hookups (30 amps) for RVs up to 42 feet, and 40 tent sites. Picnic tables, fire pits, and barbecues are provided. Drinking water, restrooms with showers, seasonal heated swimming pool, playground, horseshoes, table tennis, volleyball, group facilities, pay phone, coin laundry, and propane gas are available. Some facilities are wheelchair-accessible. Leashed pets are permitted.

Reservations, fees: Reservations are recommended. RV sites with full hookups are $35 per night, RV sites with partial hookups are $30 per night, tent sites are $20 per night, $2.50 per night for each additional vehicle,

$2.50 one-time charge per pet. Some credit cards accepted. Open year-round.

Directions: From Angels Camp, turn northeast on Highway 4 and drive 22 miles to Arnold. Continue for seven miles to the campground entrance on the left.

Contact: Golden Pines RV Resort and Campground, 209/795-2820, www.goldenpinesrvresort.com.

172 NORTH GROVE

Scenic rating: 7

in Calaveras Big Trees State Park

This is one of two campgrounds at Calaveras Big Trees State Park, the state park known for its two groves of giant sequoias (Sierra redwoods). The park covers 6,500 acres, preserving the extraordinary North Grove of giant sequoias. The grove includes the Discovery Tree. Through the years, additional acreage surrounding the grove has been added, providing a mixed conifer forest as a buffer around the giant sequoias. The trailhead for a hike on North Grove Loop is here; it's an easy 1.5-mile walk that is routed among 150 sequoias; the sweet fragrance of the huge trees fills the air. These trees are known for their massive diameter, not for their height, as is the case with coastal redwoods. Another hike, a five-miler, is in the South Grove, where the park's two largest sequoias (the Agassiz Tree and the Palace Hotel Tree) can be seen on a spur trail. A visitors center is open during peak periods, offering exhibits on the giant sequoia and natural history. The North Fork Stanislaus River runs near Highway 4, providing trout-fishing access. The Stanislaus (near the bridge) and Beaver Creek (about 10 miles away) are stocked with trout in late spring and early summer. In the winter, this is a popular spot for cross-country skiing and snowshoeing. The elevation is 4,800 feet.

Campsites, facilities: There are 51 sites for tents, 48 sites for RVs up to 30 feet (no hookups), five hike-in environmental sites, and two group sites for 40–60 people each. Fire grills, food lockers, and picnic tables are provided. Drinking water, restrooms with flush toilets and coin showers, firewood, and a dump station are available. Some facilities are wheelchair-accessible, including a nature trail and exhibits. No bicycles are allowed on the paths, but they are permitted on fire roads and paved roads. Leashed pets are permitted, but not on trails.

Reservations, fees: Reservations are accepted at 800/444-PARK (800/444-7275) or www.reserveamerica.com ($7.50 reservation fee). Sites are $20–25 per night, $6 per night for each additional vehicle, $90–135 per night for group sites, and $11–15 per night for environmental sites. Open year-round, with 12 sites available in winter.

Directions: From Angels Camp, drive east on Highway 4 for 23 miles to Arnold and then continue another four miles to the park entrance on the right.

Contact: Calaveras Big Trees State Park, 209/795-2334; Columbia State Park, 209/544-9128, www.parks.ca.gov.

173 OAK HOLLOW

Scenic rating: 7

in Calaveras Big Trees State Park

This is one of two campgrounds at Calaveras Big Trees State Park. (See the *North Grove* listing in this chapter for recreation information.)

Campsites, facilities: There are 23 sites for tents only, and 18 sites for RVs up to 30 feet (no hookups). Picnic tables, fire rings, and food lockers are provided. Drinking water and restrooms with flush toilets and coin showers are available. A dump station is available four miles away at North Grove. You can buy supplies in Dorrington or Arnold. Some facilities are wheelchair-accessible, including a nature trail and exhibits. Leashed pets are permitted in the campground, but not on trails.

Reservations, fees: Reservations are accepted at 800/444-PARK (800/444-7275) or www. reserveamerica.com ($7.50 reservation fee). Sites are $20–25 per night, $6 per night for each additional vehicle. Open March through November.

Directions: From Angels Camp, drive east on Highway 4 for 23 miles to Arnold and then continue four miles to the park entrance on the right. Continue another four miles to the campground on the right.

Contact: Calaveras Big Trees State Park, 209/795-2334; Columbia State Park, 209/588-2198, www.parks.ca.gov.

174 BEARDSLEY
Scenic rating: 6

at Beardsley Reservoir in Stanislaus National Forest

This lake is set in a deep canyon with a paved ramp, nice picnic area, and a fair beach. It is often an outstanding fishery early in the season for brown trout, and then once planted, good for catches of hatchery fish during the evening bite. In winter and spring, as soon as the gate is opened to the boat ramp access road, the fishing is best when the wind blows. This lake allows powerboats and all water sports. The water is generally warm enough for swimmers by midsummer. The camp is set at 3,400 feet elevation, but because it is near the bottom of the lake canyon, it actually feels much higher. Since the lake is a reservoir, it is subject to severe drawdowns in late summer. Bonus: There is more fishing nearby on the Middle Fork of the Stanislaus.

Campsites, facilities: There are 16 sites for tents or RVs up to 22 feet (no hookups). Fire rings are provided. Vault toilets are available.

No drinking water is available. Garbage must be packed out. Leashed pets are permitted.

Reservations, fees: Reservations are not accepted. There is no fee for camping. Open May through October, weather permitting (the road is often gated at the top of the canyon when the boat ramp road at lake level is iced over).

Directions: From Sonora, drive east on Highway 108 for about 25 miles to Strawberry and the turnoff for Beardsley Reservoir/Forest Road 52. Turn left and drive seven miles to Beardsley Dam. Continue for 0.25 mile past the dam to the campground.

Contact: Stanislaus National Forest, Summit Ranger District, 209/965-3434, fax 209/965-3372.

175 FRASER FLAT
Scenic rating: 7

on the South Fork of the Stanislaus River in Stanislaus National Forest

This camp is set along the South Fork of the Stanislaus River at an elevation of 4,800 feet. If the fish aren't biting, a short side trip via Forest Service roads will route you north into the main canyon of the Middle Fork Stanislaus. A map of Stanislaus National Forest is required for this adventure.

Campsites, facilities: There are 38 sites for tents or RVs up to 30 feet (no hookups). Picnic tables and fire grills are provided. Drinking water, vault toilets, and a wheelchair-accessible fishing pier are available. Some facilities are wheelchair-accessible. A grocery store and propane gas are nearby. Leashed pets are permitted.

Reservations, fees: Reservations are not accepted. Sites are $15 per night, $5 per night for each additional vehicle. Open May through October, weather permitting.

Directions: From Sonora, drive east on Highway 108 to Long Barn. Continue east for six

CAMPING

miles to Spring Gap Road/Forest Road 4N01. Turn left and drive three miles to the campground on the left side of the road.

Contact: Stanislaus National Forest, Mi-Wok Ranger District, 209/586-3234, fax 209/586-0643.

176 HULL CREEK

Scenic rating: 7

in Stanislaus National Forest

This obscure camp borders little Hull Creek (too small for trout fishing) at 5,600 feet elevation in Stanislaus National Forest. This is a good spot for those wishing to test out four-wheel-drive vehicles, with an intricate set of Forest Service roads available to the east. To explore that area, a map of Stanislaus National Forest is essential.

Campsites, facilities: There are 18 sites for tents or RVs up to 22 feet (no hookups). Picnic tables and fire grills are provided. Drinking water and vault toilets are available. Leashed pets are permitted.

Reservations, fees: Reservations are not accepted. Sites are $5 per night. Open May through October, weather permitting.

Directions: From Sonora, drive east on Highway 108 to Long Barn and the Long Barn Fire Station and a signed turnoff for the campground at Road 31/Forest Road 3N01. Turn right and drive 12 miles to the campground on the left side of the road.

Contact: Stanislaus National Forest, Mi-Wok Ranger District, 209/586-3234, fax 209/586-0643.

177 SUGARPINE RV PARK

Scenic rating: 5

in Twain Harte

Twain Harte is a beautiful little town, right at the edge of the snow line in winter, and right where pines take over the alpine landscape. This park is at the threshold of mountain country, with Pinecrest, Dodge Ridge, and Beardsley Reservoir nearby. It sits on 15 acres and features several walking paths. Note that only 17 of the RV sites are available for overnight campers; the other sites are rented as annual vacation leases. RVs and mobile homes are also for sale at the park.

Campsites, facilities: There are 78 sites with full hookups (20, 30, and 50 amps) for RVs up to 40 feet, 15 tent sites, and three park-model cabins. Picnic tables are provided. Restrooms with showers, cable TV, modem access, playground, seasonal swimming pool, horseshoes, volleyball, badminton, tetherball, basketball, coin laundry, group facilities, and convenience store are available. Some facilities are wheelchair-accessible. Leashed pets are permitted.

Reservations, fees: Reservations are accepted. Sites are $38 per night, $1 per pet per night, $3 per night for each additional vehicle, with exception for towed vehicles. Some credit cards accepted. Open year-round.

Directions: From Sonora, drive east on Highway 108 for 17 miles to the park on the right side of the road, three miles east of Twain Harte.

Contact: Sugarpine RV Park, 209/586-4631, fax 209/586-7738.

178 KIT CARSON

Scenic rating: 8

on the West Fork of the Carson River in
Humboldt-Toiyabe National Forest

This is one in a series of pristine, high-Sierra
camps set along the West Fork of the Carson
River. There's good trout fishing, thanks to
regular stocks from the Department of Fish
and Game. This is no secret, however, and
the area from the Highway 89 bridge on
downstream gets a lot of fishing pressure.
The elevation is 6,900 feet.

Campsites, facilities: There are 12 sites for
tents or RVs up to 22 feet (no hookups).
Picnic tables and fire grills are provided.
Drinking water and vault toilets are available. Leashed pets are permitted.

Reservations, fees: Reservations are not
accepted. Sites are $14 per night. Open
late-May through mid-September, weather
permitting.

Directions: From Sacramento, drive east on
U.S. 50 to the junction with Highway 89.
Turn south on Highway 89 and drive over
Luther Pass to the junction with Highway 88.
Turn left and drive a mile to the campground
on the left side of the road.

From Jackson, drive east on Highway 88
over Carson Pass and to the junction with
Highway 89 and then continue for a mile
to the campground on the left side of the
road.

Contact: Humboldt-Toiyabe National Forest,
Carson Ranger District, 775/882-2766, fax
775/884-8199.

179 SNOWSHOE SPRINGS

Scenic rating: 8

on the West Fork of the Carson River in
Humboldt-Toiyabe National Forest

Take your pick of this or the other three
streamside camps on the West Fork of the
Carson River. This one is at 6,100 feet elevation. Trout are plentiful but rarely grow
very large.

Campsites, facilities: There are 19 sites for
tents or RVs up to 16 feet (no hookups). Picnic
tables and fire grills are provided. Drinking
water and vault toilets are available. Leashed
pets are permitted.

Reservations, fees: Reservations are not accepted. Sites are $14 per night. Open late May
through mid-September.

Directions: From Sacramento, drive east on
U.S. 50 to the junction with Highway 89.
Turn south on Highway 89 and drive over
Luther Pass to the junction with Highway 88.
Turn left (east) and drive two miles to the
campground on the right side of the road.

From Jackson, drive east on Highway 88
over Carson Pass to the junction with Highway 89 and continue for two miles to the
campground on the right side of the road.

Contact: Humboldt-Toiyabe National Forest,
Carson Ranger District, 775/882-2766, fax
775/884-8199.

180 CRYSTAL SPRINGS

Scenic rating: 8

on the West Fork of the Carson River in
Humboldt-Toiyabe National Forest

For many people, this camp is an ideal choice.
It is set at an elevation of 6,000 feet, right
alongside the West Fork of the Carson River.
This stretch of water is stocked with trout by
the Department of Fish and Game. Crystal

Springs is easy to reach, just off Highway 88, and supplies can be obtained in nearby Woodfords or Markleeville. Grover Hot Springs State Park makes a good side-trip destination.

Campsites, facilities: There are 20 sites for tents or RVs up to 22 feet (no hookups). Picnic tables and fire grills are provided. Drinking water and vault toilets are available. Some facilities are wheelchair-accessible. Leashed pets are permitted.

Reservations, fees: Reservations are not accepted. Sites are $14 per night. Open late April to early October, weather permitting.

Directions: From Sacramento, drive east on U.S. 50 to the junction with Highway 89. Turn south on Highway 89 and drive over Luther Pass to the junction with Highway 88. Turn left (east) and drive 4.5 miles to the campground on the right side of the road.

From Jackson, drive east on Highway 88 over Carson Pass to the junction with Highway 89 and continue for 4.5 miles to the campground on the right side of the road.

Contact: Humboldt-Toiyabe National Forest, Carson Ranger District, 775/882-2766, fax 775/884-8199.

181 INDIAN CREEK RECREATION AREA
🏃‍♂️🏊🛶🍴🏕️🐎♿🚐⛺

Scenic rating: 10

near Indian Creek Reservoir and Markleeville

This beautiful campground is set amid sparse pines near Indian Creek Reservoir, elevation 5,600 feet. The campground is popular and often fills to capacity. This is an excellent lake for trout fishing, and the nearby Carson River is managed as a trophy trout fishery. The lake covers 160 acres, with a maximum speed for boats on the lake set at 5 mph. Sailing, sailboarding, and swimming are allowed. There are several good hikes in the vicinity as well. The best is a short trek, a one-mile

climb to Summit Lake, with scenic views of the Indian Creek area. Summers are dry and warm here, with high temperatures typically in the 80s, and nights cool and comfortable. (There is little shade in the summer at the group site.) Bears provide an occasional visit. The lake freezes over in winter. It is about 35 miles to Carson City, Nevada, and two miles to Markleeville.

Campsites, facilities: There are 19 sites for tents or RVs up to 30 feet (no hookups), 10 walk-in sites for tents only, and a group tent site for up to 40 people. Picnic tables and fire grills are provided. Drinking water and restrooms with flush toilets and showers are available. A boat ramp is nearby. Some facilities are wheelchair-accessible. Leashed pets are permitted.

Reservations, fees: Reservations are not accepted for individual sites but are required for the group tent site at 775/885-6000. Sites are $20 per night, double sites are $32 per night, $14–20 per night for walk-in sites, $5 per night for each additional vehicle, $50 per night for group site. Open late April through mid-November, weather permitting.

Directions: From Sacramento, drive east on U.S. 50 over Echo Summit to Meyers and Highway 89. Turn south on Highway 89 and drive to Highway 88. Turn left (east) on Highway 88/89 and drive six miles to Woodfords and Highway 89. Turn right (south) on Highway 89 and drive about four miles to Airport Road. Turn left on Airport Road and drive four miles to Indian Creek Reservoir. At the fork, bear left and drive to the campground on the west side of the lake.

From Markleeville, drive north on Highway 89 for about four miles to Airport Road. Turn right on Airport Road and drive about four miles to Indian Creek Reservoir. At the fork, bear left and drive to the campground on the west side of the lake.

Contact: Bureau of Land Management, Carson City Field Office, 775/885-6000, fax 775/885-6147.

182 HOPE VALLEY

Scenic rating: 7

near the Carson River in Humboldt-Toiyabe National Forest

The West Fork of the Carson River runs right through Hope Valley, a pretty trout stream with a choice of four streamside campgrounds. Trout stocks are made near the campgrounds during summer. The campground at Hope Valley is just east of Carson Pass, at 7,300 feet elevation, in a very pretty area. A trailhead for the Pacific Crest Trail is three miles south of the campground. The primary nearby destination is Blue Lakes, about a 10-minute drive away. Insider's note: Little Tamarack Lake, set just beyond the turnoff for Lower Blue Lake, is excellent for swimming.

Campsites, facilities: There are 20 sites for tents or RVs up to 22 feet and a group site for tents or RVs up to 22 feet that can accommodate up to 16 people. No hookups. Picnic tables and fire grills are provided. Drinking water and vault toilets are available. Leashed pets are permitted.

Reservations, fees: Reservations are accepted for individual sites and are required for the group site at 877/444-6777 or www.recreation. gov ($10 reservation fee). Sites are $14 per night, $25 per night for the group camp. Open June through September.

Directions: From Sacramento, drive east on U.S. 50 to the junction with Highway 89. Turn south on Highway 89 and drive over Luther Pass to the junction with Highway 88. Turn right (west) and drive two miles to Blue Lakes Road. Turn left (south) and drive 1.5 miles to the campground on the right side of the road.

From Jackson, drive east on Highway 88 over Carson Pass and continue east for five miles to Blue Lakes Road. Turn right (south) and drive 1.5 miles to the campground on the right side of the road.

Contact: Humboldt-Toiyabe National Forest, Carson Ranger District, 775/882-2766, fax 775/884-8199.

183 TURTLE ROCK PARK

Scenic rating: 5

near Woodfords

Because it is administered at the county level, this pretty, wooded campground, set at 6,000 feet elevation, gets missed by a lot of folks. Most vacationers want the more pristine beauty of the nearby camps along the Carson River. But it doesn't get missed by mountain bikers, who travel here every July for the "Death Ride," a wild ride over several mountain passes. The camp always fills for this event. (If it snows, it closes, so call ahead if you're planning an autumn visit.) Nearby side trips include Grover Hot Springs and the hot springs in Markleeville.

Campsites, facilities: There are 28 sites for tents or RVs up to 34 feet (no hookups). Picnic tables and fire grills are provided. Drinking water, vault toilets, and showers are available. A recreation building is available for rent. A camp host is on-site. Some facilities are wheelchair-accessible. Coin laundry, groceries, and propane gas are available within two miles. Leashed pets are permitted.

Reservations, fees: Reservations are not accepted. Sites are $10–15 per night, $3 per night for each additional vehicle. Open May through mid-October, weather permitting.

Directions: From Sacramento, drive east on U.S. 50 to the junction with Highway 89. Turn south on Highway 89 and drive over Luther Pass to the junction with Highway 88. Turn left (east) and drive to Woodfords and the junction with Highway 89. Turn south on Highway 89 and drive 4.5 miles to the park entrance on the right side of the road.

Contact: Alpine County Public Works, 530/694-2140, www.alpinecountyca.gov.

184 GROVER HOT SPRINGS STATE PARK

Scenic rating: 8

near Markleeville

This is a famous spot for folks who like the rejuvenating powers of hot springs. Some say they feel a glow about them for weeks after soaking here. When touring the South Tahoe/Carson Pass area, many vacationers take part of a day to make the trip to the hot springs. This park is set in alpine meadow at 5,900 feet elevation on the east side of the Sierra at the edge of the Great Basin, and surrounded by peaks that top 10,000 feet. The hot springs are green because of the mineral deposits at the bottom of the pools. The landscape is primarily pine forest and sagebrush. It is well known for the great fluctuations in weather, from serious blizzards to intense, dry heat, and from mild nights to awesome rim-rattling thunderstorms. High winds are occasional but legendary. During thunderstorms, the hot springs pools close because of the chance of lightning strikes. Yet they remain open in snow, even blizzards, when it can be a euphoric experience to sit in the steaming water. Note that the pools are closed for maintenance for two weeks in September. A forest fire near here remains in evidence. A 2.4-mile round-trip hike starts from the campground and continues to a series of small waterfalls. Side-trip options include a nature trail in the park and driving to the Carson River (where the water is a mite cooler) and fishing for trout.

Campsites, facilities: There are 26 sites for tents, and 50 sites for tents or RVs up to 27 feet (no hookups) and trailers up to 24 feet. Picnic tables, fire grills, and food lockers are provided. Restrooms with flush toilets and coin showers (summer only), drinking water, hot springs pool with wheelchair access, and heated swimming pool are available. A grocery store is four miles away, and a coin laundry is within 10 miles. Leashed pets are permitted.

Reservations, fees: Reservations are accepted at 800/444-PARK (800/444-7275) or www.reserveamerica.com ($7.50 reservation fee). Sites are $20–25 per night, $6 per night for each additional vehicle, pool fees are $2–5 per person per day. Open year-round, with reduced facilities in winter.

Directions: From Sacramento, drive east on U.S. 50 to the junction with Highway 89. Turn south on Highway 89 and drive over Luther Pass to the junction with Highway 88. Turn left and drive to Woodfords and the junction with Highway 89. Turn right (south) and drive six miles to Markleeville and the junction with Hot Springs Road. Turn right and drive four miles to the park entrance.

Contact: Grover Hot Springs State Park, 530/694-2248; Sierra District, 530/525-7232; pool information, 530/525-7232, www.parks.ca.gov.

185 MARKLEEVILLE

Scenic rating: 7

on Markleeville Creek in Humboldt-Toiyabe National Forest

This is a pretty, streamside camp set at 5,500 feet along Markleeville Creek, a mile from the East Fork of the Carson River. The trout here are willing, but alas, are dinkers. This area is the transition zone where high mountains to the west give way to the high desert to the east. The hot springs in Markleeville and Grover Hot Springs State Park provide good side trips.

Campsites, facilities: There are 10 sites for tents or RVs up to 20 feet (no hookups). Trailers are not recommended because of road conditions. Picnic tables and fire grills are provided. Drinking water and vault toilets are available. A grocery store and restaurant are nearby. Leashed pets are permitted.

Reservations, fees: Reservations are not accepted. Sites are $14 per night. Open late April through September, weather permitting.

Directions: From Sacramento, drive east on U.S. 50 to the junction with Highway 89. Turn south on Highway 89 and drive over Luther Pass to the junction with Highway 88. Turn left and drive to Woodfords and the junction with Highway 89. Turn south, drive six miles to Markleeville, and continue for 0.5 mile to the campground on the left side of the highway.

Contact: Humboldt-Toiyabe National Forest, Carson Ranger District, 775/882-2766, fax 775/884-8199.

186 TOPAZ LAKE RV PARK

Scenic rating: 6

on Topaz Lake, near Markleeville

Topaz Lake, set at 5,000 feet elevation, is one of the hidden surprises for California anglers. The surprise is the size of the rainbow trout, with one of the highest rates of 15- to 18-inch trout of any lake in the mountain country. All water sports are allowed on this 2,400-acre lake, and there is a swimming area. The campground itself is attractive, with a number of shade trees. The setting is on the edge of barren high desert, which also serves as the border between California and Nevada. Wind is a problem for small boats, especially in the early summer. Some of the sites here are rented for the entire season.

Campsites, facilities: There are 54 sites with full hookups (30 amps) for RVs up to 42 feet. Some sites are pull-through. Tents are allowed with RVs only, though tent-only sites are allowed during non-peak season. Picnic tables and cable TV are provided. Restrooms with coin showers, coin laundry, propane gas, small grocery store, fish-cleaning station, Wi-Fi, and modem access are available. A 40-boat marina with courtesy launch and boat-trailer

storage is available at lakeside. Some facilities are wheelchair-accessible. Leashed pets are permitted.

Reservations, fees: Reservations are recommended. Sites are $26–28 per night, $3 per person for more than two people. Monthly rates available. Some credit cards accepted. Open March through early October, weather permitting.

Directions: From Carson City, drive south on U.S. 395 for 45 miles to Topaz Lake and the campground on the left side of the road.

From Bridgeport, drive north on U.S. 395 for 45 miles to the campground on the right side of the road (0.3 mile south of the California/Nevada border).

Contact: Topaz Lake RV Park, 530/495-2357, fax 530/495-2118, www.topazlakervpark. com.

187 UPPER BLUE LAKE DAM AND EXPANSION

Scenic rating: 7

near Carson Pass

These two camps are set across the road from each other along Upper Blue Lake, and are two of five camps in the area. The trout fishing is usually quite good here in early summer. (See the *Lower Blue Lake* listing in this chapter for more information.) These camps are three miles past the Lower Blue Lake campground. The elevation is 8,400 feet.

Campsites, facilities: There are 10 sites at Upper Blue Lake Dam and 15 sites at the expansion area for tents or RVs up to 25 feet. Picnic tables and fire grills are provided at Upper Blue Lake Dam only. Drinking water and vault toilets are available. Some facilities are wheelchair-accessible. Leashed pets are permitted.

Reservations, fees: Reservations are not accepted. Sites are $17 per night, $3 per night for each additional vehicle, $1 per pet per night.

Open June through mid-September, weather permitting.

Directions: From Sacramento, drive east on U.S. 50 to the junction with Highway 89. Turn south on Highway 89 and drive over Luther Pass to the junction with Highway 88. Turn right and drive 2.5 miles to Blue Lakes Road. Turn left and drive 12 miles to the junction at the south end of Lower Blue Lake. Turn right and drive three miles to the Upper Blue Lake Dam campground on the left side of the road or the expansion area on the right.

From Jackson, drive east on Highway 88 over Carson Pass and continue east for five miles to Blue Lakes Road. Turn right (south) and drive 12 miles to a junction at the south end of Lower Blue Lake. Turn right and drive three miles to the Upper Blue Lake Dam campground on the left side of the road or the expansion area on the right.

Contact: PG&E Land Projects, 916/386-5164, www.pge.com/recreation.

188 MIDDLE CREEK AND EXPANSION

Scenic rating: 7

near Carson Pass and Blue Lakes

This tiny, captivating spot, set along the creek that connects Upper and Lower Blue Lakes, provides a take-your-pick deal for anglers. PG&E has expanded this facility and now offers a larger camping area about 200 yards from the original campground. (See the *Lower Blue Lake* listing in this chapter for more information.) The elevation is 8,200 feet.

Campsites, facilities: There are five sites for tents or RVs up to 30 feet at Middle Creek and 25 sites for tents or RVs up to 45 feet at the expansion area. No hookups. Picnic tables and fire grills are provided. Drinking water and vault toilets are available at the expansion area. Some facilities are wheelchair-accessible. Leashed pets are permitted.

Reservations, fees: Reservations are not accepted. Sites are $17 per night, $3 per night for each additional vehicle, $1 per pet per night. Open June through September, weather permitting.

Directions: From Sacramento, drive east on U.S. 50 to the junction with Highway 89. Turn south on Highway 89 and drive over Luther Pass to the junction with Highway 88. Turn right and drive 2.5 miles to Blue Lakes Road. Turn left and drive 12 miles to a junction at the south end of Lower Blue Lake. Turn right and drive 1.5 miles to the Middle Creek campground on the left side of the road and continue another 200 yards to reach the expansion area.

From Jackson, drive east on Highway 88 over Carson Pass and continue east for five miles to Blue Lakes Road. Turn right (south) and drive 12 miles (road becomes dirt) to a junction at the south end of Lower Blue Lake. Turn right and drive 1.5 miles to the Middle Creek campground on the left side of the road and continue another 200 yards to reach the expansion area.

Contact: PG&E Land Projects, 916/386-5164, www.pge.com/recreation.

189 LOWER BLUE LAKE

Scenic rating: 7

near Carson Pass

This is the high country, at 8,400 feet, where the terrain is stark and steep and edged by volcanic ridgelines, and where the deep blue-green hue of lake water brightens the landscape. Lower Blue Lake provides a popular trout fishery, with rainbow, brook, and cutthroat trout all stocked regularly. The boat ramp is adjacent to the campground. The access road crosses the Pacific Crest Trail, providing a route to a series of small, pretty, hike-to lakes just outside the edge of the Mokelumne Wilderness.

Campsites, facilities: There are 17 sites for tents or RVs up to 25 feet (no hookups). Picnic tables and fire grills are provided. Drinking water and vault toilets are available. Leashed pets are permitted.

Reservations, fees: Reservations are not accepted. Sites are $18 per night, $3 per night for each additional vehicle, $1 per pet per night, 14-day occupancy limit. Open June through September, weather permitting.

Directions: From Sacramento, drive east on U.S. 50 to the junction with Highway 89. Turn south on Highway 89 and drive over Luther Pass to the junction with Highway 88. Turn right and drive 2.5 miles to Blue Lakes Road. Turn left and drive 12 miles to a junction at the south end of Lower Blue Lake. Turn right and drive a short distance to the campground on the left side of the road.

From Jackson, drive east on Highway 88 over Carson Pass and continue east for five miles to Blue Lakes Road. Turn right (south) and drive 12 miles to a junction at the south end of Lower Blue Lake. Turn right and drive a short distance to the campground on the left.

Contact: PG&E Land Projects, 916/386-5164, www.pge.com/recreation.

190 SILVER CREEK

Scenic rating: 6

in Humboldt-Toiyabe National Forest

This pretty spot, set near Silver Creek, has easy access from Highway 4 and, in years without washouts, good fishing in early summer for small trout. It is in the remote high Sierra, east of Ebbetts Pass. A side trip to Ebbetts Pass features Kinney Lake, Pacific Crest Trail access, and a trailhead at the north end of the lake (on the west side of Highway 4) for a mile hike to Lower Kinney Lake. No bikes are permitted on the trails. The elevation is 6,800 feet.

Campsites, facilities: There are 22 sites for tents or RVs up to 22 feet (no hookups). Picnic tables and fire grills are provided. Drinking water and vault toilets are available. Some facilities are wheelchair-accessible. Leashed pets are permitted.

Reservations, fees: Reservations are accepted at 877/444-6777 or www.recreation.gov ($10 reservation fee). Sites are $15 per night. Open late May through early September, weather permitting.

Directions: From Angels Camp, drive east on Highway 4 all the way over Ebbetts Pass and continue for about six miles to the campground.

From Markleeville, drive south on Highway 89 to the junction with Highway 4. Turn west on Highway 4 (steep and winding) and drive about five miles to the campground.

Contact: Humboldt-Toiyabe National Forest, Carson Ranger District, 775/882-2766, fax 775/884-8199.

191 MOSQUITO LAKE

Scenic rating: 10

at Mosquito Lake in Stanislaus National Forest

Mosquito Lake is in a pristine Sierra setting at 8,260 feet elevation, presenting remarkable beauty for a place that can be reached by car. Most people believe that Mosquito Lake is for day-use only, and that's why they crowd into nearby Lake Alpine Campground. But it's not just for day-use, and this camp is often overlooked because it is about a mile west of the little lake. The lake is small, a pretty emerald green, and even has a few small trout in it. The camp provides a few dispersed sites.

Campsites, facilities: There are eight sites for tents or RVs up to 16 feet (no hookups). Picnic tables and fire grills are provided. Vault toilets are available. No drinking water is available. Garbage must be packed out. Leashed pets are permitted.

Reservations, fees: Reservations are not accepted. Sites are $5 per night. A free campfire permit is required from the district office. Open June through September, weather permitting.

Directions: From Angels Camp, drive east on Highway 4 to Lake Alpine and continue for about six miles to the campground on the left side of the road.

Contact: Stanislaus National Forest, Calaveras Ranger District, 209/795-1381, fax 209/795-6849.

192 HERMIT VALLEY
🏃 🛶 🐕 🚐 ⛰️

Scenic rating: 8

in Stanislaus National Forest

This tiny, remote, little-known spot is set near the border of the Mokelumne Wilderness near where Grouse Creek enters the Mokelumne River, at 7,100 feet elevation. Looking north, there is a good view into Deer Valley. A primitive road, 0.5-mile west of camp, is routed through Deer Valley north for six miles to the Blue Lakes. On the opposite (south) side of the road from the camp there is a little-traveled hiking trail that is routed up Grouse Creek to Beaver Meadow and Willow Meadow near the border of the Carson-Iceberg Wilderness.

Campsites, facilities: There are 25 sites for tents or RVs up to 16 feet (no hookups). Vault toilets are available. No drinking water is available. Garbage must be packed out. Leashed pets are permitted.

Reservations, fees: Reservations are not accepted. There is no fee for camping. A free campfire permit is required from the district office. Open June through October, weather permitting.

Directions: From Angels Camp, drive east on Highway 4 to Lake Alpine and continue for about nine miles to the campground on the left side of the road (just east of the Mokelumne

River Bridge). Note: Trailers are not recommended because of the steep access road.

Contact: Stanislaus National Forest, Calaveras Ranger District, 209/795-1381, fax 209/795-6849.

193 BLOOMFIELD
🏃 🛶 🐕 5% 🚐 ⛰️

Scenic rating: 7

in Stanislaus National Forest

This is a primitive and little-known camp set at 7,800 feet elevation near Ebbetts Pass. The North Fork Mokelumne River runs right by the camp, with good stream access for about a mile on each side of the camp. The access road continues south to Highland Lakes, a destination that provides car-top boating, fair fishing, and trailheads for hiking into the Carson-Iceberg Wilderness.

Campsites, facilities: There are 20 sites for tents or RVs up to 16 feet (no hookups). Picnic tables and fire rings are provided. Drinking water and vault toilets are available. Garbage must be packed out. Facilities and supplies are available at Lake Alpine Lodge, 25 minutes away. Leashed pets are permitted.

Reservations, fees: Reservations are not accepted. Sites are $8 per night. A free campfire permit is required from the district office. Open June through October, weather permitting.

Directions: From Angels Camp, drive east on Highway 4 to Lake Alpine and continue for about 15 miles to Forest Road 8N01 on the right side of the road (1.5 miles west of Ebbetts Pass). Turn right and drive two miles to the campground on the right side of the road. Note: Access roads are rough and not recommended for trailers.

Contact: Stanislaus National Forest, Calaveras Ranger District, 209/795-1381, fax 209/795-6849.

194 PACIFIC VALLEY
🚶 🐕 🚐 ⛺

Scenic rating: 7

in Stanislaus National Forest overlooking
Pacific Creek

This is a do-it-yourself special; that is, more
of a general area for camping than a campground, set up for backpackers heading out
on expeditions into the Carson-Iceberg Wilderness to the south. It is set at 7,600 feet
elevation along Pacific Creek, a tributary to
the Mokelumne River. The landscape is an
open lodgepole forest with nearby meadow
and a small stream. The trail from camp is
routed south and reaches three forks within
two miles. The best is routed deep into the
wilderness, flanking Hiram Peak (9,760 feet),
Airola Peak (9,938 feet), and Iceberg Peak
(9,720 feet).

Campsites, facilities: There are 15 sites for
tents or RVs up to 16 feet (no hookups). Picnic
tables and fire grills are provided. Vault toilets
are available. No drinking water is available.
Garbage must be packed out. Leashed pets
are permitted.

Reservations, fees: Reservations are not accepted. There is no fee for camping. A free
campfire permit is required from the district
office. Open June through October, weather
permitting.

Directions: From Angels Camp, drive east on
Highway 4 to Lake Alpine and continue for
eight miles to a dirt road. Turn right (south)
and drive about 0.5 mile to the campground.
Note: Trailers are not recommended because
of the rough roads.

Contact: Stanislaus National Forest, Calaveras Ranger District, 209/795-1381, fax
209/795-6849.

195 UPPER AND LOWER HIGHLAND LAKES
🚶 🏊 🛶 🚐 🐕 🚐 ⛺

Scenic rating: 9

in Stanislaus National Forest

This camp is set between Upper and Lower
Highland Lakes, two beautiful alpine ponds
that offer good fishing for small brook trout as
well as spectacular panoramic views. The boat
speed limit is 15 mph, and a primitive boat
ramp is at Upper Highland Lake. Swimming
is allowed, although the water is very cold.
The elevation at this campground is 8,600
feet, with Hiram Peak (9,760 feet) looming
to the nearby south. Several great trails are
available from this camp. Day hikes include
up Boulder Creek and Disaster Creek. For
overnight backpacking, a trail that starts at
the north end of Highland Lakes (a parking
area is available) is routed east for two miles
to Wolf Creek Pass, where it connects with
the Pacific Crest Trail; from there, turn left
or right—you can't lose. The access road is not
recommended for trailers or large RVs.

Campsites, facilities: There are 35 sites for
tents or RVs up to 16 feet (no hookups). Picnic
tables and fire grills are provided. Drinking
water and vault toilets are available. Garbage must be packed out. Leashed pets are
permitted.

Reservations, fees: Reservations are not accepted. Sites are $8 per night. Open June
through October, weather permitting.

Directions: From Angels Camp, drive east on
Highway 4 to Arnold, past Lake Alpine, and
continue for 14.5 miles to Forest Road 8N01
(one mile west of Ebbetts Pass). Turn right and
drive 7.5 miles to the campground on the right
side of the road. Note: The roads are rough
and trailers are not recommended.

Contact: Stanislaus National Forest, Calaveras Ranger District, 209/795-1381, fax
209/795-6849.

196 PINE MARTEN

Scenic rating: 8

near Lake Alpine in Stanislaus National Forest

Lake Alpine is a beautiful Sierra lake surrounded by granite and pines and set at 7,320 feet, just above where the snowplows stop in winter. This camp is on the northeast side, about a quarter mile from the shore. Fishing for rainbow trout is good in May and early June, before the summer crush. Despite the long drive to get here, the lake is becoming better known for its beauty, camping, and hiking. Lake Alpine has 180 surface acres and a 10-mph speed limit. A trailhead out of nearby Silver Valley Camp provides a two-mile hike to pretty Duck Lake and beyond into the Carson-Iceberg Wilderness.

Campsites, facilities: There are 32 sites for tents or RVs up to 27 feet (no hookups). Picnic tables and fire grills are provided. Drinking water and restrooms with flush toilets are available. A boat ramp is nearby. A grocery store, propane gas, and coin laundry are nearby. Some facilities are wheelchair-accessible. Leashed pets are permitted.

Reservations, fees: Reservations are not accepted. Sites are $20 per night. Open June through early October, weather permitting.

Directions: From Angels Camp, drive east on Highway 4 to Arnold and continue for 29 miles to Lake Alpine. Drive to the northeast end of the lake to the campground entrance on the right side of the road.

Contact: Stanislaus National Forest, Calaveras Ranger District, 209/795-1381, fax 209/795-6849.

197 SILVER VALLEY

Scenic rating: 8

on Lake Alpine in Stanislaus National Forest

This is one of four camps at Lake Alpine. Silver Valley is on the northeast end of the lake at 7,400 feet elevation, with a trailhead nearby that provides access to the Carson-Iceberg Wilderness. (For recreation information, see the *Pine Marten* listing in this chapter.)

Campsites, facilities: There are 21 sites for tents or RVs up to 16 feet (no hookups). Picnic tables and fire grills are provided. Drinking water and vault toilets are available. Some facilities are wheelchair-accessible. A boat launch, grocery store, and coin laundry are nearby. Leashed pets are permitted.

Reservations, fees: Reservations are not accepted. Sites are $20 per night. A free campfire permit is required. Open June through October, weather permitting.

Directions: From Angels Camp, drive east on Highway 4 to Arnold and continue for 29 miles to Lake Alpine. Drive to the northeast end of the lake to the campground entrance on the right side of the road. Turn right and drive 0.5 mile to the campground.

Contact: Stanislaus National Forest, Calaveras Ranger District, 209/795-1381, fax 209/795-6849.

198 LAKE ALPINE CAMPGROUND

Scenic rating: 8

on Lake Alpine in Stanislaus National Forest

BEST (

This is the campground that is in the greatest demand at Lake Alpine, and it is easy to see why. It is very small, a boat ramp is adjacent to the camp, you can get supplies at a small grocery store within walking distance, and during the evening rise you can often see the jumping trout from your campsite. Lake Alpine is one of the prettiest lakes you can drive to, set at 7,303 feet elevation amid pines and Sierra granite. A trailhead out of nearby Silver Valley Camp provides a two-mile hike to pretty Duck Lake and beyond into the Carson-Iceberg Wilderness.

Campsites, facilities: There are 25 sites for tents or RVs up to 27 feet (no hookups). Picnic tables and fire grills are provided. Drinking water, flush and vault toilets, and a boat launch are available. A grocery store, restaurant, coin showers, and a coin laundry are nearby. Some facilities are wheelchair-accessible. Leashed pets are permitted.

Reservations, fees: Reservations are not accepted. Sites are $20 per night. Open June through October, weather permitting.

Directions: From Angels Camp, drive east on Highway 4 to Arnold and continue for 29 miles to Lake Alpine. Just before reaching the lake turn right and drive 0.25 mile to the campground on the left.

Contact: Stanislaus National Forest, Calaveras Ranger District, 209/795-1381, fax 209/795-6849.

199 SILVER TIP

Scenic rating: 6

near Lake Alpine in Stanislaus National Forest

This camp is just over 0.5 mile from the shore of Lake Alpine at an elevation of 7,350 feet. Why then would anyone camp here when there are campgrounds right at the lake? Two reasons: One, those lakeside camps are often full on summer weekends. Two, Highway 4 is snowplowed to this campground entrance, but not beyond. So in big snow years when the road is still closed in late spring and early summer, you can park your rig here to camp, then hike in to the lake. In the fall, it also makes for a base camp for hunters. (See the

Lake Alpine Campground listing in this chapter for more information.)

Campsites, facilities: There are 23 sites for tents or RVs up to 27 feet (no hookups). Picnic tables and fire grills are provided. Drinking water and flush toilets are available. A boat launch is about a mile away. A grocery store, coin laundry, and coin showers are nearby. Some facilities are wheelchair-accessible. Leashed pets are permitted.

Reservations, fees: Reservations are not accepted. Sites are $20 per night. Open June through early October, weather permitting.

Directions: From Angels Camp, drive east on Highway 4 to Arnold and continue for 29 miles to Lake Alpine. A mile before reaching the lake (adjacent to the Bear Valley/Mount Reba turnoff), turn right at the campground entrance on the right side of the road.

Contact: Stanislaus National Forest, Calaveras Ranger District, 209/795-1381, fax 209/795-6849.

200 UNION RESERVOIR WALK-IN

Scenic rating: 10

northeast of Arnold in Stanislaus National Forest

Union Reservoir is set in Sierra granite at 6,850 feet. It's a beautiful and quiet lake that is kept that way with rules that mandate a 5-mph speed limit and walk-in camping only. Most of the sites provide lakeside views. Fishing is often good—trolling for kokanee salmon—but you need a boat. The setting is great, especially for canoes or other small boats. This camp was once a secret, but now it fills up quickly on weekends.

Campsites, facilities: There are 15 dispersed, primitive walk-in tent sites. Pit toilets are available. No drinking water is available. Garbage must be packed out. A boat ramp is nearby. Leashed pets are permitted.

Reservations, fees: Reservations are not accepted. There is no fee for camping. Open June through September, weather permitting.

Directions: From Angels Camp, drive east on Highway 4 for about 32 miles to Spicer Reservoir Road. Turn right and drive east for about seven miles to Forest Road 7N75. Turn left and drive three miles to Union Reservoir. There are four designated parking areas for the walk-in camps along the road.

Contact: Stanislaus National Forest, Calaveras Ranger District, 209/795-1381, fax 209/795-6849; Northern California Power Agency, 209/728-1387.

201 SPICER RESERVOIR AND GROUP CAMP

🚶 🏊 🎣 🚣 🐕 ♿ 🚐 ⛰

Scenic rating: 8

near Spicer Reservoir in Stanislaus National Forest

Set at 6,200 feet elevation and covering only 227 acres, Spicer Reservoir isn't big by reservoir standards, but it is surrounded by canyon walls and is quite pretty from a boat. Good trout fishing adds to the beauty. A boat ramp is available near the campground, and the lake speed limit is 10 mph. A trail links the east end of Spicer Reservoir to the Summit Lake trailhead, with the route bordering the north side of the reservoir. Note: This area can really get hammered with snow in big winters, so always check for access conditions in the spring and early summer before planning a trip.

Campsites, facilities: There are 60 sites for tents or RVs up to 50 feet (no hookups). There is one group site for tents or RVs up to 28 feet (no hookups) that can accommodate up to 60 people. Picnic tables and fire grills are provided. Drinking water and vault toilets, group facilities, and a primitive amphitheater are available. A boat ramp is nearby. Some facilities are wheelchair-accessible. Leashed pets are permitted.

Reservations, fees: Reservations are not accepted for individual sites, but are required for the group site at 209/295-4512. Sites are $20 per night. The group site is $140 per night. Open June through October, weather permitting.

Directions: From Angels Camp, drive east on Highway 4 for about 32 miles to Spicer Reservoir Road/Forest Road 7N01. Turn right, drive seven miles, bear right at a fork with a sharp right turn, and drive a mile to the campground at the west end of the lake.

Contact: Stanislaus National Forest, Calaveras Ranger District, 209/795-1381, fax 209/795-6849.

202 SAND FLAT-STANISLAUS RIVER

🚶 🏊 🎣 🐕 ♿ 🚐 ⛰

Scenic rating: 7

on the Clark Fork of the Stanislaus River in Stanislaus National Forest

Sand Flat campground, at 6,200 feet, is only three miles (by vehicle on Clark Fork Road) from an outstanding trailhead for the Carson-Iceberg Wilderness. The camp is used primarily by late-arriving backpackers who camp for the night, get their gear in order, then head off on the trail. The trail is routed out of Iceberg Meadow, with a choice of heading north to Paradise Valley (unbelievably green and loaded with corn lilies along a creek) and onward to the Pacific Crest Trail, or east to Clark Fork and upstream to Clark Fork Meadow below Sonora Peak. Two choices, both winners.

Campsites, facilities: There are 53 sites for tents or RVs up to 22 feet (no hookups) and 15 walk-in tent sites. Picnic tables and fire grills are provided. Drinking water and vault toilets are available. You can buy supplies in Dardanelle. Some facilities are wheelchair-accessible. Leashed pets are permitted.

Reservations, fees: Reservations are not accepted. Sites are $11 per night per vehicle.

Open May through early October, weather permitting.

Directions: From Sonora, drive east on Highway 108 past the town of Strawberry to Clark Fork Road. Turn left on Clark Fork Road and drive six miles to the campground entrance on the right side of the road.

Contact: Stanislaus National Forest, Summit Ranger District, 209/965-3434, fax 209/965-3372.

203 CLARK FORK AND CLARK FORK HORSE

Scenic rating: 8

on the Clark Fork of the Stanislaus River in Stanislaus National Forest

Clark Fork borders the Clark Fork of the Stanislaus River and is used by both drive-in vacationers and backpackers. A trailhead for hikers is 0.25 mile away on the north side of Clark Fork Road (a parking area is available here). From here the trail is routed up along Arnot Creek, skirting between Iceberg Peak on the left and Lightning Mountain on the right, for eight miles to Wolf Creek Pass and the junction with the Pacific Crest Trail. (For another nearby trailhead, see the *Sand Flat–Stanislaus River* listing in this chapter.)

Campsites, facilities: There are 88 sites for tents or RVs up to 40 feet, and at an adjacent area, 14 equestrian sites for tents or RVs up to 22 feet. No hookups. Picnic tables and fire grills are provided. Drinking water and flush toilets are available. At the equestrian site, no drinking water is available but there are water troughs. Some facilities are wheelchair-accessible. You can buy supplies in Dardanelle. Leashed pets are permitted.

Reservations, fees: Reservations are not accepted. Sites are $14–16 per night, horse camp fee is $9 per night, $5 per night for each additional vehicle. Open May through October, weather permitting.

Directions: From Sonora, drive east on Highway 108 past the town of Strawberry to Clark Fork Road. Turn left, drive five miles, turn right again, and drive 0.5 mile to the campground entrance on the right side of the road.

Contact: Stanislaus National Forest, Summit Ranger District, 209/965-3434, fax 209/965-3372.

204 FENCE CREEK

Scenic rating: 4

near the Middle Fork of the Stanislaus River in Stanislaus National Forest

Fence Creek is a feeder stream to Clark Fork, which runs a mile downstream and joins with the Middle Fork Stanislaus River en route to Donnells Reservoir. The camp sits along little Fence Creek, at 5,600 feet elevation. Fence Creek Road continues east for another nine miles to an outstanding trailhead at Iceberg Meadow on the edge of the Carson-Iceberg Wilderness.

Campsites, facilities: There are 38 sites for tents or RVs up to 22 feet (no hookups). Picnic tables and fire grills are provided. Vault toilets are available. No drinking water is available. You can buy supplies in Pinecrest about 10 miles away. Leashed pets are permitted.

Reservations, fees: Reservations are not accepted. Sites are $6 per night. Open May through mid-October, weather permitting.

Directions: From Sonora, drive east on Highway 108 about 50 miles to Clark Ford Road. Turn left and drive a mile to Forest Road 6N06. Turn left again and drive 0.5 mile to the campground on the right.

Contact: Stanislaus National Forest, Summit Ranger District, 209/965-3434, fax 209/965-3372.

205 BOULDER FLAT

Scenic rating: 7

near the Middle Fork of the Stanislaus River in Stanislaus National Forest

You want camping on the Stanislaus River? As you drive east on Highway 108, this is the first in a series of campgrounds along the Middle Fork Stanislaus. Boulder Flat is set at 5,600 feet elevation and offers easy access off the highway. Here's another bonus: This stretch of river is stocked with trout.

Campsites, facilities: There are 21 sites for tents or RVs up to 22 feet (no hookups). Picnic tables and fire grills are provided. Drinking water and vault toilets are available. You can buy supplies in Dardanelle. Some facilities are wheelchair-accessible. Leashed pets are permitted.

Reservations, fees: Reservations are not accepted. Sites are $15–17 per night, $5 per night for each additional vehicle. Open May through October, weather permitting.

Directions: From Sonora, drive east on Highway 108 past the town of Strawberry to Clark Fork Road. At Clark Fork Road, continue east on Highway 108 for a mile to the campground on the left side of the road.

Contact: Stanislaus National Forest, Summit Ranger District, 209/965-3434, fax 209/965-3372.

206 BRIGHTMAN FLAT

Scenic rating: 7

on the Middle Fork of the Stanislaus River in Stanislaus National Forest

This camp is on the Middle Fork of the Stanislaus River at 5,700 feet elevation, a mile east of Boulder Flat and two miles west of Dardanelle. (For recreation options, see the *Pigeon Flat* listing in this chapter.)

Campsites, facilities: There are 33 sites for tents or RVs up to 22 feet (no hookups). Picnic tables and fire grills are provided. Vault toilets and drinking water are available. You can buy supplies in Dardanelle. Some facilities are wheelchair-accessible. Leashed pets are permitted.

Reservations, fees: Reservations are not accepted. Sites are $12 per night, $5 per night for each additional vehicle. Open May through October, weather permitting.

Directions: From Sonora, drive east on Highway 108 past the town of Strawberry to Clark Fork Road. At Clark Fork Road continue east on Highway 108 for two miles to the campground entrance on the left side of the road.

Contact: Stanislaus National Forest, Summit Ranger District, 209/965-3434, fax 209/965-3372.

207 DARDANELLE

Scenic rating: 7

on the Middle Fork of the Stanislaus River in Stanislaus National Forest

This Forest Service camp is within walking distance of supplies in Dardanelle and is also right alongside the Middle Fork Stanislaus River. This section of river is stocked with trout by the Department of Fish and Game. The trail to see Columns of the Giants is just 1.5 miles to the east out of Pigeon Flat.

Campsites, facilities: There are 28 sites for tents or RVs up to 28 feet (no hookups). Picnic tables and fire grills are provided. Drinking water and vault toilets are available. You can buy supplies in Dardanelle. Some facilities are wheelchair-accessible. Leashed pets are permitted.

Reservations, fees: Reservations are not accepted. Sites are $17–21 per night, $5 per night for each additional vehicle. Open May through October, weather permitting.

Directions: From Sonora, drive east on Highway 108 past Strawberry to Dardanelle and the campground on the left side of the road.

Contact: Stanislaus National Forest, Summit Ranger District, 209/965-3434, fax 209/965-3372.

208 PIGEON FLAT

Scenic rating: 7

on the Middle Fork of the Stanislaus River in Stanislaus National Forest

The prime attraction at Pigeon Flat is the short trail to Columns of the Giants, a rare example of columnar hexagonal rock, similar to the phenomenon at Devils Postpile near Mammoth Lakes. In addition, the camp is adjacent to the Middle Fork Stanislaus River; trout are small here and get fished hard. Supplies are available within walking distance in Dardanelle. The elevation is 6,000 feet.

Campsites, facilities: There are nine walk-in tent sites. Picnic tables and fire grills are provided. Vault toilets are available. No drinking water is available. You can buy supplies in Dardanelle. Leashed pets are permitted.

Reservations, fees: Reservations are not accepted. Sites are $10 per night, $5 per night for each additional vehicle. Open May through October, weather permitting.

Directions: From Sonora, drive east on Highway 108 past the town of Strawberry to Dardanelle. Continue 1.5 miles east to the campground on the right side of the road, next to the Columns of the Giants Interpretive Site.

Contact: Stanislaus National Forest, Summit Ranger District, 209/965-3434, fax 209/965-3372.

209 EUREKA VALLEY

Scenic rating: 8

on the Middle Fork of the Stanislaus River in Stanislaus National Forest

There are about a half-dozen campgrounds on this stretch of the Middle Fork Stanislaus River near Dardanelle, at 6,100 feet elevation. The river runs along two sides of this campground, making it quite pretty. This stretch of river is planted with trout by the Department of Fish and Game, but it is hit pretty hard despite its relatively isolated location. A good short and easy hike is to Columns of the Giants, accessible on a 0.25-mile-long trail out of Pigeon Flat, a mile to the west.

Campsites, facilities: There are 28 sites for tents or RVs up to 22 feet (no hookups). Picnic tables and fire grills are provided. Drinking water and vault toilets are available. You can buy supplies in Dardanelle. Leashed pets are permitted.

Reservations, fees: Reservations are not accepted. Sites are $15 per night, $5 per night for each additional vehicle. Open May through October, weather permitting.

Directions: From Sonora, drive east on Highway 108 past the town of Strawberry to Dardanelle. Continue three miles east to the campground on the right.

Contact: Stanislaus National Forest, Summit Ranger District, 209/965-3434, fax 209/965-3372.

210 NIAGARA CREEK

Scenic rating: 6

in Stanislaus National Forest

This camp is set beside Niagara Creek at 6,600 feet elevation, high in Stanislaus National Forest on the western slopes of the Sierra. It provides direct access to a network of roads in national forest, including routes to Double Dome Rock and another to Eagle Meadows. So if you have a four-wheel-drive vehicle or dirt bike, this is the place to come.

Campsites, facilities: There are 10 sites for tents or RVs up to 22 feet (no hookups); some are walk-in sites. Picnic tables and fire grills are provided. A vault toilet is available. No drinking water is available. You can buy supplies in Pinecrest about 10 miles away. Leashed pets are permitted.

Reservations, fees: Reservations are not accepted. Sites are $6 per night. Open May through October, weather permitting.

Directions: From Sonora, drive east on Highway 108 to the town of Strawberry and continue for about 15 miles to Eagle Meadows Road/Forest Road 5N01 on the right. Turn right and drive 0.5 mile to the campground on the left.

Contact: Stanislaus National Forest, Summit Ranger District, 209/965-3434, fax 209/965-3372.

211 MILL CREEK
🏕️🛶🏠🚐⛺

Scenic rating: 7

on Mill Creek in Stanislaus National Forest

This pretty little camp is set along Mill Creek at 6,200 feet elevation, high in Stanislaus National Forest, near a variety of outdoor recreation options. The camp is near the Middle Fork Stanislaus River, which is stocked with trout near Donnells. For hiking, there is an outstanding trailhead at Kennedy Meadow (east of Donnells). For fishing, both Beardsley Reservoir (boat necessary) and Pinecrest Lake (shoreline prospects fair) provide two nearby alternatives.

Campsites, facilities: There are 18 sites for tents or RVs up to 22 feet (no hookups). Picnic tables and fire grills are provided. Vault toilets

are available. No drinking water is available. Leashed pets are permitted.

Reservations, fees: Reservations are not accepted. Sites are $6 per night. Open May through mid-October, weather permitting.

Directions: From Sonora, drive east on Highway 108 to Strawberry. From Strawberry continue east on Highway 108 about 13 miles to Forest Road 5N21. Turn right on Forest Road 5N21 and drive 0.1 mile to the campground access road (Forest Road 5N26) on the left.

Contact: Stanislaus National Forest, Summit Ranger District, 209/965-3434, fax 209/965-3372.

212 NIAGARA CREEK OFF-HIGHWAY VEHICLE
🏕️🛶🏠🚐⛺

Scenic rating: 6

on Niagara Creek in Stanislaus National Forest

This small, primitive camp along Niagara Creek is designed primarily for people with off-highway vehicles. Got it? It is set on Niagara Creek near Donnells Reservoir. The elevation is 6,600 feet.

Campsites, facilities: There are 10 sites for tents or RVs up to 22 feet (no hookups). Picnic tables and fire grills are provided. A vault toilet is available. No drinking water is available. You can buy supplies in Pinecrest about 10 miles away. Leashed pets are permitted.

Reservations, fees: Reservations are not accepted. Sites are $6 per night. Open May through October, weather permitting.

Directions: From Sonora, drive east on Highway 108 to Strawberry and continue for about 15 miles to Eagle Meadows Road/Forest Road 5N01. Turn right and drive 1.5 miles to the campground on the left (just after crossing the bridge at Niagara Creek).

Contact: Stanislaus National Forest, Summit Ranger District, 209/965-3434, fax 209/965-3372.

213 BAKER

Scenic rating: 7

on the Middle Fork of the Stanislaus River in
Stanislaus National Forest

Baker lies at the turnoff for the well-known
and popular Kennedy Meadow trailhead for
the Emigrant Wilderness. The camp is set
along the Middle Fork Stanislaus River, at
6,200 feet elevation, downstream a short
way from the confluence with Deadman
Creek. The trailhead, with a nearby horse
corral, is another two miles farther on the
Kennedy Meadow access road. From here
it is a 1.5-mile hike to a fork in the trail;
right will take you two miles to Relief Reservoir, 7,226 feet, and left will route you
up Kennedy Creek for five miles to pretty
Kennedy Lake, just north of Kennedy Peak
(10,716 feet).

Campsites, facilities: There are 44 sites for
tents or RVs up to 22 feet (no hookups). Picnic
tables and fire grills are provided. Drinking
water and vault toilets are available. You can
buy supplies in Dardanelle. Some facilities
are wheelchair-accessible. Leashed pets are
permitted.

Reservations, fees: Reservations are not accepted. Sites are $17–34 per night, $5 per
night for each additional vehicle. Open May
through mid-October, weather permitting.

Directions: From Sonora, drive east on Highway 108 past Strawberry to Dardanelle. From
Dardanelle, continue 5.5 miles east to the
campground on the right side of the road at
the turnoff for Kennedy Meadow.

Contact: Stanislaus National Forest, Summit Ranger District, 209/965-3434, fax
209/965-3372.

214 DEADMAN

Scenic rating: 7

on the Middle Fork of the Stanislaus River in
Stanislaus National Forest

This is a popular trailhead camp and an ideal
jump-off point for backpackers heading into
the adjacent Emigrant Wilderness. The elevation is 6,200 feet. The camp is a short distance
from Baker (see the *Baker* listing in this chapter for hiking destinations).

Campsites, facilities: There are 17 sites for
tents or RVs up to 22 feet (no hookups). Picnic
tables and fire grills are provided. Drinking
water and vault toilets are available. You can
buy supplies in Dardanelle. Some facilities
are wheelchair-accessible. Leashed pets are
permitted.

Reservations, fees: Reservations are not accepted. Sites are $17–34 per night, $5 per
night for each additional vehicle. Open May
through early October, weather permitting.

Directions: From Sonora, drive east on Highway 108 past the town of Strawberry to Dardanelle. From Dardanelle, continue 5.5 miles
east to the Kennedy Meadow turnoff. Drive a
mile on Kennedy Meadow Road to the campground, which is opposite the parking area for
Kennedy Meadow Trail.

Contact: Stanislaus National Forest, Summit Ranger District, 209/965-3434, fax
209/965-3372.

215 BOOTLEG

Scenic rating: 6

on the Walker River in Humboldt-Toiyabe
National Forest

Location is always key, and easy access off U.S.
395, the adjacent West Walker River, and good
trout stocks in summer make this a popular
spot. (See the *Chris Flat* and *Sonora Bridge*

listings in this chapter for more information.) Note that this camp is on the west side of the highway, and anglers will have to cross the road to gain fishing access. The elevation is 6,600 feet.

Campsites, facilities: There are 63 sites for tents or RVs up to 35 feet (no hookups). Picnic tables and fire grills are provided. Drinking water and flush toilets are available. Leashed pets are permitted.

Reservations, fees: Reservations are accepted at 877/444-6777 or www.recreation.gov ($10 reservation fee). Sites are $17 per night, $6 per night for each additional vehicle. Open early May through mid-September, weather permitting.

Directions: From Carson City, drive south on U.S. 395 to Coleville and then continue south for 13 miles to the campground on the west side of the highway (six miles north of the junction of U.S. 395 and Highway 108).

Contact: Humboldt-Toiyabe National Forest, Bridgeport Ranger District, 760/932-7070, fax 760/932-5899.

216 CHRIS FLAT

🏃 🚣 🏕 🚙 ⛺

Scenic rating: 7

on the Walker River in Humboldt-Toiyabe National Forest

This is one of two campgrounds set along U.S. 395 next to the West Walker River, a pretty trout stream with easy access and good stocks of rainbow trout. The plants are usually made at two campgrounds, resulting in good prospects here at Chris Flat and west on Highway 108 at Sonora Bridge. The elevation is 6,600 feet.

Campsites, facilities: There are 15 sites for tents or RVs up to 30 feet (no hookups). Picnic tables and fire grills are provided. Drinking water (shut off during freezing temperatures) and vault toilets are available. Leashed pets are permitted.

Reservations, fees: Reservations are accepted at 877/444-6777 or www.recreation.gov ($10 reservation fee). Sites are $17 per night, $6 per night for each additional vehicle. Open April through mid-November, weather permitting.

Directions: From Carson City, drive south on U.S. 395 to Coleville and then continue south for 15 miles to the campground on the east side of the road (four miles north of the junction of U.S. 395 and Highway 108).

Contact: Humboldt-Toiyabe National Forest, Bridgeport Ranger District, 760/932-7070, fax 760/932-5899.

217 SONORA BRIDGE

🏃 🚣 🏕 🚙 ⛺

Scenic rating: 7

near the Walker River in Humboldt-Toiyabe National Forest

The West Walker River is a pretty stream, flowing over boulders and into pools, and each year this stretch of river is well stocked with rainbow trout by the Department of Fish and Game. One of several campgrounds near the West Walker, Sonora Bridge is set at 6,800 feet elevation, about 0.5 mile from the river. The setting is in the transition zone from high mountains to high desert on the eastern edge of the Sierra Nevada.

Campsites, facilities: There are 23 sites for tents or RVs up to 35 feet (no hookups). Picnic tables and fire grills are provided. Drinking water and vault toilets are available. Leashed pets are permitted.

Reservations, fees: Reservations are accepted at 877/444-6777 or www.recreation.gov ($10 reservation fee). Sites are $15 per night, $6 per night for each additional vehicle. Open mid-May through mid-October, weather permitting.

Directions: From north of Bridgeport, at the junction of U.S. 395 and Highway 108, turn west on Highway 108 and drive one mile to the campground on the left.

Contact: Humboldt-Toiyabe National Forest, Bridgeport Ranger District, 760/932-7070, fax 760/932-5899.

218 LEAVITT MEADOWS
🏃 🛶 🐴 🚐 ⛺

Scenic rating: 9

on the Walker River in Humboldt-Toiyabe National Forest

While Leavitt Meadows sits right beside Highway 108, a little winding two-laner, there are several nearby off-pavement destinations that make this camp a winner. The camp is set in the high eastern Sierra, east of Sonora Pass at 7,000 feet elevation, where Leavitt Creek and Brownie Creek enter the West Walker River. There is a pack station for horseback riding nearby. For four-wheel-drive owners, the most popular side trip is driving four miles west on Highway 108, then turning south and driving four miles to Leavitt Lake, where the trout fishing is sometimes spectacular, if you're trolling a gold Cripplure.

Campsites, facilities: There are 16 sites for tents or RVs up to 30 feet (no hookups). Picnic tables, food lockers, and fire grills are provided. Drinking water and vault toilets are available. Leashed pets are permitted.

Reservations, fees: Reservations are accepted at 877/444-6777 or www.recreation.gov ($10 reservation fee). Sites are $15 per night, $6 per night for each additional vehicle. Open April through mid-October, weather permitting.

Directions: From the junction of Highway 108 and U.S. 395 north of Bridgeport, turn west on Highway 108 and drive approximately seven miles to the campground on the left side of the road.

Contact: Humboldt-Toiyabe National Forest, Bridgeport Ranger District, 760/932-7070, fax 760/932-5899.

219 OBSIDIAN
🏃 🛶 🐴 🚐 ⛺

Scenic rating: 6

on Molybdenite Creek in Humboldt-Toiyabe National Forest

This primitive, little-known camp at 7,800 feet elevation is set up for backpackers, with an adjacent trailhead providing a jump-off point into the wilderness; wilderness permits are required. The trail is routed up the Molybdenite Creek drainage and into the Hoover Wilderness.

Campsites, facilities: There are 14 sites for tents or RVs up to 30 feet (no hookups). Picnic tables and fire grills are provided. Vault toilets are available. No drinking water is available. Garbage must be packed out. Leashed pets are permitted.

Reservations, fees: Reservations are accepted at 877/444-6777 or www.recreation.gov ($10 reservation fee). Sites are $10 per night, $6 per night for each additional vehicle. Open June through October, weather permitting.

Directions: At the junction of U.S. 395 and Highway 108 (13 miles north of Bridgeport), drive south a short distance on U.S. 395 to an improved dirt road and a sign that says "Little Walker River Road." Turn west and drive four miles to the campground.

Contact: Humboldt-Toiyabe National Forest, Bridgeport Ranger District, 760/932-7070, fax 760/932-5899.

220 CASCADE CREEK
🐴 🚐 ⛺

Scenic rating: 6

in Stanislaus National Forest

This campground is set along Cascade Creek at an elevation of 6,000 feet. A Forest Service road about a quarter mile west of camp on the south side of the highway provides a side trip three miles up to Pikes Peak, at 7,236 feet.

Campsites, facilities: There are 14 sites for tents or RVs up to 22 feet (no hookups). Picnic tables and fire rings are provided. Pit and vault toilets are available. No drinking water is available. Supplies are available in Dardanelle. Leashed pets are permitted.

Reservations, fees: Reservations are not accepted. Sites are $6 per night. Open May through October, weather permitting.

Directions: From Sonora, drive east on Highway 108 to Strawberry and continue for 11 miles to the campground on the left side of the road.

Contact: Stanislaus National Forest, Summit Ranger District, 209/965-3434, fax 209/965-3372.

TAHOE HIKING

© ANN MARIE BROWN

BEST HIKES

《 Butt-Kickers
Beacroft Trail, **page 140.**

《 Fall Colors
Fallen Leaf Lake Trail, **page 160.**

《 Hikes with a View
Rubicon Trail, **page 152.**

《 Kids
Rainbow and Lake of the Sky Trails, **page 157.**
Angora Lakes Trail, **page 160.**

《 Meadow Hikes
Carson Pass to Echo Lakes Resort (PCT), **page 174.**
Eagle Meadow to Dardanelle, **page 186.**

《 Self-Guided Nature Walks
Rainbow and Lake of the Sky Trails, **page 157.**
Trail of the Gargoyles, **page 187.**

《 Short Backpack Trips
Winnemucca Lake from Woods Lake, **page 176.**

《 Waterfalls
Grouse Falls, **page 144.**

《 Wheelchair-Accessible Trails
Sierra Discovery Trail, **page 135.**

《 Wildflowers
Lake Margaret, **page 169.**

HIKING

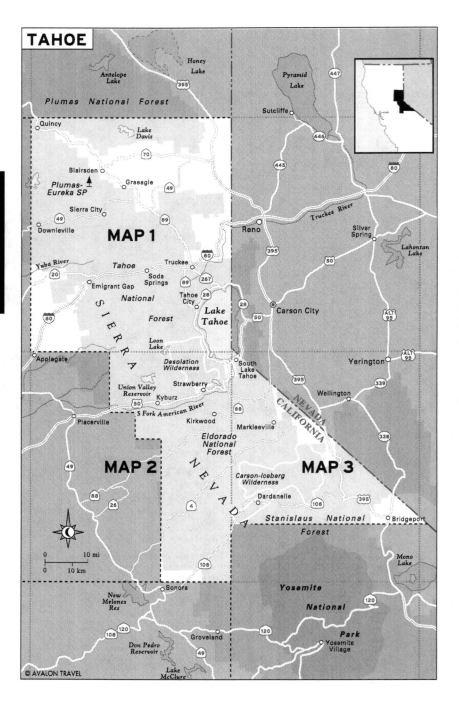

TAHOE

Map 1

Hikes 1-51

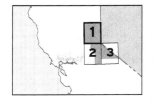

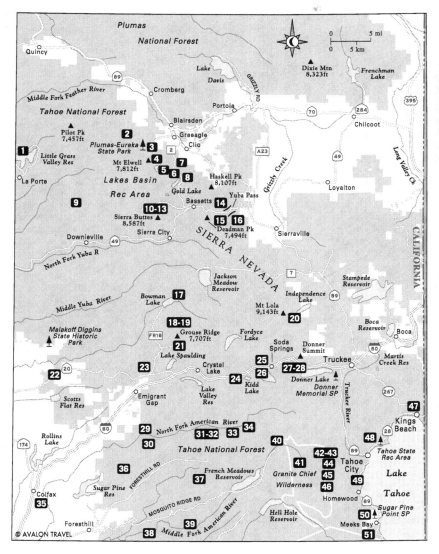

Map 2

Hikes 52-84

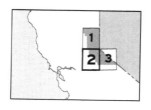

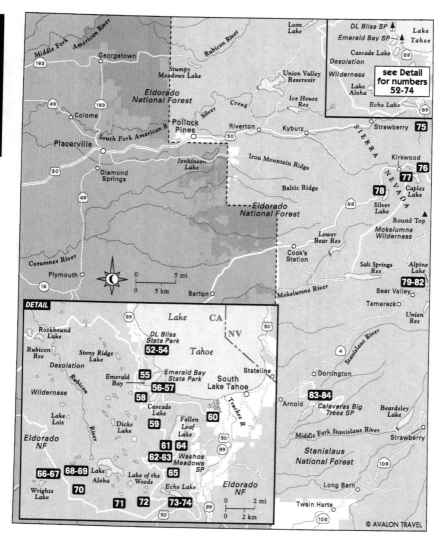

Map 3

Hikes 85-111

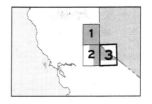

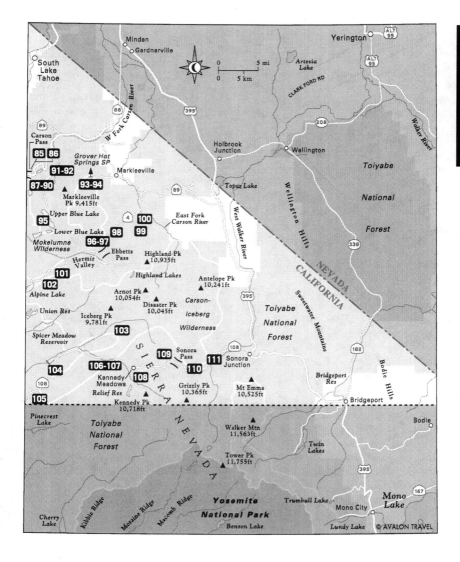

HIKING

1 FOWLER PEAK TO BUCKS SUMMIT (PCT)

26.0 mi one-way / 3.0 days 👣4 ⛰6

at Fowler Peak north of Little Grass Valley Reservoir in Plumas National Forest

Most Pacific Crest Trail (PCT) hikers will want to sprint through this section of trail. From Fowler Peak trailhead, it passes through Plumas National Forest country until reaching the southern border of the Bucks Lake Wilderness. It starts quite nicely, dropping down to the Middle Fork Feather River (3,180 feet), a great trout stream with an excellent footbridge to get you across a gorge. Enjoy it, because the rest of this route won't exactly have you writing postcards home. It climbs from the Middle Fork Feather to 6,955-foot Lookout Rock, a long, dry pull, and then drops down to Bucks Creek. Most of this region is dry rattlesnake country, so watch your step, and time your water stops.

To continue north on the PCT, see the *Bucks Summit to Feather River (PCT)* hike in *Moon California Hiking.* If you are walking this trail in reverse, see the *Yuba River to Fowler Peak (PCT)* hike in this chapter to continue south.

User Groups: Hikers, dogs, and horses. No mountain bikes. No wheelchair access.

Permits: A wilderness permit (free) is required. Parking and access are free.

Maps: For a map, ask the U.S. Forest Service for Tahoe and Plumas National Forests. For topographic maps, ask the USGS for Onion Valley, Dogwood Peak, and Bucks Lake.

Directions: From Oroville, take Highway 162 east for eight miles to Highway 174 (Forbestown Road and the junction signed Challenge/LaPorte). Turn right on Forbestown Road and drive east to Highway 120/Quincy-LaPorte Road. Turn left and drive past LaPorte to Little Grass Valley Road. Turn left on Little Grass Valley Road and drive to Black Rock Campground and Forest Road 94. Bear left on Forest Road 94 and drive three miles to Forest Road 22N27. Turn right and drive four miles to the parking area.

Contact: Plumas National Forest, Feather River Ranger District, 875 Mitchell Avenue, Oroville, CA 95965-4699, 530/534-6500, www.fs.fed.us/r5—click on Forest Offices.

2 EUREKA PEAK LOOP

3.0 mi / 2.0 hr 👣3 ⛰10

in Plumas-Eureka State Park east of Quincy

The panoramic view of the Sierra Nevada from Eureka Peak (elevation 7,447 feet) includes all the peaks of the Gold Lakes Basin. Mount Elwell (7,818 feet) is the most prominent to the south. Plumas National Forest to the north and west is crowned by Blue Nose Mountain (7,290 feet), Stafford Mountain (7,019 feet), and Beartrap Mountain (7,232 feet). It's the vista that compels people to make the climb—a serious three-mile loop, and the first half is a grunt to the top. The trailhead starts at Eureka Lake, (elevation 6,300 feet). It then climbs 1,150 feet—a good, hard pull to the top. Many people start this trail by accident after seeing the trailhead sign while visiting the lake. That's a mistake. The trip should be planned. Bring plenty of water and snacks to enjoy from the summit.

User Groups: Hikers only. No dogs, horses, or mountain bikes. No wheelchair facilities.

Permits: No permits are required. Access and parking are free. In the future, a vehicle fee may be charged.

Maps: A brochure and trail map is available for a fee from Plumas-Eureka State Park at the address below. For a topographic map, ask the USGS for Johnsville.

Directions: From Sacramento, take I-80 east to Truckee and the exit for Highway 89 North. Turn north on Highway 89 and go past the town of Clio to County Road A14 (Graeagle-Johnsonville Road). Turn left (west) and drive six miles to the park entrance. Continue several miles to Eureka Lake (the road is rough, and high-clearance vehicles are recommended).

The trailhead is located at the north end of Eureka Lake.

Contact: Plumas-Eureka State Park, 310 Johnsville Road, Blairsden, CA 96103, 530/836-2380, www.parks.ca.gov—click on Find A Park.

3 UPPER JAMISON TRAIL
8.2 mi / 1.0-2.0 days   🏃3   ⛰9

in Plumas-Eureka State Park on the northern boundary of Gold Lakes Basin, east of Quincy

There's no reason to rush your way through this trail, which passes Grass, Jamison, and Rock Lakes. Rather, take your time at it, stopping to enjoy the lakes along the way. A good option is to take this route and turn it into an overnight backpacking trip. The trail provides a glimpse of the beauty of the northern section of Lakes Basin Recreation Area, a country of alpine lakes and beveled granite mountains.

From the trailhead at the Jamison Mine building, start the trip by taking Grass Lake Trail. It follows along Little Jamison Creek. Note that a 100-foot cutoff trail provides a route to Little Jamison Falls. Back on the trail, you will climb 1.75 miles (from the parking area) to Grass Lake, with the trail skirting the east side of the lake. For those on a day hike, this is far enough. However, we urge you to forge onward. It's another two miles to Jamison Lake, with the trail climbing more steeply, then crossing the creek twice before arriving at the outlet of Jamison Lake. Another 0.25 mile will route you over to Rock Lake, a pretty sight below Mount Elwell (elevation 7,818 feet). Several good trail campsites are available at Rock, Jamison, and Grass Lakes and are usually occupied on weekends. Note that the first half mile of trail is located in the state park, and the remainder is in Plumas National Forest.

User Groups: Hikers, dogs, horses, and mountain bikes. No wheelchair facilities.

Permits: No permits are required. Access and parking are free. In the future, a vehicle fee may be charged.

Maps: A brochure and trail map is available for a fee from Plumas-Eureka State Park at the address below. For a topographic map, ask the USGS for Johnsville.

Directions: From Sacramento, take I-80 east to Truckee and the exit for Highway 89 North. Take that exit, turn north on Highway 89, and drive past the town of Clio to County Road A14 (Graeagle-Johnsonville Road), Turn left (west) and drive 4.5 miles to a dirt road that is signed Jamison Mine–Grass Lake Mine Complex (before reaching the Jamison Creek Bridge). Turn left and drive on the dirt road for 1.5 miles to the Jamison Mine Complex. The trailhead starts at the far end of the parking lot.

Contact: Plumas-Eureka State Park, 310 Johnsville Road, Blairsden, CA 96103, 530/836-2380, www.parks.ca.gov—click on Find A Park.

4 MOUNT ELWELL TRAIL
6.0 mi / 3.5 hr   🏃3   ⛰10

at Smith Lake in Gold Lakes Basin south of Quincy

This is one of the truly great hikes in the north Sierra. From atop Mount Elwell (7,818 feet), you're surrounded by the Gold Lakes Basin, a wildland filled with alpine lakes and granite mountains. You'll find yourself dreaming of the days when you might visit them. This trail is a good way to start. It begins at the Smith Lake trailhead and passes near Smith Lake (6,079 feet) on Smith Lake Trail, climbing all the way—2,018 feet over the course of three miles—to the top of Mount Elwell. It makes a great day trip for folks staying at the Gray Eagle Lodge. Though few go onward to Mount Elwell, the trip can be extended simply enough. The trail continues past Mount Elwell, descending 0.75 mile to the Long Lake Trail junction, then another mile to a four-wheel-drive route. From this junction, you can also make a loop back to the Smith Lake trailhead by descending to Long Lake and continuing north three miles on Long Lake Trail.

HIKING

User Groups: Hikers, dogs, mountain bikes, and horses. No wheelchair facilities.

Permits: No permits are required. Parking and access are free.

Maps: A trail map is available for a fee at the Beckwourth Ranger District. For a map, ask the U.S. Forest Service for Plumas National Forest. For a topographic map, ask the USGS for Gold Lake.

Directions: From Sacramento, take I-80 east to Truckee and the exit for Highway 89 North. Take that exit, turn north on Highway 89, and drive to Clio and continue a short distance north on Highway 89 to Forest Road 24 (Gold Lake Highway). Turn left (west) on Gold Lake Highway and drive five miles to the sign for Gray Eagle Lodge. Turn right and drive 0.5 mile to the Smith Lake trailhead.

Contact: Plumas National Forest, Beckwourth Ranger District, P.O. Box 7, Mohawk Road, Blairsden, CA 96103, 530/836-2575, www .fs.fed.us/r5—click on Forest Offices.

⑤ BEAR LAKES LOOP
5.6 mi / 3.0 hr   🏃3 ⛰10

north of Sierra City

Long Lake is one of the celestial settings in the heavenly Gold Lakes Basin. It's the feature destination of this hike, a good tromp that includes some steep, rocky portions. The trailhead is just past the Lakes Basin Campground (elevation 6,300 feet). From here, the trail is clear and well maintained but requires a huff and a puff of a mile. Here you'll see the turnoff for 0.25-mile spur trail to Long Lake, one mile to little Silver Lake, 0.75 mile to Cub Lake, and another 0.5 mile to Little Bear and Big Bear Lakes, and then 0.75 mile back to the trailhead. Long Lake is always a surprise to newcomers, since it's much larger than most high-country lakes and is very pretty. The trail skirts along the southeast shoreline.

Special Note: Camping is permitted only at the Lakes Basin Campground. No camping is permitted at either Long or Silver Lakes.

User Groups: Hikers, dogs, mountain bikes, and horses. No wheelchair facilities.

Permits: No permits are required. Parking and access are free.

Maps: A trail map is available for a fee at the Beckwourth Ranger District at the address below. For a map, ask the U.S. Forest Service for Plumas National Forest. For a topographic map, ask the USGS for Gold Lake.

Directions: From Sacramento, take I-80 east to Truckee and the exit for Highway 89 North. Take that exit, turn north on Highway 89, and drive to Clio and continue a short distance north on Highway 89 to Forest Road 24 (Gold Lake Highway). Turn left on Gold Lake Highway and proceed about six miles until you see the sign for the Long Lake trailhead and Lakes Basin Campground, on the left (west) side of the road.

Contact: Plumas National Forest, Beckwourth Ranger District, P.O. Box 7, Mohawk Road, Blairsden, CA 96103, 530/836-2575, www .fs.fed.us/r5—click on Forest Offices.

⑥ ROUND LAKE TRAILHEAD
1.4 mi / 1.0 hr   🏃1 ⛰8

on the southern boundary of Gold Lakes Basin north of Sierra City

The 0.7-mile hike to Big Bear Lake is an easy, popular, and pretty walk. It is most commonly taken by visitors staying at Gold Lake Lodge. The trailhead is located alongside the parking lot next to the road to the lodge, and the trail itself is actually a closed road to Round Lake. It becomes a trail within a few hundred yards when routed west to Big Bear Lake, the first in a series of beautiful alpine lakes in the Gold Lakes Basin. Although most day users return after a picnic at Big Bear Lake, the trip can easily be extended, either west to Round Lake or Silver Lake or north to Long Lake. Most of this country is in the 6,000- to 7,000-foot elevation range and is high granite filled with alpine lakes.

User Groups: Hikers, dogs, mountain bikes, and horses. No wheelchair facilities.

Permits: No permits are required. Parking and access are free.

Maps: A trail map is available for a fee from Beckwourth Ranger District at the address below. For a map, ask the U.S. Forest Service for Plumas National Forest. For a topographic map, ask the USGS for Gold Lake.

Directions: From Sacramento, take I-80 east to Truckee and the exit for Highway 89 North. Take that exit, turn north on Highway 89, and drive to Clio and continue a short distance north on Highway 89 to Forest Road 24 (Gold Lake Highway). Turn left (west) on the Gold Lake Highway and drive seven miles until you see the sign for Round Lake Trail. Turn right and continue to the parking area.

Contact: Plumas National Forest, Beckwourth Ranger District, P.O. Box 7, Mohawk Road, Blairsden, CA 96103, 530/836-2575, www .fs.fed.us/r5—click on Forest Offices.

7 FRAZIER FALLS TRAIL
1.0 mi / 1.0 hr   🏃1 ⛰10

north of Sierra City

Frazier Falls is a 178-foot, silver-tasseled waterfall that tumbles out of a chute into a rocky basin. It is like a miniature version of Feather Falls that is located near Lake Oroville. The trail is completely wheelchair-accessible and is a breeze, a 0.5-mile romp on a gentle route that leads to the scenic, fenced overlook of the falls. The best time to visit is early summer, when snowmelt from the high country is peaking, filling Frazier Falls like a huge fountain. In addition, wildflowers along the trail in early summer add a splash of color, with violet lupine the most abundant. The road to the trailhead is paved all the way, the hike is easy, the falls are beautiful, and as you might expect, thousands of people make the trip every summer.

User Groups: Hikers, wheelchairs, and dogs. No ATVs, mountain bikes, or horses. Wheelchair facilities are available.

Permits: No permits are required. Parking and access are free.

Maps: A trail map is available for a fee from Beckwourth Ranger District at the address below. For a map, ask the U.S. Forest Service for Plumas National Forest. For a topographic map, ask the USGS for Gold Lake.

Directions: From Sacramento, take I-80 east to Truckee and the exit for Highway 89 North. Take that exit, turn north on Highway 89, and drive to Clio and continue a short distance north on Highway 89 to Forest Road 24 (Gold Lake Highway). Turn left (west) on the Gold Lake Highway and drive until you see the sign for Frazier Falls. Turn left and drive four miles to the trailhead, on the left.

Note: If you continue west on Gold Lake Highway for several miles, you will see another trailhead sign for Frazier Falls; it can also be reached on this route, but the road is rough and unpaved.

Contact: Plumas National Forest, Beckwourth Ranger District, P.O. Box 7, Mohawk Road, Blairsden, CA 96103, 530/836-2575, www .fs.fed.us/r5—click on Forest Offices.

8 HASKELL PEAK TRAIL
3.0 mi / 2.0 hr   🏃3 ⛰10

north of Highway 49 in Tahoe National Forest

Haskell Peak is one of the great but unknown lookouts. On clear days, visitors can see many mountains both nearby and distant, including Mount Shasta and Mount Lassen, in Northern California; Mount Rose, in Nevada; and the closer Sierra Buttes. To get this view requires a 1,100-foot climb over the course of 1.5 miles, topping out at the 8,107-foot summit. The trail climbs at a decent, steady grade through heavy forest for the first mile. It then flattens and reaches an open area, where Haskell Peak comes into view. From here it's only a 0.25-mile (but very steep) climb to the top. You'll discover that Haskell Peak is the flume of an old volcano and has many unusual volcanic-rock formations. You'll also discover that just about nobody knows about this great hike. A fire lookout was once perched here, but it's gone now. Elevations range from 7,000 feet to 8,107 feet.

User Groups: Hikers, dogs, horses, and mountain bikes. No wheelchair facilities.

Permits: No permits are required. Parking and access are free.

Maps: For a map, ask the U.S. Forest Service for Tahoe National Forest. For a topographic map, ask the USGS for Clio.

Directions: From Sacramento, take I-80 east to Truckee and the exit for Highway 89 North. Take that exit, turn north on Highway 89, and drive to Sierraville and Highway 49. Turn left on Highway 49 and drive 10 miles to Bassetts and the Gold Lake Highway. Turn right on Gold Lake Highway and drive 3.7 miles to Forest Road 9 (Haskell Peak Road). Turn right and drive 8.4 miles. The trailhead is on the left; parking is available on either side of the road.

Contact: Tahoe National Forest, Nevada City/Downieville Ranger Districts, 15924 Highway 49, Camptonville, CA 95922, 530/288-3231, www.fs.fed.us/r5—click on Forest Offices.

⑨ CHIMNEY ROCK TRAIL
5.0 mi / 2.5 hr   🏃2 ⛰5

north of Downieville in Tahoe National Forest

Chimney Rock is a huge volcanic cone that's 12 feet in diameter at its base, and it rises nearly straight up for 25 feet. The great views from the top are well worth the trip. The elevations are roughly 6,400 to 6,800 feet. Yet brace yourself, because this little patch of land has undergone considerable change. First, the trail surface was hardened in 1999. In turn, off-highway-vehicle (OHV) users started showing up in force, especially with dirt bikes. Now nearly 50 percent of the trail users are OHV users, and 50 percent are mountain bikers—and between them, they

have driven out the hikers. The Downieville area in general has been taken over by mountain bikes, and hikers looking for a natural, harmonious experience often encounter a pack of bikes. When that happens, it's "Adios, never to return." This trip was once a quiet spectacle, with side ventures around Needle Point and Rattlesnake Peak. Now you cringe when you hear the thunder of oncoming fast traffic. It's like all the problems of city driving have been transported to a mountain trail.

User Groups: Hikers, dogs, mountain bikes, horses, and OHVs (primarily motorcycles). No wheelchair facilities.

Permits: No permits are required. Parking and access are free.

Maps: A trail map is available for a fee at the Downieville Ranger District. For a map, ask the U.S. Forest Service for Tahoe National Forest. For a topographic map, ask the USGS for Mount Fillmore.

Directions: From Sacramento, take I-80 east to Auburn and Highway 49. Turn north on Highway 49 and drive to Nevada City and continue on Highway 49 (it jogs to the left in Nevada City, then narrows) for about 40 miles to an old cannon displayed on the right side of the road (.25 mile before reaching Downieville). Turn right at the cannon onto an unsigned road, make a U-turn back to Highway 49, and drive a short distance back to Saddleback Road. Turn right on Saddleback Road. (Note: When driving on Highway 49 toward Downieville, do not attempt to turn left across traffic to reach Saddleback Road. It is dangerous and illegal.) Continue north on Saddleback Road for eight miles to a five-way intersection. Drive straight through to Road 25-23-1 and continue for 2.6 miles to Road 25-23-1-2 (look for the Chimney Rock Trail sign). Bear right on Road 25-23-1-2 and drive 0.5 mile to an intersection and head straight through. Continue another mile to a turnout on the left side of the road. Park here and hike in 0.6 mile to the trailhead. The total mileage from Downieville is 13 miles.

Note: The last sections of the road are quite rough.

Contact: Tahoe National Forest, Nevada City/ Downieville Ranger Districts, 15924 Highway 49, Camptonville, CA 95922, 530/288-3231, www.fs.fed.us/r5—click on Forest Offices.

10 BUTCHER RANCH TRAIL
8.0 mi / 5.0 hr   🏃4 ⛰6

west of Packer Lake in Tahoe National Forest

This used to be a great hike, a picture of harmony and beauty. It still is for the few who are here at dawn and get it done before all the mountain bikes show up. The place is overrun now by mountain bikes and motorcycles and weekends are often intolerable. Hikers have virtually been driven out to the point that hiker usage is down below 10 percent of users. This place was once a place of peace and harmony, a mountain canyon paradise where wildflowers were abundant, fishing was good, and a side trip would take hikers to a pristine stream with gorgeous deep pools. No more.

Elevations range from 6,200 to 4,320 feet. The trail follows the contour of Butcher Creek for 1.5 miles to the confluence of Pauley and Butcher Ranch Creeks. You then parallel Pauley Creek, with its deep and beautiful pools. On the way down, you'll drop nearly 2,000 feet over the course of four miles. Try not to laugh on your way down; what goes down must come up, and on the return, you'll be wondering why you ever talked yourself into this trip, especially if you run into a few motorcycles or a pack of mountain bikes heading downhill.

User Groups: Off-highway vehicles, mountain bikes, hikers, dogs, and horses. No wheelchair facilities.

Permits: No permits are required. Parking and access are free.

Maps: A trail map is available for a fee at the Downieville Ranger District. For a map, ask the U.S. Forest Service for Tahoe National Forest. For a topographic map, ask the USGS for Sierra City.

Directions: From Sacramento, take I-80 east to Truckee and the exit for Highway 89 North. Take that exit, turn north on Highway 89, and drive to Sierraville and Highway 49. Turn left on Highway 49 and drive 10 miles to Bassetts and Gold Lake Highway. Turn right (north) on Gold Lake Highway and drive 1.4 miles to Sardine Lake Road. Turn left on Sardine Lake Road and drive a short distance. Cross the Salmon Creek Bridge and continue 0.3 mile to Packer Lake Road. Turn right on Packer Lake Road and drive 2.5 miles to a fork (near Packer Lake). Take the left fork (Packer Saddle Road/Forest Road 93), drive 2.1 miles, and look for the sign for Sierra Buttes Lookout. Turn left, drive 0.5 mile, and bear right; then continue 0.5 mile to a fork and sign for Butcher Ranch. Take the right fork (Forest Road 93-3) and drive 0.7 mile to a sign for the trailhead. Note: The road is quite steep and is only recommended for high-clearance or four-wheel-drive vehicles. Otherwise, park at the sign for the trailhead and hike 0.5 mile to the trailhead.

Contact: Tahoe National Forest, Nevada City/ Downieville Ranger Districts, 15924 Highway 49, Camptonville, CA 95922, 530/288-3231, www.fs.fed.us/r5—click on Forest Offices.

11 PAULEY CREEK TRAIL
12.0 mi / 2.0 days   🏃4 ⛰8

west of Packer Lake in Tahoe National Forest

The Pauley Creek Trail encompasses a land where there are streamside camps, spectacular wildflowers in early summer, and good trout fishing. Pauley Creek is a beautiful stream, and this trail is the best way to see it. Wildlife is also abundant in this watershed. The trailhead is difficult to reach, and the return hike out of the canyon back to the trailhead involves a 1,800-foot climb. Elevations range from 6,200 to 4,400 feet.

Warning: Weekends are horrendous for dealing with high-speed mountain bikes and noisy motorcycles. We've received numerous complaints regarding inconsiderate trail sharing with hikers, so consider timing your trip during the week instead.

User Groups: Hikers, dogs, horses, mountain bikes, and off-highway vehicles. No wheelchair facilities.

Permits: No permits are required. Parking and access are free.

Maps: A trail map is available for a fee at the Downieville Ranger District. For a map, ask the U.S. Forest Service for Tahoe National Forest. For topographic maps, ask the USGS for Downieville, Sierra City, and Gold Lake.

Directions: From Sacramento, take I-80 east to Truckee and the exit for Highway 89 North. Take that exit, turn north on Highway 89, and drive to Sierraville and Highway 49. Turn left on Highway 49 and drive 10 miles to Bassetts and Gold Lake Highway. Turn right (north) on Gold Lake Highway and drive 1.4 miles to Sardine Lake Road. Turn left on Sardine Lake Road and drive a short distance. Cross the Salmon Creek Bridge and continue 0.3 mile to Packer Lake Road. Turn right on Packer Lake Road and drive 2.5 miles to a fork (near Packer Lake). Take the left fork (Packer Saddle Road/Forest Road 93), drive 2.1 miles, and look for the sign for Sierra Buttes Lookout. Turn left, drive 0.5 mile, bear right, and drive 0.5 mile to Forest Road 93-3. Bear right and drive 2.5 miles to a sign that says Gold Valley OHV Route. Turn left and drive 1.5 miles to an intersection. Bear left and cross Pauley Creek, then drive 0.25 mile to a Y-intersection. Bear left and drive 0.25 mile to the trailhead, at the end of the road.

Note: The access road is quite steep and is only recommended for high-clearance or four-wheel-drive vehicles. Otherwise, park at the sign for the trailhead and hike 0.5 mile to the trailhead.

Contact: Tahoe National Forest, Nevada City/Downieville Ranger Districts, 15924 Highway 49, Camptonville, CA 95922, 530/288-3231, www.fs.fed.us/r5—click on Forest Offices.

12 DEER LAKE TRAIL
5.0 mi / 3.5 hr

west of Packer Lake in Tahoe National Forest

Most lakes are green, but Deer Lake is the deepest azure blue you can imagine, and with the spectacular Sierra Buttes in the background, it's easy to understand why this trip is so popular. It gets some of the heaviest use of any trail in this section of Tahoe National Forest. It's a 2.5-mile hike to the lake, climbing 1,000 feet and topping out at 7,110 feet. Elevations range from 6,080 to 7,110 feet.

From the trailhead, you'll climb through a basin and get a sweeping view of the massive Sierra Buttes and the surrounding forested slopes. As you head on, you'll cross a signed spur trail, a 0.25-mile route to Grass Lake. It's well worth the short detour, but approach quietly, because deer are common here. Then it's onward, over the ridge and down to Deer Lake. On warm evenings, the brook trout leave countless circles while feeding on surface insects. This hike has it all and that's why it often includes so many other people. Good news for hikers: Mountain bikes are few, and off-highway-vehicle use is prohibited.

User Groups: Hikers, dogs, horses, and mountain bikes. No wheelchair facilities.

Permits: No permits are required. Parking and access are free.

Maps: A trail map is available for a fee at the Downieville Ranger District. For a map, ask the U.S. Forest Service for Tahoe National Forest. For a topographic map, ask the USGS for Sierra City.

Directions: From Sacramento, take I-80 east to Truckee and the exit for Highway 89 North. Take that exit, turn north on Highway 89, and drive to Sierraville and Highway 49. Turn left on Highway 49 and drive 10 miles to Bassetts and Gold Lake Highway. Turn right (north) on to Gold Lake Highway and drive 1.4 miles to Sardine Lake Road. Turn left on Sardine Lake Road and drive a short distance. Cross the Salmon Creek Bridge and continue 0.3 mile to Packer Lake Road. Turn right on Packer Lake Road and drive 2.5 miles to the trailhead. Parking is available in the Packsaddle camping area just opposite the trailhead.

Contact: Tahoe National Forest, Nevada City/ Downieville Ranger Districts, 15924 Highway 49, Camptonville, CA 95922, 530/288-3231, www.fs.fed.us/r5—click on Forest Offices.

13 SIERRA BUTTES TRAIL
5.0 mi / 3.5 hr   🏃4 ⛰10

near Packer Lake in Tahoe National Forest

The Sierra Buttes Lookout Station, sitting at 8,587 feet and with a railed stairway to its top, provides a destination for one of California's best day hikes and greatest viewpoints. Stand here one time, and you'll never forget it the rest of your life. The trip starts above Packer Lake, at 6,220 feet. The trail starts by climbing through a series of shaded switchbacks to 6,700 feet, tracing the ridge that eventually leads to the summit, crowned by a series of jagged crags. On the way, you will rise to the rim of a mountain bowl that frames Sardine Lake off to the east. You will climb 2,367 feet to reach the top. The trail traces this rim to the lookout and is capped by three stairways that seem to project into wide-open space. Climbing it is an astounding sensation, almost like climbing the cable at Half Dome. The lookout itself also juts out into space with a grated deck. You scan miles and miles of Sierra mountain country, from Mount Lassen in the north all the way to the Tahoe Rim to the south, with a highlight being Union Valley Reservoir. Because the walkway around the lookout is grated, when you look straight down, you can see past your boots to open air. A bizarre sensation for many, this can even cause spatial disorientation.

User Groups: Hikers, dogs, and horses. No mountain bikes (except on jeep trail). No wheelchair access.

Permits: No permits are required. Parking and access are free.

Maps: A trail map is available for a fee from the Downieville Ranger District. For a map, ask the U.S. Forest Service for Tahoe National Forest. For a topographic map, ask the USGS for Sierra City.

Directions: From Sacramento, take I-80 east to Truckee and the exit for Highway 89 North. Take that exit, turn north on Highway 89, and drive to Sierraville and Highway 49. Turn left on Highway 49 and drive 10 miles to Bassetts and Gold Lake Highway. Turn right on Gold Lake Highway and drive 1.4 miles to Sardine Lake/Packer Lake Road. Turn left, cross a small bridge, and bear right on Packer Lake Road. Continue past Packer Lake and bear left at a fork, following the signs to a trailhead for the Pacific Crest Trail (do not bear right at a jeep road). Continue to a small parking area. The trail starts as a jeep trail next to the parking area (then becomes trail on the ridge).

Contact: Tahoe National Forest, Nevada City/ Downieville Ranger Districts, 15924 Highway 49, Camptonville, CA 95922, 530/288-3231, www.fs.fed.us/r5—click on Forest Offices.

14 CHAPMAN CREEK TRAIL
3.0 mi / 2.0 hr   🏃2 ⛰7

east of Sierra City in Tahoe National Forest

Chapman Creek is a babbling brook that you can walk alongside, or you can stop to picnic near it, fish a little in it, or do absolutely nothing. That's right, nothing. It's that kind of place. The trailhead, elevation 5,840 feet, is set at a campground, providing easy access. Outside of campers, few others know of it. The trail winds easily along the contours of Chapman Creek under the canopy of a dense forest, rising gently along the way. It climbs to 6,400 feet, 560 feet in a span of 1.5 miles. The river is the lifeblood for a variety of birds and wildlife, but few visitors make the trip for that reason. Rather they come to stroll and let their minds wander and be free.

User Groups: Hikers, dogs, horses, and mountain bikes. No wheelchair facilities.

Permits: No permits are required. Parking and access are free.

Maps: For a map, ask the U.S. Forest Service for Tahoe National Forest. For a topographic map, ask the USGS for Sierra City.

Directions: From Sacramento, take I-80 east to Truckee and the exit for Highway 89 North. Take that exit, turn north on Highway 89, and drive to Sierraville and Highway 49. Turn left on Highway 49 and drive over Yuba Pass and continue for four miles to the Chapman Creek Campground, on the right. The trailhead and a parking area are located at the north end of the campground.

Contact: Tahoe National Forest, Nevada City/Downieville Ranger Districts, 15924 Highway 49, Camptonville, CA 95922, 530/288-3231, www.fs.fed.us/r5—click on Forest Offices.

15 WILD PLUM LOOP/ HAYPRESS CREEK

6.0 mi / 1.0 day   🏃3 ⛰8

east of Sierra City in Tahoe National Forest

For the properly inspired, a canyon with a hidden stream and a waterfall that's surrounded by old-growth red fir make this a wonderful day hike. Why must you be properly inspired? Because the trail climbs from 4,400 feet up Haypress Creek to 5,840 feet, a 1,440-foot rise over just three miles. The trail starts out almost flat for the first 0.5 mile, and then it crosses over Haypress Creek on a footbridge. There's an excellent view of the Sierra Buttes in this area. Continue on Haypress Creek Trail, where you rise past a rocky area and into forest. You pass evidence of logging activity where the trail turns to road for a short spell. Don't despair. The trail soon enters an old-growth forest. It then contours along Haypress Canyon, and

then passes by a lovely waterfall. This hike makes a great day trip with a picnic lunch, and trail use is typically quite light. Note that on the return trip, you turn right on the Pacific Crest Trail to complete the loop. Walk 0.5 mile and turn left at the Wild Plum Loop sign to return.

User Groups: Hikers, dogs, and horses. No mountain bikes. No wheelchair facilities.

Permits: No permits are required. Parking and access are free.

Maps: For a map, ask the U.S. Forest Service for Tahoe National Forest. For a topographic map, ask the USGS for Haypress Valley.

Directions: From Sacramento, take I-80 east to Truckee and the exit for Highway 89 North. Take that exit, turn north on Highway 89, and drive to Sierraville and Highway 49. Turn left on Highway 49 and drive 12 miles (past Bassetts) to Wild Plum Road (near the eastern end of Sierra City) at the sign for Wild Plum Campground. Drive one mile on this road to the Wild Plum trailhead parking area. Walk through the campground to its upper loop, walk around a locked gate, and continue up the road 0.25 mile to the Wild Plum Loop Trail Sign. Walk 0.25 mile to the intersection with the Pacific Crest Trail, turn left, and cross a bridge over Haypress Creek. Continue for 200 yards to the trailhead, on the right.

Contact: Tahoe National Forest, Nevada City/Downieville Ranger Districts, 15924 Highway 49, Camptonville, CA 95922, 530/288-3231, www.fs.fed.us/r5—click on Forest Offices.

16 YUBA RIVER TO FOWLER PEAK (PCT)

51.0 mi one-way / 4.0 days 🏃4 ⛰9

in Tahoe National Forest, off Highway 49 east of Sierra City

Pristine alpine lakes and high mountain lookouts highlight this section of the Pacific Crest Trail. Although nearly as beautiful as the section of trail south near Tahoe, this stretch gets far less use. It starts at the Yuba River, and in the first two miles, it climbs an endless series of switchbacks up the back side of the Sierra Buttes. This is a long, grueling climb on exposed terrain with a great reward. Note that the spur trail up to the Sierra Buttes Fire Lookout is an additional 1,400-foot climb, but it furnishes one of the top lookouts in California. The trail then heads north. It skirts past the western border of the Gold Lakes Basin, where a dozen high alpine lakes make for easy side trips and camps. With some terrible switchbacks, the PCT passes Mount Gibraltar (7,343 feet), Stafford Mountain (7,019 feet), and Mount Etna (7,163 feet), and flanks below Pilot Peak (7,457 feet). It then heads along the western slope, eventually reaching the Fowler Peak trailhead.

To continue north on the PCT, see the *Fowler Peak to Bucks Summit (PCT)* hike in this chapter. If you are walking this trail in reverse, see the *Donner Pass to the Yuba River (PCT)* hike in this chapter.

User Groups: Hikers, dogs, and horses. No mountain bikes. No wheelchair access.

Permits: A wilderness permit (free) is required. Parking and access are free.

Maps: For a map, ask the U.S. Forest Service for Tahoe National Forest. For topographic maps, ask the USGS for Haypress Valley, Sierra City, Mount Fillmore, and Onion Valley.

Directions: From Sacramento, take I-80 east to Truckee and the exit for Highway 89 North. Take that exit, turn north on Highway 89, and drive to Sierraville and Highway 49. Turn left on Highway 49 and drive 12 miles (passing Bassetts) to the eastern end of Sierra City. Look for the Pacific Crest Trail access sign and park on the right (north) side of the road.

Contact: Tahoe National Forest, Nevada City/ Downieville Ranger Districts, 15924 Highway 49, Camptonville, CA 95922, 530/288-3231, www.fs.fed.us/r5—click on Forest Offices.

17 GROUSE RIDGE TRAIL (SAWMILL TO EAGLE LAKES)

6.0-16.5 mi / 1.0-2.0 days 🏃3 ⛰9

in Tahoe National Forest north of Emigrant Gap

This is a gorgeous hike. The Grouse Ridge Trail weaves up and down from a mountain crest, connecting Sawmill Lake to the north with the Eagle Lakes, for a one-way distance of 8.25 miles. The beauty of this hike is the number of side trips along the way that you can take to make your choice of visits at a half dozen lakes. In fact, we often use Grouse Ridge Trail as a jump-off point to take short and spectacular day hikes. The elevation varies from 6,160 to 6,400 feet, with the ups and downs coming in short yet serious spurts. From Sawmill Lake, climb up a timbered slope to a ridge and a turnoff for Rock Lake, which is worth a visit itself. You then pass Shotgun Lake (it's actually a wet meadow) and continue to Middle Lake, Crooked Lakes, and Milk Lake (gorgeous!). The views are divine much of the way.

Special Note: At Sawmill Lake, the trail crosses the spillway of the dam, which may be impassable in late spring when high water spills into Canyon Creek.

User Groups: Hikers, dogs, horses, and mountain bikes. No wheelchair facilities.

Permits: A campfire permit (free) is required for overnight use. Parking and access are free.

Maps: For a map, ask the U.S. Forest Service for Tahoe National Forest. For topographic maps, ask the USGS for Cisco Grove and English Mountain.

Directions: From Auburn, take I-80 east for 45 miles to the Highway 20 exit. Take that exit, head west, and drive four miles to Bowman Lake Road (Forest Road 18). Turn right on Bowman Lake Road and drive 16 miles to Bowman Lake. Turn right and drive along Bowman Lake to Faucherie Lake Road. Turn right on Faucherie Lake Road and drive 0.5 mile to the north end of Sawmill Lake and the trailhead.

HIKING

Contact: Tahoe National Forest, Nevada City/Downieville Ranger Districts, 15924 Highway 49, Camptonville, CA 95922, 530/288-3231, www.fs.fed.us/r5—click on Forest Offices; Big Bend Visitors Center, Tahoe National Forest, 530/426-3609.

18 LINDSEY LAKES TRAIL

7.0 mi / 3.0 hr   🏃2   ⛰7

in Tahoe National Forest north of Emigrant Gap

The highlight of Lindsey Lakes Trail is that it intersects with other trails, including the beautiful Grouse Ridge Trail, and is set in a gorgeous landscape that features Sierra alpine beauty. But the trail itself from Lindsey Lakes to Rock Lake is a service road closed to public vehicle traffic, so you're hiking up a road. This 3.5-mile trail dead-ends after climbing past the three Lindsey Lakes, and it offers a great optional side trip. From the trailhead at Lower Lindsey Lake (elevation 6,160 feet), hike up to the other lakes on a short trail (it's quite steep in several places) before topping out at 6,400 feet. The route gets medium use and accesses good swimming holes with cold water, but the fishing is poor. The best fishing in this basin is at nearby Culbertson Lake, where you can make a wonderful side trip by hiking out to Rock Lake and up to Bullpen Lake. Another side trip from Lindsey Lakes Trail is Crooked Lakes Trail.

User Groups: Hikers, dogs, and horses. Mountain bikes not advised. No wheelchair facilities.

Permits: No permits are required. Parking and access are free.

Maps: For a map, ask the U.S. Forest Service for Tahoe National Forest. For topographic maps, ask the USGS for English Mountain and Graniteville.

Directions: From Auburn, take I-80 east for 45 miles, then take the Highway 20 exit and drive four miles to Bowman Lake Road (Forest Road 18). Turn right and drive 8.5 miles north until you see a sign that says Lindsey Lake, Feely Lake, Carr Lake. Turn right and follow the signs to the parking area for Lindsey Lake. The road can be rough for the last 0.5 mile; high-clearance vehicles are advised.

Contact: Tahoe National Forest, Nevada City/Downieville Ranger Districts, 15924 Highway 49, Camptonville, CA 95922, 530/288-3231, www.fs.fed.us/r5—click on Forest Offices; Big Bend Visitors Center, Tahoe National Forest, 530/426-3609.

19 PENNER LAKE

4.5 mi / 3.0 hr   🏃3   ⛰10

at Carr Lake in Tahoe National Forest north of Emigrant Gap

The Round Lake Trail accesses a series of Sierra lakes (including Island Lake and Penner Lake), and is extremely beautiful, but it is also very popular, even crowded at the trailhead on weekends. From the trailhead at Feely Lake (elevation 6,720 feet), the route heads east, climbing first to Island Lake. This lake, named for the little rocky islands sprinkled about, has several good campsites. Turn left when you reach Island Lake and walk 1.5 miles on Crooked Lakes Trail through a fir forest to Penner Lake. The last half mile is uphill, but nothing serious. Penner Lake is one of the crown jewels of the Grouse Ridge area. Along with Island Lake, it has the most scenic beauty, is great for swimming, and is ideal for picnics or just gazing and taking in the mountain panorama. It is best experienced on an early weekday summer morning.

User Groups: Hikers, dogs, mountain bikes, and horses. No wheelchair facilities.

Permits: No permits are required. Parking and access are free.

Maps: For a map, ask the U.S. Forest Service for Tahoe National Forest. For topographic maps, ask the USGS for English Mountain and Graniteville.

Directions: From Auburn, take I-80 east for 45 miles, then take the Highway 20 exit and drive four miles to Bowman Lake Road (Forest Road 18). Turn right and drive 8.5 miles north until you see a sign that says Lindsey Lake, Feely Lake, Carr Lake. Turn right and follow the signs to the parking area at Carr Lake. Continue on foot to the trailhead at Feely Lake. Sections of the road can be rough; four-wheel-drive vehicles are advised.

Contact: Tahoe National Forest, Nevada City/Downieville Ranger Districts, 15924 Highway 49, Camptonville, CA 95922, 530/288-3231, www.fs.fed.us/r5—click on Forest Offices; Big Bend Visitors Center, Tahoe National Forest, 530/426-3609.

20 DONNER PASS TO THE YUBA RIVER (PCT)

38.0 mi one-way / 3.0 days 🏃3 ⛰7

from Highway 80 to Highway 49 in
Tahoe National Forest

Though not one of the more glamorous sections of the Pacific Crest Trail, this stretch is hardly a stinker. For the most part, it follows a crest connecting a series of small mountaintops before dropping down to Jackson Meadow Reservoir and Highway 49. Some good views are to be had on the first leg of the trail, so many that some PCT hikers begin to take them for granted after awhile. Here the trail is routed past Castle Peak (elevation 9,103 feet), Basin Peak (9,015 feet), and Lacey Mountain (8,214 feet). Covering this much terrain makes for an ambitious first day, perhaps with stops at Paradise Lake or White Rock Lake. As the trail drops to Jackson Meadow Reservoir, the views end, but in time you'll catch sight of the lake; surrounded by firs, it is quite pretty. The PCT then skirts the east side of the reservoir, passes several drive-to campgrounds, heads through Bear Valley (not *the* Bear Valley), and drops steeply to Milton Creek and four miles beyond that to Loves Falls at Highway 49.

To continue north on the PCT, see the *Yuba River to Fowler Peak (PCT)* hike in this chapter. If you are walking this trail in reverse, see the *Barker Pass to Donner Pass (PCT)* hike in this chapter.

User Groups: Hikers, dogs, and horses. No mountain bikes. No wheelchair facilities.

Permits: A campfire permit (free) is required for overnight use. Parking and access are free.

Maps: For a map, ask the U.S. Forest Service for Tahoe National Forest. For topographic maps, ask the USGS for Norden, Soda Springs, Webber, Haypress Valley, Independence Lake, and English Mountain.

Directions: From Auburn, take I-80 east to the Boreal/Donner Summit and the signed exit for Pacific Crest trailhead parking area. Take that exit to parking. There is no hiker parking in the Donner Summit rest area.

Contact: Tahoe National Forest, Sierraville Ranger District, 317 South Lincoln Street, P.O. Box 95, Sierraville, CA 96126, 530/994-3401, www.fs.fed.us/r5—click on Forest Offices.

21 GLACIER LAKE

10.0 mi / 1.0 day 🏃3 ⛰10

in Tahoe National Forest north of Emigrant Gap

In just a few hours you can be transported to heaven. Some people, however, call it Glacier Lake. It is only a five-mile hike to get here, a pristine and peaceful high Sierra setting that can make you feel as if you're three days out on a backpacking expedition. The small lake is set in a rockbound bowl with the Black Buttes looming nearby. The tree cover is sparse, and the rock cover is abundant. To get there, start your hike by heading east on Round Lake Trail at Carr Lake, and hike almost three miles. You will pass a series of lakes, including Feely Lake, Island Lake, Round Lake, and Milk Lake. Then you'll drop down into forest and meadow landscape and reach a trail junction. Continue east on Glacier Lake Trail and continue through a meadow and some forest. Here

HIKING

you start a gradual climb, passing a small lake before entering a rocky area and then dropping down to the pretty lake. Several backpacking campsites are available.

Note that the map of Tahoe National Forest does not show the direct route to Glacier Lake. Our suggested unmapped route climbs up through a beautiful canyon. The map, on the other hand, shows the trail routed up a hot, exposed route on Sandy Ridge.

Another note is that cows are often present in the lower meadow portions of the route, near the trail junction. A certain black-and-white cow is known to adopt female hikers, following for up to a mile, staring with lonely brown eyes as if saying, "Momma." Whatever you do, don't wear a cowbell around your neck.

Great side trips are also available. It is a one-mile hike north to the Five Lakes Basin and a 1.5-mile hike south to Beyers Lake. The elevations here range from 5,500 to 7,000 feet.

User Groups: Hikers, dogs, and horses. Mountain bikes strongly discouraged. No wheelchair facilities.

Permits: No permits are required. Parking and access are free.

Maps: For a map, ask the U.S. Forest Service for Tahoe National Forest. For topographic maps, ask the USGS for Cisco Grove and English Mountain.

Directions: From Auburn, take I-80 east for 45 miles, then take the Highway 20 exit and drive four miles to Bowman Lake Road (Forest Road 18). Turn right and drive 8.5 miles north until you see a sign that says Lindsey Lake, Feely Lake, Carr Lake. Turn right and follow the signs to the parking area at Carr Lake. Continue on foot to the trailhead at Feely Lake. Sections of the road can be rough; four-wheel-drive vehicles are advised.

Contact: Tahoe National Forest, Nevada City/Downieville Ranger Districts, 15924 Highway 49, Camptonville, CA 95922, 530/288-3231, www.fs.fed.us/r5—click on Forest Offices; Big Bend Visitors Center, Tahoe National Forest, 530/426-3609.

22 PIONEER TRAIL

1.0-24.0 mi / 0.5 hr-2.0 days 🏃2 6

east of Nevada City, off of Highway 20 in Tahoe National Forest

Hiking the Pioneer Trail is like taking a history lesson as you trace the route of the first wagon road, opened by emigrants and gold seekers in 1850. Along the way are three campgrounds for backpackers, but the trail is better suited for mountain biking. In fact, it has become almost an exclusive biking trip, but its historical significance still merits inclusion in this book.

From the trailhead at Five Mile House (elevation 3,500 feet), the trail heads east for 15 miles to Bear Valley, gaining 2,000 feet. You will pass Central House (once a stagecoach stop); White Cloud and Skillman Flat (former mill sites, one burned down); and the Omega Overlook, which provides a view of a huge hydraulic gold-mining operation. The CalTrans Omega rest area has a parking area, a restroom, and a viewing platform perched over the South Yuba River Canyon. From the Omega Overlook, you will get dramatic views of the Yuba River and the surrounding granite cliffs.

Note: The mountain bike traffic is high on this trail. While we admire bikers who make the round-trip, it seems a high percentage use the one-way trip downhill from Omega rest area to Five Mile House. When encountering other trail users, remember to demonstrate the utmost courtesy: Bikers should always dismount and walk when passing hikers.

User Groups: Hikers, dogs, mountain bikes, and horses. No wheelchair facilities.

Permits: A campfire permit (free) is required for overnight use. Parking and access are free.

Maps: For a map, ask the U.S. Forest Service for Tahoe National Forest. For a topographic map, ask the USGS for Washington.

Directions: From Nevada City, drive about seven miles east on Highway 20 to the trailhead, across from Lone Grave. If the parking lot there is full, additional parking and trail access are available at Skillman Flat, Upper Burlington Ridge, Harmony Ridge Market, the Omega rest area, and the Washington Overlook trailhead—all located to the east of Highway 20.

Contact: Tahoe National Forest, Nevada City/ Downieville Ranger Districts, 15924 Highway 49, Camptonville, CA 95922, 530/288-3231, www.fs.fed.us/r5—click on Forest Offices; Big Bend Visitors Center, Tahoe National Forest, 530/426-3609.

23 SIERRA DISCOVERY TRAIL
1.0 mi / 0.5 hr   👫1 ⛰8

off Highway 20 near Lake Spaulding

BEST (

The waterfall at Bear River is your destination on this easy, short, and nearly flat trail that is accessible to wheelchair users (with a bit of assistance). This is not the wilderness. Much of the trail is pavement, soil cement, or compressed gravel. It is designed as an interpretive loop walk, with information about ecosystems, wildlife, geology, and cultural history available as the trail winds through a forest of pines and incense cedars. This is an ideal mountain walk for seniors, youngsters, or the physically challenged. Bear River Falls is short but wide and is well framed by a forest canopy.

User Groups: Hikers, dogs, and wheelchairs (with assistance). No horses or mountain bikes. Dogs permitted, but rangers strongly discourage bringing them on this trail.

Permits: No permits are necessary. Parking and access are free.

Maps: For a topographic map, ask the USGS for Blue Canyon.

Directions: From Auburn, drive east on I-80 for 45 miles. Take the Highway 20 exit heading west and drive four miles to Bowman Lake Road. Turn right and drive 0.6 mile to the Sierra Discovery Trail parking lot, on the left side of the road.

Contact: Pacific Gas & Electric, 800/743-5000, www.pge.com.

24 LOCH LEVEN LAKES
7.2 mi / 4.0 hr   👫3 ⛰7

south of Cisco Grove in Tahoe National Forest

Most people would like to know what heaven is like but are not very willing to sign up for the trip. This trip to Loch Leven Lakes, however, won't be your final resting place, yet it provides a glimpse of what heaven might resemble. The 3.5-mile hike to Loch Leven Lakes provides sweeping vistas of ridges and valleys, gorgeous high alpine meadows, and glaciated mountain terrain with a series of perfect lakes. As hikers get deeper into the wildlands here, the lakes become progressively more beautiful and pristine. The lakes themselves are clear and blue, set in granite, and speckled with boulders—the perfect picnic site.

The trail starts at 5,680 feet then works its way upward on a moderate grade to the southwest. Granite outcrops are numerous, and huge boulders (deposited by receding glaciers) lie sprinkled among Jeffrey pine and lodgepole pine. The trail crosses a creek and railroad tracks, then climbs through a cool forest. Here the trail becomes steeper, climbing 800 feet in 1.25 miles. It then tops the summit and descends gently to Lower Loch Leven Lake (2.5 miles from the trailhead). Many people stop here, content to just take in the surroundings. But you can forge on for another mile, circling Middle Loch Leven Lake (2.8 miles from the trailhead) and heading east up to High Loch Leven Lake (3.6 miles from the trailhead), at 6,800 feet. At the south end of Lower Loch Leven Lake, turn left at the trail junction to see Middle and High Loch Leven Lakes (turning right at the junction will route you to Salmon Lake, a less-crowded alternative). Once you've come this far, beautiful High Loch Leven is an easy trip and a must-do.

But this hike is not without frustration: The first hour involves a continuous climb with the echo of I-80 traffic in the background. You do not escape the noise until you top the ridge. Elevations range from 5,680 feet to 6,850 feet

HIKING

at the ridge, a gain of 1,070 feet. With access so easy off I-80, the area can become inundated with people on summer weekends. With no trailhead quota, the numbers can affect the sense of wilderness.

Fishing is fair during the evening bite, and there are backcountry campgrounds at each lake. Restrooms are available at the trailhead (a plus). The trail is generally open for hiking from early June to November, weather permitting; it's not marked for winter use and can be difficult to find in snow conditions.

User Groups: Hikers, dogs, and horses. Mountain bikes not advised. No wheelchair facilities.

Permits: No permits are required. Parking and access are free.

Maps: For a map, ask the U.S. Forest Service for Tahoe National Forest. For a topographic map, ask the USGS for Cisco Grove.

Directions: From Sacramento, take I-80 east into the Sierra Nevada and to the Big Bend exit. Take that exit and then turn left on Hampshire Rocks Road. Follow the signs to the Big Bend Visitors Center, located adjacent to the highway. The parking area and trailhead are about 0.2 mile east of the visitors center. The trailhead is on the opposite side of the road from the parking area.

From Reno, take I-80 west to the Cisco Grove exit. Take that exit and turn right on Hampshire Rocks Road. Continue as above.

Contact: Tahoe National Forest, Nevada City/Downieville Ranger Districts, 15924 Highway 49, Camptonville, CA 95922, 530/288-3231, www.fs.fed.us/r5—click on Forest Offices; Big Bend Visitors Center, Tahoe National Forest, 530/426-3609.

25 LOWER LOLA MONTEZ LAKE

6.0 mi / 3.0 hr   🏃2 ⛰8

in Tahoe National Forest near Soda Springs

The hike to Lower Lola Montez Lake is a bad choice for a July or August weekend afternoon. That is because it's so easy, partly because it's

right off the highway, and partly because the trail is favored by mountain bikers. So get this one in focus: For hikers who enjoy peace and quiet, this is definitely an off-season trail, best left for the days of autumn, when the vacationers have abandoned Lake Tahoe. The path cuts through Toll Mountain Estates, a private community, and is a mix of wide dirt roads and single-track trails. The first 0.25 mile is on single track; then you reach a dirt road and turn right, cross Castle Creek, and continue until the road becomes single track again. And so it goes. Luckily, the route is marked all the way, and with all the people who visit here, it's unlikely you'll get lost and not be found. The good news is that the Lower Lola Montez Lake is popular for a reason; it's a beautiful alpine lake set at 7,200 feet but shallow enough to warm up for swimming. Fishing is half decent but is best early in the year.

User Groups: Hikers, dogs, horses, and mountain bikes. No wheelchair facilities.

Permits: No permits are required. Parking and access are free.

Maps: For a map, ask the U.S. Forest Service for Tahoe National Forest. For topographic maps, ask the USGS for Soda Springs and Norden.

Directions: From Auburn, take I-80 east for 55 miles to Soda Springs. Take the Soda Springs/Norden exit and cross over the overpass to the north side of the freeway. Follow the paved road east, past the fire station for 0.3 mile to the trailhead parking area.

Contact: Tahoe National Forest, Truckee Ranger District, 9646 Donner Pass Road, Truckee, CA 96161, 530/587-3558, www.fs.fed.us/r5—click on Forest Offices; Big Bend Visitors Center, Tahoe National Forest, 530/426-3609.

26 PALISADE CREEK TRAIL TO HEATH FALLS

10.0 mi / 6.0 hr   🏃3 ⛰10

In Tahoe National Forest near Soda Springs

The hike to Heath Falls is like going on vacation on your credit card. You can have all the fun you want, but when you return home, you have to pay up. That's because the trip to the Heath Falls Overlook is downhill nearly all the way, dropping 1,700 feet over five miles, through stunning alpine scenery that will have you smiling the whole time. The return trip is a long and steady five-mile climb back uphill, so be sure you have plenty of food, water, and energy left for it.

The trail begins at the dam between the two Cascade Lakes, the first of many lakes you'll see on this trip. The big hunk of imposing rock you have to walk around is 7,704-foot Devils Peak. Take the right fork signed for the North Fork American River, and get ready for a steady diet of granite, lakes, and vistas. At 2.2 miles, the trail leaves the rocks behind and enters the forest, switchbacking downhill for two miles to the Palisade Creek Bridge. Look for an unsigned junction 300 yards beyond it, where Heath Falls Overlook Trail heads east. Follow it for 0.5 mile to the trail's end, at a vista of the American River's Heath Falls. Camping is prohibited along this trail because much of it runs through private property, so after enjoying the falls overlook, you've got to make the long climb home. Hope you have at least one Power Bar left.

User Groups: Hikers, dogs, and horses. No mountain bikes. No wheelchair facilities.

Permits: No permits are required. Parking and access are free.

Maps: For a map, ask the U.S. Forest Service for Tahoe National Forest. For topographic maps, ask the USGS for Soda Springs and Norden.

Directions: From Auburn, drive east on I-80 for 55 miles to Soda Springs. Take the Soda Springs/Norden exit and follow Old Highway 40 east

for 0.8 mile to Soda Springs Road. Turn south (right) and drive for another 0.8 mile to Pahatsi Road. Turn right. Pahatsi Road turns to dirt in 0.2 mile, and its name changes to Kidd Lakes Road. At 1.5 miles, you'll reach a fork. Continue straight for 2.3 more miles, passing Kidd Lake on your left and the Royal Gorge Devils Lookout Warming Hut on your right. Take the left fork after the warming hut and drive 0.5 mile farther. The trailhead, signed as Palisade Creek Trail, is on the north side of Cascade Lakes.

Contact: Tahoe National Forest, Truckee Ranger District, 9646 Donner Pass Road, Truckee, CA 96161, 530/587-3558, www.fs.fed.us/r5—click on Forest Offices; Big Bend Visitors Center, Tahoe National Forest, 530/426-3609.

27 WARREN LAKE

14.0 mi / 2.0 days   🏃4 ⛰9

In Tahoe National Forest near Donner Summit

The first 1.6 miles of this trail follow the same route as the Summit Lake Trail (see next listing), along the PCT access trail and underneath I-80. But Warren Lake hikers will take the left fork where Summit Lake hikers go right. Whereas Summit Lake Trail is an easy stroll in the park, Warren Lake Trail climbs 1,500 feet and then drops 1,500 feet, which you must repeat on the return trip. The elevation change means you part company with most casual hikers. The route climbs through lodgepole pine and red fir forest to a saddle at three miles, where there are excellent views (you can see where you're going to be hiking next). Then the trail drops gently over the next 3.5 miles, into a wide valley basin that has a mix of volcanic and glaciated rocks. Wildflowers abound on the valley floor. After a brief climb to a ridge, the final mile is a steep descent, dropping 1,000 feet to Warren Lake, where you'll find many campsites on the lake's west and south sides. Note that just before you reach the top of the ridge, about 1.3 miles from Warren Lake, there is a left spur trail that leads to Devils Oven Lake. It's a good day hike for the following day.

User Groups: Hikers, dogs, horses, and mountain bikes. No wheelchair facilities.

Permits: No permits are required. Parking and access are free.

Maps: For a map, ask the U.S. Forest Service for Tahoe National Forest. For a topographic map, ask the USGS for Norden.

Directions: From Auburn, take I-80 east for 60 miles to the Castle Peak Area/Boreal Ridge Road exit just west of Donner Summit. Exit the freeway; turn right and then immediately left. Drive 0.4 mile to the trailhead for Donner Summit and the Pacific Crest Trail.

Contact: Tahoe National Forest, Truckee Ranger District, 9646 Donner Pass Road, Truckee, CA 96161, 530/587-3558, www .fs.fed.us/r5—click on Forest Offices; Big Bend Visitors Center, Tahoe National Forest, 530/426-3609.

28 SUMMIT LAKE TRAIL
4.0 mi / 2.0 hr   🏃2 ⛰9

in Tahoe National Forest near Donner Summit

The Summit Lake Trail is a quick and easy leg-stretcher and a great hike for families, leading two miles to a pretty alpine lake at 7,400 feet. It is crowded on weekends and those who are not fit complain the little climb is harder than they expected. Start hiking from the PCT trailhead, heading east and roughly paralleling the freeway. Watch carefully for an intersection 0.5 mile in. You must turn left and follow the PCT Access Trail north (signed for Castle Pass and Peter Grubb Hut), through a tunnel underneath I-80. (This is not the most scenic part of the trip, but it's not as bad as it sounds.) Once you're on the north side of the freeway, you'll reach a trail fork. Bear right for Summit Lake and Warren Lake, then start to climb a bit. The trail alternates through fir forest and occasional open ridges, with some excellent views to the south and

east. At 1.6 miles, you'll see another trail fork: Warren Lake to the left, and Summit Lake to the right. Bear right, and finish out your walk to the lake's edge, where you can drop in a fishing line if you wish.

User Groups: Hikers, dogs, horses, and mountain bikes. No wheelchair facilities.

Permits: No permits are required. Parking and access are free.

Maps: For a map, ask the U.S. Forest Service for Tahoe National Forest. For a topographic map, ask the USGS for Norden.

Directions: From Auburn, take I-80 east for 60 miles to the Castle Peak Area/Boreal Ridge Road exit just west of Donner Summit. Exit the freeway, turn right, and then immediately left. Drive 0.4 mile to the trailhead for Donner Summit and the Pacific Crest Trail.

Contact: Tahoe National Forest, Truckee Ranger District, 9646 Donner Pass Road, Truckee, CA 96161, 530/587-3558, www .fs.fed.us/r5—click on Forest Offices; Big Bend Visitors Center, Tahoe National Forest, 530/426-3609.

29 EUCHRE BAR TRAIL
6.0 mi / 3.5 hr   🏃3 ⛰8

on the North Fork American River near Baxter in Tahoe National Forest

A river runs through almost every Sierra gulch and canyon, and so it is with this portion of the North Fork American River. From the trailhead, the route winds steeply down to the river and Euchre Bar, where a suspension footbridge crosses the water. The trail then leads upriver for 2.4 miles, along an excellent stretch of water for fishing, camping, panning for gold, and swimming (cold). If you want a lesson in pain, continue hiking another five miles. You'll climb the old Dorer Ranch Road, passing mining ruins and abandoned equipment from the Gold Rush era, gaining 2,000 feet in elevation through this dry, dusty country. Correct: This is an old mining trail.

User Groups: Hikers, dogs, and horses. Mountain bikes not advised. No wheelchair facilities.

Permits: Campfire permits are required for overnight use. Parking and access are free.

Maps: For a map, ask the U.S. Forest Service for Tahoe National Forest. For topographic maps, ask the USGS for Dutch Flat and Westville.

Directions: From Auburn, take I-80 east to the Alta exit. Take that exit from Alta to Morton. Turn right on Morton, then turn left on Casa Loma and continue until you see the sign for the Rawhide Mine. Turn right at the sign and drive 0.75 mile past the second railroad crossing to a parking area. The trailhead is 0.1 mile beyond the parking area.

Contact: Tahoe National Forest, Nevada City/ Downieville Ranger Districts, 15924 Highway 49, Camptonville, CA 95922, 530/288-3231, www.fs.fed.us/r5—click on Forest Offices.

User Groups: Hikers, dogs, and horses. Mountain bikes not advised. No wheelchair facilities.

Permits: No permits are required. Parking and access are free.

Maps: For a map, ask the U.S. Forest Service for Tahoe National Forest. For a topographic map, ask the USGS for Westville.

Directions: Take I-80 to Auburn and the exit for Foresthill/Foresthill Road. Take that exit, turn east on Foresthill Road, and drive 16 miles to Foresthill. Continue another 13 miles northeast (the road becomes Foresthill Divide Road) to Humbug Ridge Road (Forest Road 66). Turn left and drive three miles north to the trailhead.

Contact: Tahoe National Forest, Nevada City/ Downieville Ranger Districts, 15924 Highway 49, Camptonville, CA 95922, 530/288-3231, www.fs.fed.us/r5—click on Forest Offices.

30 ITALIAN BAR TRAIL
4.5 mi / 3.5 hr   5 / 8

near the North Fork American River in Tahoe National Forest

Miners in the 1850s were like mountain goats, and they knew the most direct route between two points was a straight line. As a result, this route—which miners once used to reach the North Fork American River—is almost straight down going in and straight up coming out, gaining 3,000 feet in elevation over the course of 2.25 miles. It's about as fun as searching for a tiny gold nugget on the beach. As you head down from the trailhead at 5,400 feet, you get little help from switchbacks. The trail ends at the river, and from there, you must scramble and hop from rock to rock along the riverbanks. Eventually you end up at a secluded spot where all seems perfect—until you start the hike back. When you face the 3,000-foot climb out, you will wonder how you ever talked yourself into doing this hike.

31 MUMFORD BAR TRAIL
6.5 mi / 1.0 day   4 / 8

near the North Fork American River in Tahoe National Forest

You'd have to be part mountain goat and part idiot to want to try this hike. Guess how we know? The trail leads almost straight down to the North Fork American River for more than 3.25 miles, and you know what that means. Right—it's almost straight up coming back. (Guess those gold miners were plenty of both.)

From the trailhead at 5,360 feet, the first mile of trail follows an old four-wheel-drive route that deteriorates and then drops down to the river canyon at 2,640 feet. This stretch of river is designated as "wild and scenic" and is quite pretty, with good canyon views and fishing spots. Consider extending your walk by taking American River Trail (see next listing) and staying overnight. Otherwise you will have to climb back out of the canyon on the same day, something even most mountain goats or gold miners would choose not to do.

User Groups: Hikers, dogs, and horses. Mountain bikes are not advised. No wheelchair facilities.

Permits: No permits are required. Parking and access are free.

Maps: For a map, ask the U.S. Forest Service for Tahoe National Forest. For topographic maps, ask the USGS for Duncan Peak and Westville.

Directions: Take I-80 to Auburn and the exit for Foresthill/Foresthill Road. Take that exit, turn east on Foresthill Road, and drive 16 miles to Foresthill. Continue another 17 miles northeast (the road becomes Foresthill Divide Road) to the Mumford trailhead, on the left side of the road.

Contact: Tahoe National Forest, Foresthill Ranger District, 22830 Foresthill Road, Foresthill, CA 95631, 530/367-2224, www.fs.fed.us/r5—click on Forest Offices.

32 AMERICAN RIVER TRAIL
15.2 mi / 2.0 days　　　🏃5 ⛰9

on the North Fork American River
east of Foresthill in Tahoe National Forest

A 90-minute hike from the Mumford Bar trailhead (see previous listing) gets you down into a steep canyon and alongside the beautiful and remote North Fork American River. There you turn right and start hiking upstream on American River Trail. This is what you came for, the chance to walk along a pristine stretch of river on a steady, easy grade. You will pass old mining sites and abandoned cabins, alternating between dense vegetation and pretty river views. This trail makes a great getaway, and hikers can enjoy exploring and trout fishing. Nothing is perfect, and this hike does have some drawbacks: It crosses two creeks, Tadpole and New York, which are difficult, even dangerous, to ford when running high during the snowmelt in spring and early sum-

mer. A mile upriver of Tadpole Creek and then again at New York Creek, the trail runs adjacent to private property. Check your map and stay on the trail in these places. And the hike back out of the canyon to your car is a terrible grunt, going from 2,640 feet along the river up to 5,360 feet. That is a gain of 2,720 feet in just 3.25 miles.

Special Note: The Mumford trailhead is also accessible from Sailor Flat Trail (see listing in this chapter).

User Groups: Hikers, dogs, and horses. Mountain bikes not advised. No wheelchair facilities.

Permits: A campfire permit (free) is required for overnight use. Parking and access are free.

Maps: For a map, ask the U.S. Forest Service for Tahoe National Forest. For a topographic map, ask the USGS for Duncan Peak.

Directions: Take I-80 to Auburn and the exit for Foresthill/Foresthill Road. Take that exit, turn east on Foresthill Road, and drive 16 miles to Foresthill. Continue another 17 miles northeast (the road becomes Foresthill Divide Road) to the Mumford trailhead, on the left side of the road.

Contact: Tahoe National Forest, Foresthill Ranger District, 22830 Foresthill Road, Foresthill, CA 95631, 530/367-2224, www.fs.fed.us/r5—click on Forest Offices.

33 BEACROFT TRAIL
4.5 mi / 1.0 day　　　🏃5 ⛰9

near the North Fork American River
in Tahoe National Forest

BEST ◖

The Beacroft Trail is the "no-option" option to hiking down to the North Fork American River. The trailhead is located four miles beyond the Mumford trailhead, and after having reviewed the steep descent and climb required for that hike, you might want to look elsewhere for an easier route down. That's where Beacroft Trail comes in. Still, it isn't a much of an option, requiring an even more hellacious effort: it drops 3,240 feet in only 2.25 miles. The trip back up will have you howling. How can such a short trail be so steep? Ask the people who built the darn thing; those gold miners apparently had neither an abundance of useful gray matter between their ears nor much gold to carry on the return trip. OK, so you head down the canyon, then what? When you reach the river, turn left on American River Trail, which traces some of the most beautiful, accessible portions of this stream. Even here you face an obstacle. Within the first mile, you must cross New York Creek, a difficult (and sometimes dangerous) ford when full of snowmelt in early summer.

User Groups: Hikers, dogs, and horses. Mountain bikes are not advised. No wheelchair facilities.

Permits: No permits are required. Parking and access are free.

Maps: For a map, ask the U.S. Forest Service for Tahoe National Forest. For a topographic map, ask the USGS for Duncan Peak.

Directions: Take I-80 to Auburn and the exit for Foresthill/Foresthill Road. Take that exit, turn east on Foresthill Road and drive 16 miles to Foresthill. Continue another 19 miles northeast (the road becomes Foresthill Divide Road) to the trailhead, on the left side of the road (one mile past Secret House Campground).

Contact: Tahoe National Forest, Foresthill Ranger District, 22830 Foresthill Road, Foresthill, CA 95631, 530/367-2224, www.fs.fed.us/r5—click on Forest Offices.

34 SAILOR FLAT TRAIL
6.5 mi / 1.0 day   5   ⛺ 10

near the North Fork American River
in Tahoe National Forest

There are several trailheads heading for Sailor Flat Trail on the Foresthill side of Foresthill Road that provide access to the North Fork

American River. But this is the most distant, most remote, and, yes, most difficult. In turn, it is the least traveled. The Sailor Flat trailhead lies at the end of the road, out in the middle of nowhere, at an elevation of 6,400 feet; yet the remains of a long-abandoned gold stamp mill still stand nearby. The hike starts out easily enough—the first 1.5 miles follow an old mining road on which hikers will confront nothing serious. Don't be fooled though. The trail becomes much steeper, with switchback after switchback leading down into the canyon. When you reach the river at 3,360 feet, you will have dropped 3,040 feet in only 3.25 miles. You can explore farther by turning left (west) on American River Trail, which traces the most beautiful sections of this river, heading downstream past meadows, canyon views, and good spots to fish and pan for gold.

Special Note: With a shuttle vehicle and a partner, you can create a one-way hike covering 15.6 miles. From Sailor Flat trailhead, hike down to American River Trail, turn left, hike along the river to Mumford Bar, make a left turn, and hike out to Foresthill Road (see preceding hikes).

User Groups: Hikers, dogs, and horses. Mountain bikes not advised. No wheelchair facilities.

Permits: No permits are required. Parking and access are free.

Maps: For a map, ask the U.S. Forest Service for Tahoe National Forest. For topographic maps, ask the USGS for Royal Gorge and Duncan Peak.

Directions: Take I-80 to Auburn and the exit for Foresthill/Foresthill Road. Take that exit, turn east on Foresthill Road, and drive 16 miles to Foresthill. Continue another 25 miles northeast (the road becomes Foresthill Divide Road) to Sailor Flat Road. Turn left and drive one mile north to the trailhead.

Contact: Tahoe National Forest, Foresthill Ranger District, 22830 Foresthill Road, Foresthill, CA 95631, 530/367-2224, www.fs.fed.us/r5—click on Forest Offices.

HIKING

35 STEVENS TRAIL
9.0 mi / 5.0 hr

near Colfax

The Stevens Trail is a surprisingly lush and peaceful trail that leaves noisy I-80 in Colfax and drops down into the canyon of the North Fork American River. The features here are gentle terrain and long-distance canyon and stream views.

After parking, walk 1.3 miles, starting with a gentle climb, and keep a sharp eye off to the left, where a pretty waterfall is hidden just off the trail. From the ridge, continue on a gentle downhill path, descending 1,200 feet over the course of 4.5 miles if you choose to head all the way to the river. The return trip is up but is well graded and not too difficult for most hikers. The biggest problem here is timing. This is no fun on a summer afternoon, with 90-degree temperatures and an afternoon climb out of a canyon. Regardless, this is a great trip for many, especially for those cruising the interstate who desire a quick getaway into a pretty setting where the highway traffic seems like a million miles away.

You can also see the railroad line that was built by Chinese laborers dangling in rope-strung baskets from the cliffs above. In the spring, you will also pass blooming wildflowers and buckeye trees. The trail is well signed, except the section you take to see the waterfall. This trail was registered in 2002 as a National Historic Trail. It was originally part of a livery trail from the town of Iowa Hill to Colfax (the entire historic route is no longer connected).

User Groups: Hikers, dogs, horses, and mountain bikes. No wheelchair facilities.

Permits: No permits are necessary. Parking and access are free.

Maps: For a topographic map, ask the USGS for Colfax.

Directions: From Sacramento, drive east on I-80 for 45 miles to Colfax and the Colfax/Grass Valley exit. Take that exit and drive a short distance to a stop sign at North Canyon Way (a frontage road). Turn left at the stop sign and drive east 0.7 mile to the trailhead parking area.

Contact: Bureau of Land Management, Folsom Field Office, 63 Natoma Street, Folsom, CA 95630, 916/985-4474, www.ca.blm.gov—click on Field Offices.

36 GREEN VALLEY TRAIL
4.5 mi / 1.0 day

on the North Fork American River
near Sugar Pine Reservoir

It's amazing what people will go through to create a space that feels like their own. Hikers can do just that on Green Valley Trail by finding an idyllic spot along the North Fork American River and soaking up the serenity. But the price is steep, and the return trip will put you through more punishment than is typically handed out at Folsom Prison.

The trip starts at a little-known trailhead near Sugar Pine Reservoir (elevation 4,080 feet). From there, Green Valley Trail is steep and often rocky, dropping 2,240 feet in 2.25 miles before reaching the river. We do not advise extending your trip from here. It is possible to continue downriver a short way, or to cross the river (good luck) and hike upstream into Green Valley. However, these sections of the trail are in very poor condition, and the upstream route crosses private property owned by people who don't take kindly to visitors.

User Groups: Hikers, dogs, and horses. Mountain bikes are not advised. No wheelchair facilities.

Permits: No permits are required. Parking and access are free.

Maps: For a map, ask the U.S. Forest Service for Tahoe National Forest. For a topographic map, ask the USGS for Dutch Flat.

Directions: Take I-80 to Auburn and the exit for Foresthill/Foresthill Road. Take that exit, turn east on Foresthill Road, and drive 16 miles to Foresthill. Continue another seven miles (it becomes Foresthill Divide Road) to Forest Road 10. Turn left on Forest Road 10 (Sugar Pine Road) and drive five miles to Sugar Pine Dam. Continue one mile past the dam to Elliot Ranch Road (just past the entrance to Sugar Pine Campground, on the right). Turn north on Elliot Ranch Road and drive three miles to the trailhead.

Contact: Tahoe National Forest, Foresthill Ranger District, 22830 Foresthill Road, Foresthill, CA 95631, 530/367-2224, www .fs.fed.us/r5—click on Forest Offices.

37 FOREST VIEW TRAIL
1.5 mi / 0.75 hr   🏃1 ⛰9

in Tahoe National Forest east of Foresthill

Giant sequoias, the world's largest trees, attract many visitors to this easy, well-maintained interpretive trail that leads through California's northernmost grove of sequoias. It is set at 5,200 feet on Mosquito Ridge Road. The trail meanders through virgin old-growth forest, home to a half dozen truly monster-sized trees. Along the 0.5-mile Big Trees Interpretive Trail are 16 stops marked with numbers that coincide with numbered listings in a brochure that's available at the trailhead, allowing visitors to take an interesting and informative self-guided tour of the fascinating history of these massive trees. Linked with Forest View Trail, the entire loop extends 1.5 miles. Despite the long drive to the trailhead on Mosquito Ridge, the trail gets quite a bit of use. The drive in provides views of an expansive foothill landscape before entering the conifers.

User Groups: Hikers and dogs. No horses or mountain bikes. No wheelchair facilities.

Permits: No permits are required. Parking and access are free.

Maps: Free interpretive brochures are available at the trailhead. For a map, ask the U.S. Forest Service for Tahoe National Forest. For

a topographic map, ask the USGS for Greek Store.

Directions: Take I-80 to Auburn and the exit for Foresthill/Foresthill Road. Take that exit, turn east on Foresthill Road, and drive 16 miles to Foresthill and Mosquito Ridge Road. Turn right (east) on Mosquito Ridge Road and drive 23 miles to the trailhead.

Contact: Tahoe National Forest, Foresthill Ranger District, 22830 Foresthill Road, Foresthill, CA 95631, 530/367-2224, www .fs.fed.us/r5—click on Forest Offices.

38 WESTERN STATES TRAIL/ MICHIGAN BLUFF TO DEADWOOD SEGMENT
4.0 mi / 2.5 hr   🏃3 ⛰7

in Tahoe National Forest east of Foresthill

The attraction here is beautiful Eldorado Canyon, where you can fish for trout and camp along Eldorado Creek. From the trailhead at 3,520 feet, the trail quickly drops about two miles into the canyon. Switchbacks lead to a footbridge over Eldorado Creek. Extend the trip by crossing the bridge and hiking up the other side of the canyon to scenic views of the rugged topography.

Special Note: The Michigan Bluff Trail is a section of the Western States Trail, which spans from Squaw Valley to Auburn.

User Groups: Hikers, dogs, horses, and mountain bikes. No wheelchair facilities.

Permits: No permits are required. Parking and access are free.

Maps: For a map, ask the U.S. Forest Service for Tahoe National Forest. For a topographic map, ask the USGS for Michigan Bluff.

Directions: Take I-80 to Auburn and the exit for Foresthill/Foresthill Road. Take that exit, turn east on Foresthill Road, and drive 16 miles to Foresthill. Continue northeast (it becomes Foresthill Divide Road) and look for the signed turnoff to Michigan Bluff. Turn right on Michigan Bluff Road and drive five miles to Michigan Bluff. The trailhead is located about 0.25 mile east of Michigan Bluff, at the end of the road.

Contact: Tahoe National Forest, Foresthill Ranger District, 22830 Foresthill Road, Foresthill, CA 95631, 530/367-2224, www .fs.fed.us/r5—click on Forest Offices.

39 GROUSE FALLS

1.0 mi / 0.5 hr   🏃1 ⛰10

in Tahoe National Forest near Foresthill

BEST (

Some waterfalls are simply mind-boggling in their beauty, and some provide the centerpiece of a beautiful setting. Grouse Falls is one of the latter. The hike is a 15-minute walk through old-growth forest to a viewing deck. From here you're looking out over a deep and wide canyon with absolutely no sign of human development. The waterfall is about 0.5 mile away across the canyon; it's several hundred feet long, and when it's running full, it can seem like a scene out of Yosemite. The overlook is a wooden platform with benches where you can sit and admire the beauty. You don't see or hear immense Grouse Falls until just before you come out to the overlook, and when you do, it can be a shock to your system.

User Groups: Hikers, dogs, horses, and mountain bikes. No wheelchair facilities.

Permits: No permits are necessary. Parking and access are free.

Maps: For a map, ask the U.S. Forest Service for Tahoe National Forest. For a topographic map, ask the USGS for Michigan Bluff.

Directions: Take I-80 to Auburn and the exit for Foresthill/Foresthill Road. Take that exit, turn east on Foresthill Road, and drive 16 miles to Foresthill and Mosquito Ridge Road. Turn right (east) on Mosquito Ridge Road and drive 19 miles to Peavine Road (Road 33). Turn left on Peavine Road and drive 5.5 miles to the Grouse Falls turnoff, on the left. Turn left and drive 0.5 mile to the trailhead.

Contact: Tahoe National Forest, Foresthill Ranger District, 22830 Foresthill Road, Foresthill, CA 95631, 530/367-2224, www .fs.fed.us/r5—click on Forest Offices.

40 WESTERN STATES TRAIL/ McGUIRE SEGMENT

7.8 mi / 4.0 hr   🏃2 ⛰8

at French Meadows Reservoir in Tahoe National Forest

The McGuire Trail has become a favorite side trip for families visiting or camping at French Meadows Reservoir (elevation 5,290 feet). The trail traces the north shore of the lake, poking in and out of timber. It then rises up an easy grade to the top of Red Star Ridge (5,600 feet) and provides good views of the reservoir below. French Meadows is a beautiful and large lake, covering nearly 2,000 acres when full. It is stocked each year with more than 30,000 trout that join a healthy population of resident brown trout and holdovers from stocks of rainbow trout from prior years. Water drawdowns are a common problem in late summer, as they expose many stumps and boulders, creating a navigational hazard for boaters.

User Groups: Hikers, dogs, horses, and mountain bikes. No wheelchair facilities.

Permits: No permits are required. Parking and access are free.

Maps: For a map, ask the U.S. Forest Service for Tahoe National Forest. For a topographic map, ask the USGS for Bunker Hill.

Directions: Take I-80 to Auburn and the exit for Foresthill/Foresthill Road. Take that exit, turn east on Foresthill Road, and drive 16 miles to Foresthill and Mosquito Ridge Road. Turn right (east) on Mosquito Ridge Road and drive 40 miles to the French Meadows Reservoir Dam. Cross the dam, turn left (still Mosquito Ridge Road), and drive 3.5 miles to the trailhead, near McGuire Boat Ramp.

Contact: Tahoe National Forest, Foresthill Ranger District, 22830 Foresthill Road,

Foresthill, CA 95631, 530/367-2224, www
.fs.fed.us/r5—click on Forest Offices.

41 POWDERHORN TRAIL
TO HELL HOLE

13.0 mi one-way / 2.0 days 🏃‍♀️5 ⛰️9

in the Granite Chief Wilderness east of
Hell Hole Reservoir in Tahoe National Forest

This is a difficult trek that traverses the Sierra
crest, east to west, Tahoe to Hell Hole. The
Hell Hole Trail requires hikers to have wilderness skills and, worst of all, to be prepared
for a difficult stream crossing and traversing
a landslide. Sound fun? Who said anything
about fun?

Start at the remote Powderhorn trailhead,
set at 6,400 feet on the boundary of the Granite Chief Wilderness. From there, you hike
four miles down to Diamond Crossing (ford-
ing Powderhorn Creek), where you will meet
Hell Hole Trail. Shortly after turning left, you
will have to cross Five Lakes Creek, a difficult
and sometimes dangerous endeavor, especially
during snowmelt. After crossing, you will descend to Little Buckskin Creeks (two more
fords, both a lot easier than the first one) and
into Steamboat Canyon. Approximately 0.5
mile from Steamboat Canyon, hikers face a
slippery landslide that demands caution. The
trail then drops toward the Rubicon River and
Hell Hole Reservoir.

Do you yearn for a challenging trek in a
very remote high-mountain wilderness setting? This is it.

Special Notes: The stream crossings required on this hike can be life threatening during periods of high snowmelt and runoff.

For a day hike or a weekend camping trip,
start the trail at the Hell Hole Dam and walk
three miles to a hike-in camp set at the head
of the lake.

User Groups: Hikers, dogs, and horses. No
mountain bikes. No wheelchair facilities.

Permits: A campfire permit (free) is required

for overnight use. Parking and access are
free.

Maps: For a map, ask the U.S. Forest Service
for Tahoe National Forest. For a topographic
map, ask the USGS for Wentworth Springs.

Directions: From Truckee, take Highway 89
south and drive to Tahoe City. Turn right on
Highway 89 (along Lake Tahoe) and drive four
miles to the Kaspian Picnic Area and Blackwood Canyon Road. Turn right (west) on
Blackwood Canyon Road and drive 2.3 miles.
Cross the creek and continue for another 4.8
miles to Barker Pass and the trailhead.

Contact: Tahoe National Forest, Truckee
Ranger District, 9646 Donner Pass Road,
Truckee, CA 96161, 530/587-3558, www
.fs.fed.us/r5—click on Forest Offices.

42 GRANITE CHIEF TRAIL
TO TINKER KNOB

14.0 mi / 8.0 hr or 2.0 days 🏃‍♀️4 ⛰️10

in Tahoe National Forest near Squaw Valley

Tinker Knob is not an easy summit to at-
tain, but those who reach it always remember it. From the Squaw Valley Fire Station,
it's a demanding 3.5-mile hike to the intersection of the Granite Chief Trail and the
Pacific Crest Trail. The total gain is 2,000
feet; most of the climb is forested, but there
are occasional openings with views of Lake
Tahoe and surrounding peaks. When at
last you gain the PCT (at 8,200 feet), turn
right (north) toward Tinker Knob. Now it's
another 3.5 miles, most of it on an easier,
winding grade along the top of a ridge, with
only one surprising, cruel stretch in which
you must drop downhill and then climb up
again. The last section of trail is a series of
switchbacks up to the Tinker Knob Saddle,
then it's a brief 0.25-mile climb to the summit of Tinker Knob, at 8,950 feet. You like
views? How about this one—a head-swiveling
vista of Anderson Peak, Painted Rock, Silver
Peak, the American River Canyon, Donner

Lake, and Lake Tahoe. To cut some mileage off your trip, hike this trail as a shuttle trip, leaving one car at the Coldstream trailhead near Donner Memorial State Park. (It's at the horseshoe bend in the railroad tracks at the end of Coldstream Creek access road.) The Coldstream Trail meets the PCT just below the summit of Tinker Knob, so after gaining the summit via the route described above, follow Coldstream Trail four miles down to its trailhead. This makes an 11-mile one-way hike with a shuttle.

User Groups: Hikers, dogs, horses, and mountain bikes. No wheelchair facilities.

Permits: No permits are required. Parking and access are free.

Maps: For a map, ask the U.S. Forest Service for Tahoe National Forest. For topographic maps, ask the USGS for Tahoe City and Granite Chief.

Directions: From Truckee, take Highway 89 south and drive about 8 miles to Squaw Valley Road. Turn right on Squaw Valley Road and drive 2.2 miles to the Squaw Valley Fire Station. The trail begins on its east side. You must leave your car in the large parking lot by the ski lift buildings, not by the fire station. Walk back across the bridge to the trailhead.

Contact: Tahoe National Forest, Truckee Ranger District, 9646 Donner Pass Road, Truckee, CA 96161, 530/587-3558, www .fs.fed.us/r5—click on Forest Offices.

43 GRANITE CHIEF TRAIL TO EMIGRANT PASS
12.0 mi / 7.0 hr

in Tahoe National Forest near Squaw Valley

The Granite Chief Trail begins at the Squaw Valley Fire Station (at 6,200 feet) and climbs, climbs, and climbs some more until it reaches the Pacific Crest Trail 3.5 miles later. This is why many hikers choose to ride the tram at Squaw Valley to reach the PCT, then start hiking around from there. But not you... you

like a challenge, right? Well, in either case, see you at the top.

You'll climb 2,000 feet over those 3.5 miles, roughly paralleling Squaw Creek and mostly in the woods. When you reach the PCT, turn left (south) toward Twin Peaks. The view of Lake Tahoe and its cobalt blue waters is stunning. Still ascending, hike for one mile on the PCT to the eastern flank of Granite Chief Peak (elevation 9,086 feet). Finally you begin to descend, and in one more mile you reach an intersection with Western States Trail. Turn left and take a 0.5-mile walk to visit the Watson Monument, a stone marker at Emigrant Pass. You probably won't stay long if you arrive in the afternoon: Although the views are lovely, the wind is usually fierce by midday.

User Groups: Hikers, dogs, horses, and mountain bikes. No wheelchair facilities.

Permits: No permits are required. Parking and access are free.

Maps: For a map, ask the U.S. Forest Service for Tahoe National Forest. For topographic maps, ask the USGS for Tahoe City and Granite Chief.

Directions: From Truckee, take Highway 89 south and drive about 8 miles to Squaw Valley Road. Turn right on Squaw Valley Road and drive 2.2 miles to the Squaw Valley Fire Station. The trail begins on its east side. You must leave your car in the large parking lot by the ski lift buildings, not by the fire station. Walk back across the bridge to the trailhead.

Contact: Tahoe National Forest, Truckee Ranger District, 9646 Donner Pass Road, Truckee, CA 96161, 530/587-3558, www .fs.fed.us/r5—click on Forest Offices.

44 FIVE LAKES
4.2 mi / 2.0 hr

in the Granite Chief Wilderness near Alpine Meadows

Some say that this trek into the Granite Chief Wilderness is too easy, and they may be right.

Although the trail has a moderately steep grade, it's mercifully short, which makes it incredibly popular with hikers, especially on weekends. Make your trip in the off-season or during the week, and definitely make this a day trip instead of an overnight in order to minimize impact at the five granite-bound lakes.

The first 0.5 mile is the steepest grade. The next 0.75 mile continues uphill more gradually to the top of a ridge. Switchbacks make it manageable, but there is almost no shade along the route as you climb 1,000 feet. At 1.8 miles, you reach the Granite Chief Wilderness boundary and enter a land of red fir, white fir, and rocks. A signed junction 0.25 mile farther points you to the left toward the lakes, with your trail heading directly downhill to the largest of them. From there, you can follow numerous side trails to the four other lakes, all east of the big one. Most people don't go any farther than the first big lake, where the swimming is excellent. The shallow water is clear and warm. Remember: Minimize your impact in this heavily traveled area. The Five Lakes are set at 7,400 feet.

User Groups: Hikers, dogs, and horses. No mountain bikes. No wheelchair facilities.

Permits: No permits are required for day hiking. Parking and access are free.

Maps: For a map, ask the U.S. Forest Service for Tahoe National Forest. For topographic maps, ask the USGS for Tahoe City and Granite Chief.

Directions: From Truckee, take Highway 89 south and drive about 10 miles to Alpine Meadows Road. Turn right on Alpine Meadows Road and drive two miles to the trailhead, on the right. Park along the road.

Contact: Tahoe National Forest, Truckee Ranger District, 9646 Donner Pass Road, Truckee, CA 96161, 530/587-3558, www .fs.fed.us/r5—click on Forest Offices.

45 WARD CREEK TRAIL
6.0 mi / 3.0 hr   🥾1 ⛰9

in Tahoe National Forest near Tahoe City

Ward Creek Trail may seem rather tame compared to some of the more famous hikes at Lake Tahoe. There's no stellar waterfall, no drop-dead gorgeous lake views, no towering granite monoliths. But then again, there are no crowds either. For many, the trade-off is a good one. The route passes through fields of mule's ears and forests of sugar pines, with enough open sections to provide wide-open views of the surrounding mountain ridges.

The trail begins as an old dirt road, paralleling Ward Creek for 1.5 miles to a washed-out bridge and a Road Closed sign. Cross the creek on logs and continue hiking, now on a single track. The trail climbs a little higher above Ward Creek, then enters a dense, lovely pine forest. You can go as far as you like (the trail continues to Twin Peaks, 5.3 miles from the trailhead), but for the mileage suggested above, turn around when you are about 0.5 mile into the trees and take an easy stroll home.

User Groups: Hikers, dogs, horses, and mountain bikes. No wheelchair facilities.

Permits: No permits are required. Parking and access are free.

Maps: For a map, ask the U.S. Forest Service for Lake Tahoe Basin Management Unit. For a topographic map, ask the USGS for Tahoe City.

Directions: From Truckee, take Highway 89 south and drive to Tahoe City. Turn right on Highway 89 and drive 2 miles to Pineland Drive (just north of Kilner Park). Turn right on Pineland Drive and go 0.5 mile to Twin Peaks Drive. Turn left and drive 1.7 miles. (Twin Peaks Drive becomes Ward Creek Boulevard.) At 1.7 miles, park in the pullout on the left side of the highway and begin hiking at the gated dirt road, Forest Service Road 15N62. If the gate is open, you can drive inside and park along the dirt road.

Contact: Lake Tahoe Basin Management

Unit, 35 College Drive, South Lake Tahoe, CA 96150, 530/543-2600, www.fs.fed.us/r5—click on Forest Offices; Visitors Center (open only in summer), 530/543-2674.

46 ELLIS PEAK

6.0 mi / 3.5 hr

in Tahoe National Forest near Tahoe City

This short but steep trek leads to the top of Ellis Peak and to fabulous views of Lake Tahoe, Granite Chief and Desolation Wildernesses, and Hell Hole Reservoir. There is a total 1,300-foot elevation gain to the peak (at 8,740 feet), but the route is beautiful all the way, with close-up wildflowers rivaling the far-off views. The initial climb is a bit steep, but there is plenty of shade on this stretch. Then, for 1.5 miles, the route follows a sunny ridgeline with wide-open vistas, revealing Lake Tahoe to the east and Hell Hole Reservoir to the west. The perspective from this ridgeline alone is worth the trip. Plus, mule's ears and other wildflowers bloom in profusion all around your ankles.

After traversing the ridgeline, head downhill (surprise!) through the forest, dropping 400 feet in elevation. When you come to a wide dirt road, bear left to begin the trek to Ellis Peak. In 0.25 mile, you'll see a short left spur to tiny Ellis Lake, a worthy side trip of about 50 yards. If you ignore the spur and stay on the main trail for another 100 yards, you'll reach an old dirt road, where you turn east (left). In 0.25 mile, you come to Knee Ridge, from which the summit of Ellis Peak is plainly visible. Go for it. Note that the only downer along this route is that some of it is accessible to off-road-vehicle riders and mountain bikers, although we saw none of the former on our trip, and the latter were extremely courteous.

User Groups: Hikers, dogs, horses, and mountain bikes. No wheelchair facilities.

Permits: No permits are required. Parking and access are free.

Maps: For a map, ask the U.S. Forest Service for Lake Tahoe Basin Management Unit. For a topographic map, ask the USGS for Homewood.

Directions: From Truckee, take Highway 89 south and drive to Tahoe City. Turn right on Highway 89 and drive four miles south to Forest Service Road 03 (unsigned Barker Pass Road). Turn right (west) and drive seven miles to the summit of Barker Pass. The trailhead is on the left (south) side of the road.

Contact: Lake Tahoe Basin Management Unit, 35 College Drive, South Lake Tahoe, CA 96150, 530/543-2600, www.fs.fed.us/r5—click on Forest Offices; Visitors Center (open only in summer), 530/543-2674.

47 STATELINE LOOKOUT

1.0 mi / 0.5 hr

off Highway 28 near Crystal Bay

For years we avoided this trail because we thought it was just a tourist attraction, located at the lookout tower that straddles the Nevada and California state line. It turns out that *we* were the dumb tourists, because this little trail is great. You can learn all about the cultural history of Lake Tahoe's north shore—which includes stories of timber, railroads, casinos, and resorts—as well as a little about the natural history of the area. After you walk the short self-guided trail, be sure to check out the views of Lake Tahoe from the telescopes located at the lookout (elevation 7,017 feet). Or, hey, forget the telescopes and just look with your own eyes. Either way, the view is unforgettable.

User Groups: Hikers, wheelchairs, and dogs. No horses or mountain bikes.

Permits: No permits are required. Parking and access are free.

Maps: For a map, ask the U.S. Forest Service for Lake Tahoe Basin Management Unit. For a topographic map, ask the USGS for Kings Beach.

Directions: From Truckee, take Highway 89 south and drive to Tahoe City and Highway 28. Turn left on Highway 28 and drive six miles to Reservoir Drive (just east of the old Tahoe Biltmore Casino). Turn left (north) and drive to Lake View Avenue. Turn right and drive through a residential area and continue to Forest Service Road 1601 (at an unmarked iron gate). Turn left on Forest Service Road 1601, park at the gate, and walk 0.5 mile to the lookout. Parking is limited.

Contact: Lake Tahoe Basin Management Unit, 35 College Drive, South Lake Tahoe, CA 96150, 530/543-2600, www.fs.fed.us/ r5—click on Forest Offices; Visitors Center (open only in summer), 530/543-2674.

48 BURTON CREEK LOOP
5.0 mi / 2.5 hr   🏃1 ⛰8

off Highway 28 near Tahoe City

At more than 2,000 acres, Burton Creek is Lake Tahoe's second-largest state park, so you might wonder why few people have ever heard of it. It's because the park has no visitors center, no campground, no entrance kiosk, and, unfortunately, no trail signs or official map. What really matters is that it has no crowds—a major bonus at Lake Tahoe. A five-mile loop trip is possible in the park, starting near North Tahoe High School and wandering through a mix of fir and pine forest, open meadows, and creekside riparian habitat. Although the trail is not signed, there are numbers painted at most intersections, which help you stay on track. The loop starts 0.25 mile from the trailhead; you can hike it in either direction. Just make sure you remember what the spur trail that leads from the loop back to the trailhead looks like; otherwise you may walk right past it on your return trip. Some advice: If you're visiting this park in summer, stop in at the campground at Tahoe State Recreation Area,

across Highway 28 from the turnoff to Burton Creek State Park. Check with the kiosk to see if they have any updated trail information on Burton Creek.

User Groups: Hikers, leashed dogs, horses, and mountain bikes. No wheelchair facilities.

Permits: No permits are required. Parking and access are free.

Maps: For a topographic map, ask the USGS for Tahoe City.

Directions: From Truckee, take Highway 89 south and drive to Tahoe City and Highway 28. Turn left on Highway 28 and drive 2.3 miles to Old Mill Road. Turn left and drive 0.4 mile to Polaris Road. Turn left on Polaris Road and drive 0.5 mile to North Tahoe High School and the dirt road by the school parking lot. Park alongside the dirt road. Be careful not to block the gate.

Contact: Tahoe State Recreation Area, P.O. Box 266, Tahoma, CA 96142, 530/525-7232 or 530/583-3074, fax 530/525-0138.

49 BARKER PASS TO DONNER PASS (PCT)
31.4 mi one-way / 3.0 days 🏃3 ⛰8

from Barker Pass to Donner Pass

The trailhead at Barker Pass (7,650 feet), is one of the best anywhere. It provides direct access to the Granite Chief Wilderness to the north or the Desolation Wilderness to the south. Heading north on the PCT, the trip starts with a climb of 800 feet to enter Granite Chief. Once on the ridge, you're rewarded with 360-degree views of this high-mountain landscape, a mix of volcanic rock and granite ridges, much of it above tree line. Though hikers don't face the long, sustained climbs so common in the southern Sierra, it's enough of a roller-coaster ride to require hikers to be in excellent shape. The trail cuts the flank of Ward Peak, at 8,470 feet, then switchbacks steeply down to Five Lakes and Five Lakes Creek (where there's good camping). The trail then continues up and down canyons all the way to Donner Pass. You can expect to see lots of hikers, because along the way, you'll pass near two ski resorts (Alpine Meadows and Squaw Valley), where hikers can use the ski lifts in the summer to gain easy elevation to the ridgeline, rather than having to grind out long, all-day climbs. Before making the final push to Donner Pass, a descent of more than 1,000 feet, hikers can enjoy breathtaking views of Donner Lake and the miles of surrounding high country.

To continue north on the PCT, see the *Donner Pass to the Yuba River (PCT)* hike in this chapter. If you are walking this trail in reverse, see the *Echo Lakes Resort to Barker Pass (PCT)* hike in this chapter.

User Groups: Hikers, dogs, and horses. No mountain bikes. No wheelchair facilities.

Permits: A backcountry permit is required for traveling through various wilderness and special-use areas that the trail traverses. In addition, a campfire permit is required for the use of portable camp stoves or the building of campfires (where allowed). To make it simple, you can contact the national forest, Bureau of Land Management (BLM), or national park office at your point of entry for a combined permit that is good for traveling through multiple-permit areas during your dates of travel.

Maps: For topographic maps, ask the USGS for Emerald Bay, Rockbound Valley, Homewood, Tahoe City, Granite Chief, and Norden.

Directions: To reach the Barker Pass trailhead: From Truckee, take Highway 89 south and drive to Tahoe City. Turn right on Highway 89 and drive south to Kaspian Picnic Grounds (0.5 north of Tahoe Pines) and Forest Road 15N03. Turn right (west) and drive seven miles to the trailhead.

For the Donner Pass trailhead: From Truckee, drive west on I-80 and exit at Castle Peak Area/Boreal Ridge, just west of the Donner Summit roadside rest area. The sign for the Pacific Crest trailhead is what you're looking

for, and it's located on the south side of the highway.

Contact: Tahoe National Forest, Truckee Ranger District, 9646 Donner Pass Road, Truckee, CA 96161, 530/587-3558, www .fs.fed.us/r5—click on Forest Offices; Lake Tahoe Basin Management Unit, 35 College Drive, South Lake Tahoe, CA 96150, 530/543-2600, www.fs.fed.us/r5—click on Forest Offices; Visitors Center (open only in summer), 530/543-2674.

🔟 GENERAL CREEK TO LILY POND

7.0 mi / 3.5 hr

in Sugar Pine Point State Park
near Lake Tahoe

Marshy Lily Pond is a pretty, serene spot. This trail starts in Sugar Pine Point State Park and follows a flat open stretch of General Creek and then leads gently uphill through the forest to the Lily Pond. Most of the trail is part of a popular cross-country skiing loop in the winter, which means it's on a dirt road. At 2.5 miles from the campground, at the far end of the loop, you'll see the single-track turnoff signed for Lily Pond and Lost Lake. It's a one-mile hike through a rocky, dense forest to the pond, which is indeed covered with lilies. On your return, you can always take the south side of the loop for variety, then turn left on the bridge over General Creek to return to the start of the loop.

There are a couple key factors to enjoying this walk: If you're not staying in the General Creek Campground, the day-use parking area is more than 0.5 mile from campsite No. 149, where the trail begins. To make this walk to the trailhead more pleasant, be sure to take the single-track trail from the parking lot instead of walking along the paved camp road. The trail is somewhat hidden from view, so if you don't see it, ask the attendant in the entrance kiosk where it is. Next, when you finally meet up with the loop, be sure to take the north side of it, which is prettier than the south side, with lots of big sugar pines interspersed with Jeffreys and lodgepoles. The south side is mostly open meadows. This was the site of the 1960 Olympics biathlon.

User Groups: Hikers and mountain bikes. No dogs or horses. No wheelchair facilities.

Permits: No permits are required. A day-use fee of $6 is charged per vehicle.

Maps: A map of Sugar Pine Point State Park is available for a fee at the entrance station. A Lake Tahoe map is available for a fee from Tom Harrison Maps. For a topographic map, ask the USGS for Homewood.

Directions: From Truckee, take Highway 89 south and drive to Tahoe City. Turn right on Highway 89 and drive south eight miles to the General Creek Campground entrance on the right. Turn right and park in one of the day-use areas by the entrance kiosk, then walk into the campground to site No. 149 and the start of the trail. You can walk into the camp on the park road or take the single-track trail that leads from the parking lot.

Contact: Sugar Pine Point State Park, P.O. Box 266, Tahoma, CA 96142, 530/525-7982, www.parks.ca.gov—click on Find A Park.

51 MEEKS CREEK TRAIL TO RUBICON LAKE

15.0 mi / 1.0-2.0 days

In the Desolation Wilderness

This trek into the Desolation Wilderness is a moderate backpacking trip that's loaded with alpine lakes and classic Tahoe scenery. In summer, plan on sharing the trail with lots of other folks The trip starts as you hike on a closed dirt road (Road 14N42) that leads from the Desolation Wilderness sign near Meeks Bay for 1.3 level miles to a trail sign for Phipps Pass and Tahoe-Yosemite Trail. Bear right here and begin the gradual climb to a chain of alpine lakes. You hike parallel to Meeks Creek on a

gently climbing trail, and pass the wilderness boundary at 2.5 miles. You're in forest most of the time, so don't expect a lot of panoramic views, but then again, don't expect any brutal, sunny, exposed ascents. Cross Meeks Creek and continue straight to Lake Genevieve, at 4.5 miles. The lake is shallow but provides swimming. The trail then climbs up to larger Crag Lake, then continues to climb farther to small, lily-covered Shadow Lake. (A right fork beyond Crag Lake leads to small Hidden Lake, less than 0.25 mile off the main trail; it's a good side trip.) From Shadow Lake, it's a mile farther to Stony Ridge Lake, the largest of this series of lakes, and then yet another mile to Rubicon Lake, 7.5 miles from the trailhead and with a total elevation gain of only 2,000 feet. The main steep stretch is right at the end, between Stony Ridge Lake and Rubicon Lake. Campsites can be found at most all of the lakes, but Rubicon Lake is the preferred site, since it's the most scenic of the group.

User Groups: Hikers, dogs, and horses. No mountain bikes. No wheelchair facilities.

Permits: Permits are required year-round for both day and overnight use. Day hikers may obtain a free permit from a ranger station or may self-issue at most major trailheads. Backpackers camping in Desolation Wilderness are subject to trailhead quotas. There is a $5 reservation fee, plus $5 per person for one night, $10 per person for two or more nights up to 14 days (nonrefundable). Children ages 12 and under are free. Golden Passes do not apply to personal-use permits. For groups, the cost of a single permit will not exceed $100.

Maps: For a map, ask the U.S. Forest Service for Desolation Wilderness or Lake Tahoe Basin Management Unit. A Lake Tahoe or Desolation Wilderness map is also available from Tom Harrison Maps. For topographic maps, ask the USGS for Homewood and Rockbound Valley.

Directions: From Truckee, take Highway 89 south and drive to Tahoe City. Turn right on Highway 89 and drive south for 10 miles to Meeks Bay Resort. Look for a small dirt parking lot across from the resort, on the west side of the highway, and park there. The trailhead is well marked.

Contact: Lake Tahoe Basin Management Unit, 35 College Drive, South Lake Tahoe, CA 96150, 530/543-2600, www.fs.fed.us/r5—click on Forest Offices; Visitors Center (open only in summer), 530/543-2674.

52 RUBICON AND LIGHTHOUSE LOOP

2.0 mi / 1.0 hr   🥾1 ⛺10

in D. L. Bliss State Park on the west shore of Lake Tahoe

If you're visiting Lake Tahoe, you should not leave the area without sampling at least a piece of this magnificent pathway. The trail edges along the steep cliffs on the west side of the lake and provides sweeping lake views. An excellent short trip on the Rubicon is this loop, which starts from Calawee Cove Beach, at D. L. Bliss State Park. Although the hike has very little elevation gain, it's not for those who are afraid of heights, because there are 100-foot drop-offs along the trail's edge, leading straight down to Lake Tahoe. Cables are in place in some sections to keep people from falling off the trail. Hike 0.25 mile to a spur trail leading to the old lighthouse (don't bother with the spur; there's nothing to see), then continue beyond it for another 0.5 mile. The lake and mountain views are mind-boggling every step of the way. Bear right at the trail junction and walk to a parking lot, where you can pick up Lighthouse Trail and loop back to Calawee Cove Beach. On the other hand, if you want to see those lake vistas one more time, forget about the loop and just head back the way you came. Not everybody is up for hiking the entire length of Rubicon Trail (see next listing).

User Groups: Hikers only. No dogs, horses, or mountain bikes. No wheelchair facilities.

Permits: No permits are required. A day-use fee of $6 is charged per vehicle.

Maps: A map of D. L. Bliss State Park is available for a fee at the entrance station. A Lake Tahoe map is available for a fee from Tom Harrison Maps. For a topographic map, ask the USGS for Emerald Bay.

Directions: From South Lake Tahoe, take Highway 89 north past Emerald Bay and continue a short distance to the entrance road for D. L. Bliss State Park. Turn right and drive 0.5 mile to the entrance station and continue for 0.7 mile to a fork. Turn right and drive another 0.7 mile to Calawee Cove Beach and the parking lot. The Rubicon Trail begins on the far side of the lot. If this lot is full, you will have to use one of the other day-use parking lots in the park.

Contact: D. L. Bliss State Park, P.O. Box 266, Tahoma, CA 96142, 530/525-7277 or 530/525-7232, www.parks.ca.gov—click on Find A Park.

53 RUBICON TRAIL

9.0 mi / 5.0 hr   🥾2 ⛺10

in D. L. Bliss State Park on the west shore of Lake Tahoe

BEST (

The Rubicon Trail is the premier Lake Tahoe day hike. Accept no substitutes. If you want the best scenery that Lake Tahoe offers, this is the trail to hike. The only problem? Right—it's you and about a zillion other hikers. If you possibly can, walk this trail in the off-season (late September is great), and do it on a weekday. Better yet, do it at dawn or dusk. Then get ready for eye-popping, film-burning scenery as you gaze out across the surface and deep into the depths of sparkling, clear, 12-mile-wide Lake Tahoe and the rim of mountains that surround it. The trail stays close to the lake edge and has very little elevation change, just some mild ups and downs, holding steady near 6,300 feet. Highlights include Rubicon

Point, Emerald Point, Emerald Bay, Fannette Island, Vikingsholm Castle, and Eagle Point. If you stop for a picnic, don't be surprised if several little ground squirrels visit you, hoping for a hand-out. If you prefer, you can start and end your Rubicon hike at Vikingsholm: Leave your car in the Emerald Bay Overlook parking lot, hike down to Vikingsholm, and then head north to the boat-in campground and beyond. But note that finding room in the parking lot in summer is nearly impossible except for those arriving very early in the day. In addition, you'll add on nearly two miles round-trip getting from the parking lot to Vikingsholm, during which there is a 600-foot elevation change.

Note: If you start the hike at Calawee Cove Beach, just after setting out on the Rubicon Trail, be sure to take the left fork, which will keep you on Rubicon Trail.

User Groups: Hikers only. No dogs, horses, or mountain bikes. No wheelchair facilities.

Permits: No permits are required. A day-use fee of $6 is charged per vehicle.

Maps: A map of D. L. Bliss State Park is available for a fee at the entrance station. A Lake Tahoe map is available for a fee from Tom Harrison Maps. For a topographic map, ask the USGS for Emerald Bay.

Directions: From South Lake Tahoe, take Highway 89 north past Emerald Bay and continue a short distance to the entrance road for D. L. Bliss State Park. Turn right and drive 0.5 mile to the entrance station, then continue for 0.7 mile to a fork. Turn right and drive another 0.7 mile to Calawee Cove Beach and the parking lot. The Rubicon Trail begins on the far side of the lot. If this lot is full, you will have to use one of the other day-use parking lots in the park.

Contact: D. L. Bliss State Park, P.O. Box 266, Tahoma, CA 96142, 530/525-7277 or 530/525-7232, www.parks.ca.gov—click on Find A Park.

54 BALANCING ROCK
1.0 mi / 0.5 hr

in D. L. Bliss State Park on the west shore of Lake Tahoe

The Balancing Rock is a big hunk of granite that has been a curiosity at Lake Tahoe for eons. It's a 130-ton rock that sits balanced on a small rock pedestal, like a giant golf ball on an itty-bitty golf tee. The trail's interpretive brochure explains that eventually erosion will wear away the pedestal and cause the Balancing Rock to lose its balance, but Tahoe lovers have been awaiting this event forever, and it still hasn't happened. In addition to Balancing Rock, the trail shows off many of the plants and trees of the Tahoe area. It's a good learning experience for both kids and adults.

User Groups: Hikers only. No dogs, horses, or mountain bikes. No wheelchair facilities.

Permits: No permits are required. A day-use fee of $6 is charged per vehicle.

Maps: A map of D. L. Bliss State Park is available for a fee at the entrance station. A Lake Tahoe map is available for a fee from Tom Harrison Maps. For a topographic map, ask the USGS for Emerald Bay.

Directions: From South Lake Tahoe, take Highway 89 north past Emerald Bay and continue a short distance to the entrance road for D. L. Bliss State Park. Turn right and drive 0.5 mile to the entrance station, then continue for 0.7 mile to a fork. Turn left and drive 0.25 mile to the Balancing Rock parking lot, on the left.

Contact: D. L. Bliss State Park, P.O. Box 266, Tahoma, CA 96142, 530/525-7277 or 530/525-7232, www.parks.ca.gov—click on Find A Park.

55 VIKINGSHOLM

2.0 mi / 1.0 hr

in Emerald Bay State Park on the west shore
of Lake Tahoe

If you can take this walk very early in the
morning, and preferably on a weekday, you'll
experience the incredible beauty that has made
Lake Tahoe the revered vacation destination
that it is. If you take this walk at almost any
other time, be prepared for a lot of company.
Although the destination of this one-mile trail
(really a dirt road) is Vikingsholm, a Viking
castle built by an heiress in 1929, the beauty
lies in the scenery spread out before you as you
hike downhill. You'll see spectacular Fannette
Island and the deep blue waters of Emerald Bay,
and you'll travel through an old-growth cedar
and pine forest. You even gain access to some of
Lake Tahoe's coveted sandy shoreline. Although
visitors have to pay a buck to tour the inside
of the castle, you can hike to it for free and
add on a side trip to the base of 150-foot Eagle
Falls, situated 0.25 mile from Vikingsholm. For
many people, the surprise on this trail is that
the return hike has a 500-foot elevation gain.
What, you mean we have to breathe hard?

Special Note: Be sure to arrive early. By
midmorning on weekends, visitors are forced
to park up to two miles away.

User Groups: Hikers only. No dogs, horses, or
mountain bikes. No wheelchair facilities.

Permits: No permits are required. A fee of $6
is charged per vehicle. There is a fee to tour
the inside of the castle.

Maps: A map of Emerald Bay and D. L. Bliss
State Parks is available for a fee at the visitors
center at Vikingsholm. A Lake Tahoe map is
available for a fee from Tom Harrison Maps.
For a topographic map, ask the USGS for
Emerald Bay.

Directions: From South Lake Tahoe, take
Highway 89 north and drive nine miles to
the Emerald Bay Overlook parking lot on the
east side of Highway 89. The trail begins from
the lake side of the parking lot.

Contact: Emerald Bay State Park, P.O. Box
266, Tahoma, CA 96142, 530/525-7277 or
530/525-7232, www.parks.ca.gov—click on
Find A Park.

56 UPPER EAGLE FALLS AND EAGLE LAKE

2.0 mi / 1.0 hr

off Highway 89 near South Lake Tahoe

This is one of the most popular hikes in the
entire Tahoe region, perhaps number two
only to the trail to Vikingsholm. A sign by
the restroom at the Eagle Falls Picnic Area
points hikers to Upper Eagle Falls Trail. Unfortunately this is something of a "designer"
path, with natural granite cut into flagstone-
like stairs and an elaborate wooden bridge
that escorts visitors over the top of the falls.
Still it's a beautiful walk, best taken early in
the morning and during the week, when the
masses aren't around. The waterfall pours
right under the hikers' bridge. (If you want
to see the "other" Eagle Falls, the one that
drops right along Highway 89, see the previous listing). Immediately after the bridge, the
designer aspect of the trail ends as you enter
the Desolation Wilderness and climb 400
feet in less than a mile to reach rocky Eagle
Lake, surrounded by granite cliffs. People
fish and picnic here; some even try to swim
in the icy water.

User Groups: Hikers and dogs. No horses or
mountain bikes. No wheelchair facilities.

Permits: Day hikers must fill out a free permit
at the wilderness trailhead. A $6 parking fee
is charged per vehicle.

Maps: For a map, ask the U.S. Forest Service
for Desolation Wilderness or Lake Tahoe
Basin Management Unit. A Lake Tahoe map
is available for a fee from Tom Harrison Maps.
For a topographic map, ask the USGS for Emerald Bay.

Directions: From South Lake Tahoe, take
Highway 89 north and drive 8.5 miles to the

Eagle Falls Picnic Area and trailhead. Turn left into the parking area, or park in the roadside pullout just north of the picnic area on the west side of Highway 89.

Contact: Lake Tahoe Basin Management Unit, 35 College Drive, South Lake Tahoe, CA 96150, 530/543-2600, www.fs.fed.us/ r5—click on Forest Offices; Visitors Center (open only in summer), 530/543-2674.

57 VELMA LAKES
10.0 mi / 5.0 hr   👫3 ⛰9

in the Desolation Wilderness

The Velma Lakes are classic Desolation: gorgeous, alpine jewels. This route follows the trail to Eagle Falls and Eagle Lake (see previous listing) for the first mile, then climbs through a rugged, glaciated landscape, with only occasional hardy lodgepole pines and twisted junipers providing meager shade. The lack of trees and the abundance of rock mean wide-open views and plenty of granite drama: Welcome to the Sierra high country.

At three miles, you intersect the trail heading southwest (left) to Dicks Lake, but you should head northwest (right) for Velma Lakes. Your trail heads directly to Middle Velma Lake (in one mile), the most popular of the lakes. It has several granite islands and is favored for swimming. You can take a left cutoff just before Middle Velma Lake and head south to Upper Velma Lake in 0.5 mile, or follow a use trail north along a creek to Lower Velma Lake (on your right, also 0.5 mile away).

Note that hikers can also begin the Velma Lakes hike from the trailhead at Bayview Campground, but then they miss out on seeing Eagle Lake and a world-class view of Tahoe. Remember to bring your sunscreen because the rocky trail to the Velma Lakes is exposed and open.

User Groups: Hikers and dogs. No horses or mountain bikes (the Bayview Trail provides access for horses; contact Tahoe Basin National Forest). No wheelchair facilities. To reach Velma Lakes, equestrians must access from another trailhead; Bayview trailhead is the best for this.

Permits: Permits are required year-round for both day and overnight use. Day hikers may obtain a free permit from a ranger station or may self-issue at most major trailheads. Backpackers camping in Desolation Wilderness are subject to trailhead quotas. There is a $5 reservation fee, plus $5 per person for one night, $10 per person for two or more nights up to 14 days (nonrefundable). Children ages 12 and under are free. Golden Passes do not apply to personal-use permits. For groups, the cost of a single permit will not exceed $100. A $6 parking fee is charged per vehicle.

Maps: For a map, ask the U.S. Forest Service for Desolation Wilderness or Lake Tahoe Basin Management Unit. A Lake Tahoe or Desolation Wilderness map is available from Tom Harrison Maps. For topographic maps, ask the USGS for Emerald Bay and Rockbound Valley.

Directions: From South Lake Tahoe, take Highway 89 north and drive 8.5 miles to the Eagle Falls Picnic Area and trailhead. Turn left into the parking area or park in the roadside pullout just north of the picnic area, on the west side of Highway 89.

Contact: Lake Tahoe Basin Management Unit, 35 College Drive, South Lake Tahoe, CA 96150, 530/543-2600, www.fs.fed.us/ r5—click on Forest Offices; Visitors Center (open only in summer), 530/543-2674.

58 CASCADE FALLS
2.0 mi / 1.0 hr   👫1 ⛰10

off Highway 89 near South Lake Tahoe

This trail is the best easy hike at Lake Tahoe. It's short and flat enough for almost anybody to make the trip, including young children, but it still feels like wilderness. The one-mile trail leads to the brink of a stunning 200-foot cascade that drops into the southwest end of Cascade Lake.

From the trailhead at Bayview Campground, take the left fork signed for Cascade Falls. In five minutes, you get tremendous views of Cascade Lake (elevation 6,464 feet) below to your left. Then you start to hear and see the falls. The trail disintegrates as it nears the waterfall's edge, and hikers with children shouldn't get too close. But no matter; the best views are actually farther back on the trail. Upstream of the falls are some lovely pools surrounded by wide shelves of granite. Make sure you visit in spring or early summer, when the waterfall is flowing full and wide, because by August, it loses its drama.

User Groups: Hikers and dogs. No horses or mountain bikes. No wheelchair facilities.

Permits: No permits are required. Parking and access are free.

Maps: For a map, ask the U.S. Forest Service for Lake Tahoe Basin Management Unit. A Lake Tahoe map is available for a fee from Tom Harrison Maps. For a topographic map, ask the USGS for Emerald Bay.

Directions: From South Lake Tahoe, take Highway 89 north and drive 7.5 miles to the Bayview Campground. Turn left and drive to the far end of the campground to the trailhead parking area. If it's full, park on the shoulder of Highway 89 by the campground entrance.

Contact: Lake Tahoe Basin Management Unit, 35 College Drive, South Lake Tahoe, CA 96150, 530/543-2600, www.fs.fed.us/r5—click on Forest Offices; Visitors Center (open only in summer), 530/543-2674.

59 MOUNT TALLAC (TALLAC TRAILHEAD)

9.0 mi / 6.0 hr   🚶5 ⛰10

in the Desolation Wilderness
near Fallen Leaf Lake

Mount Tallac towers over Lake Tahoe and provides one of the most beautiful lookouts in North America. From the 9,375-foot summit, you look down on Fallen Leaf Lake, Cascade Lake, Emerald Bay, Lake Tahoe, and beyond to Mount Rose on the eastern Tahoe rim. To the west are miles of Desolation Wilderness.

But you pay dearly: You climb 2,600 feet over the final three miles, plus another 900-foot climb in the first 1.5 miles. From the trailhead, you make the first butt-kicker climb for 1.7 miles to Floating Island Lake. You get excellent views of Fallen Leaf Lake and Lake Tahoe along the way. Then it's another 0.7 mile to a trail junction just before Cathedral Lake, where a trail from Fallen Leaf Lake joins this trail. Cathedral Lake is a good rest stop before making the final ascent to the top of Mount Tallac, a 2.4-mile butt-kicker of a climb on a rocky trail. It's made somewhat easier by a continuous and inspiring parade of vistas, including long looks at Gilmore Lake, Susie Lake, and Lake Aloha. The trail ends 0.25 mile below the summit, where it meets the other Mount Tallac trail coming from Gilmore Lake. Bear right, and boulder hop your way to the top. Note that Mount Tallac can also be reached from the Gilmore Lake trailhead and is a far different trek with the same ending. See the *Gilmore Lake* hike in this chapter.

User Groups: Hikers and dogs. No horses or mountain bikes. No wheelchair facilities.

Permits: Permits are required year-round for both day and overnight use. Day hikers may obtain a free permit from a ranger station or may self-issue at most major trailheads. Backpackers camping in Desolation Wilderness are subject to trailhead quotas. There is a $5 reservation fee, plus $5 per person for one night, $10 per person for two or more nights up to 14 days (nonrefundable). Children ages 12 and under are free. Golden Passes do not apply to personal-use permits. For groups, the cost of a single permit will not exceed $100.

Maps: For a map, ask the U.S. Forest Service for Desolation Wilderness. A Lake Tahoe or Desolation Wilderness map is also available for a fee from Tom Harrison Maps. For a topographic map, ask the USGS for Emerald Bay.

Directions: From South Lake Tahoe, take Highway 89 north and drive 3.8 miles to the signed turnoff for Mount Tallac and Camp Concord (on the left, across the highway from the sign for Baldwin Beach). Drive 0.4 mile to the trailhead spur. Turn left and drive 0.6 mile to the trailhead.

Contact: Lake Tahoe Basin Management Unit, 35 College Drive, South Lake Tahoe, CA 96150, 530/543-2600, www.fs.fed.us/ r5—click on Forest Offices; Visitors Center (open only in summer), 530/543-2674.

60 RAINBOW AND LAKE OF THE SKY TRAILS
0.5 mi / 0.5 hr   👫1 ⛰8

in Tahoe National Forest
near South Lake Tahoe

BEST (

Several short interpretive walks begin at the Lake Tahoe Visitors Center. The best is the Rainbow Trail and Lake of the Sky Trail. You can hike them both from the same starting point at the visitors center and combine an interesting nature lesson with a walk along Lake Tahoe's shoreline for exceptional scenery and views.

Start with Rainbow Trail, which leads from the visitors center's west side and takes you to Taylor Creek and its Stream Profile Chamber. The creek is where thousands of kokanee salmon come to spawn in the fall, and visitors can view them through the glass walls of the profile chamber. You can also see them the ordinary way, just by peering into the creek as you walk. Then loop back to the visitors center and pick up Lake of the Sky Trail. You'll pass by Taylor Creek Marsh on your way to Tallac Point and Tahoe's shoreline. In summer, people go swimming at this sandy stretch of beach.

User Groups: Hikers and wheelchair users. No dogs, horses, or mountain bikes.

Permits: No permits are required. Parking and access are free.

Maps: For a map, ask the U.S. Forest Service for Lake Tahoe Basin Management Unit. A free forest recreation newspaper is also available. A Lake Tahoe map is available for a fee from Tom Harrison Maps. For a topographic map, ask the USGS for Emerald Bay.

Directions: From South Lake Tahoe, take Highway 89 north and drive three miles to the Lake Tahoe Visitors Center turnoff, on the right. Turn right and drive to the visitors center parking lot, where the trails begin.

Contact: Lake Tahoe Basin Management Unit, 35 College Drive, South Lake Tahoe, CA 96150, 530/543-2600, www.fs.fed.us/ r5—click on Forest Offices; Visitors Center (open only in summer), 530/543-2674.

61 MOUNT TALLAC LOOP (GLEN ALPINE TRAILHEAD)
11.6 mi / 7.5 hr   👫3 ⛰10

in the Desolation Wilderness
near Fallen Leaf Lake

You can hike to the top of 9,735-foot Mount Tallac for the world-class view from either of two trailheads. This trip from Glen Alpine is more gradual than the route from the Tallac trailhead (see the *Mount Tallac (Tallac Trailhead)* listing in this chapter). Start at the Glen Alpine trailhead, elevation 6,560 feet, and follow the main trail, which is lined with large, cobblestone-like rocks. It's a difficult walking surface for many, but fortunately, the surface flattens out shortly beyond the first mile. At the Grass Lake and Gilmore Lake junction, 1.5 miles in, bear right. Get ready for a well-graded series of switchbacks climbing out of Glen Alpine Canyon, with some shade (but not quite enough) to keep you somewhat refreshed. A good rest stop is at Gilmore Lake, 3.5 miles in, where you can stretch your hamstrings and munch a snack. From there, it's just under two miles to the top of Mount Tallac, climbing steeply up its

HIKING

smooth back side. This is the toughest part of the trail, and it slows down a lot of casual hikers. The official trail ends just below the summit; you must scramble over and around boulders for the last 0.25 mile to reach the top. The vista here is one of the finest in North America. Enjoy the eye-popping views of the Desolation Wilderness, Fallen Leaf Lake, Lake Tahoe, and Mount Rose.

You have a choice on how to return to your car. You can simply return the way you came. Or you can turn this into a loop hike. But to make this a loop hike, be prepared for a knee-jarring descent down the front face of Mount Tallac. From the summit, head back down the Glen Alpine Trail and look for another trail heading east, toward Fallen Leaf Lake. Just past tiny Cathedral Lake, 2.3 miles from the summit, bear right at the fork (it's easy to miss) and continue downhill to Stanford Camp; walk through the camp, and pick up the road to Glen Alpine trailhead. A short stint on the road will deposit you back at your car.

User Groups: Hikers and dogs. No horses or mountain bikes. No wheelchair facilities.

Permits: Permits are required year-round for both day and overnight use. Day hikers may obtain a free permit from a ranger station or may self-issue at most major trailheads. Backpackers camping in Desolation Wilderness are subject to trailhead quotas. There is a $5 reservation fee, plus $5 per person for one night, $10 per person for two or more nights up to 14 days (nonrefundable). Children ages 12 and under are free. Golden Passes do not apply to personal-use permits. For groups, the cost of a single permit will not exceed $100.

Maps: For a map, ask the U.S. Forest Service for Desolation Wilderness. A Lake Tahoe or Desolation Wilderness map is also available for a fee from Tom Harrison Maps. For a topographic map, ask the USGS for Echo Lake.

Directions: From South Lake Tahoe, take Highway 89 north and drive 2.9 miles to Fallen Leaf Lake Road. Turn left and drive 4.8 miles on a narrow road past the Fallen Leaf Marina to a fork. Take the left fork on Road

1216, signed for Lily Lake and the Desolation Wilderness. Drive 0.7 mile to the trailhead, at the road's end.

Contact: Lake Tahoe Basin Management Unit, 35 College Drive, South Lake Tahoe, CA 96150, 530/543-2600, www.fs.fed.us/r5—click on Forest Offices; Visitors Center (open only in summer), 530/543-2674.

62 GILMORE LAKE

7.6 mi / 4.0 hr

in the Desolation Wilderness
near Fallen Leaf Lake

If you only have time to day-hike to one destination near South Lake Tahoe, Gilmore Lake is an excellent choice. Everything about it is a classic Lake Tahoe and Desolation Wilderness trip, a roundup of the best the area has to offer. You get to visit a scenic alpine lake, and along the way, you are treated to fields of wildflowers, mountain vistas, conifer forests, and more. Of course, we're not the only ones who like this trail, so all the usual disclaimers apply about timing your trip for the off-season or during the week.

With that said, take off from the Glen Alpine trailhead and hike down the road past the private cabins. The rocky road eventually becomes a rocky trail. This cobblestone-like stretch is by far the worst part of the hike; the rocks make it rough going for hikers' ankles and knees. Bear right at the junction with Grass Lake Trail, 1.5 miles in, where the trail surface improves dramatically. Get ready to do the majority of this trail's climbing, heading for more trail junctions at nearly three miles in, where paths lead off to the left, to Susie and Heather Lakes. Bear right instead for Gilmore Lake, the largest lake in this area between Fallen Leaf Lake and Lake Aloha. You'll reach it at 3.5 miles, with a total 1,700-foot elevation gain. Despite the fact that hundreds of people cruise by Gilmore Lake each day on their way to climb Mount Tallac, few take the time to hang out for long by the lake's sapphire-blue waters. The lake, ringed by grassy, flower-filled meadows, manages to stay secluded and pristine.

User Groups: Hikers and dogs. No horses or mountain bikes. No wheelchair facilities.

Permits: Permits are required year-round for both day and overnight use. Day hikers may obtain a free permit from a ranger station or may self-issue at most major trailheads. Backpackers camping in Desolation Wilderness are subject to trailhead quotas. There is a $5 reservation fee, plus $5 per person for one night, $10 per person for two or more nights up to 14 days (nonrefundable). Children ages 12 and under are free. Golden Passes do not apply to personal-use permits. For groups, the cost of a single permit will not exceed $100.

Maps: For a map, ask the U.S. Forest Service for Desolation Wilderness. A Lake Tahoe or Desolation Wilderness map is also available for a fee from Tom Harrison Maps. For a topographic map, ask the USGS for Emerald Bay.

Directions: From South Lake Tahoe, take Highway 89 north and drive 2.9 miles to Fallen Leaf Lake Road. Turn left and drive 4.8 miles on a narrow road past the Fallen Leaf Marina to a fork. Take the left fork on Road 1216, signed for Lily Lake and the Desolation Wilderness. Drive 0.7 mile to the trailhead, at the road's end.

Contact: Lake Tahoe Basin Management Unit, 35 College Drive, South Lake Tahoe, CA 96150, 530/543-2600, www.fs.fed.us/r5—click on Forest Offices; Visitors Center (open only in summer), 530/543-2674.

63 SUSIE AND HEATHER LAKES
10.0 mi / 5.0 hr 🚶3 ⛺9

in the Desolation Wilderness
near Fallen Leaf Lake

Many people believe they must visit the beautiful Desolation Wilderness to see the rugged alpine beauty of the Tahoe wildlands. Not so. This trip, a day hike to Susie and Heather Lakes, is a perfect example.

The trail to Susie and Heather Lakes begins as a rocky road and passes some summer cabins and a waterfall on Glen Alpine Creek. At 1.2 miles, the road ends near an old resort and you'll see a sign for Gilmore, Susie, and Grass Lakes. Start to climb, and shortly, you'll enter the Desolation Wilderness boundary. You can take the short left cutoff to little Grass Lake (adding one mile each way to your trip) or continue straight, which is signed for Susie, Heather, and Aloha Lakes. At four miles, you'll reach the eastern shore of Susie Lake, then hike alongside it and around the lake's southern edge to continue another mile to Heather Lake. The granite-lined lake is deep and wide, and is set in a landscape of classic high Sierra scenery.

User Groups: Hikers, dogs, and horses. No mountain bikes. No wheelchair facilities.

Permits: Permits are required year-round for both day and overnight use. Day hikers may obtain a free permit from a ranger station or may self-issue at most major trailheads. Backpackers camping in Desolation Wilderness are subject to trailhead quotas. There is a $5 reservation fee, plus $5 per person for one night, $10 per person for two or more nights up to 14 days (nonrefundable). Children ages 12 and under are free. Golden Passes do not apply to personal-use permits. For groups, the cost of a single permit will not exceed $100.

Maps: For a map, ask the U.S. Forest Service for Desolation Wilderness. A Lake Tahoe or Desolation Wilderness map is also available for a fee from Tom Harrison Maps. For a topographic map, ask the USGS for Emerald Bay.

Directions: From South Lake Tahoe, take Highway 89 north and drive 2.9 miles to Fallen Leaf Lake Road. Turn left and drive 4.8 miles on a narrow road past the Fallen Leaf Marina to a fork. Take the left fork on Road 1216, signed for Lily Lake and the Desolation Wilderness. Drive 0.7 mile to the trailhead, at the road's end.

Contact: Lake Tahoe Basin Management

Unit, 35 College Drive, South Lake Tahoe, CA 96150, 530/543-2600, www.fs.fed.us/r5—click on Forest Offices; Visitors Center (open only in summer), 530/543-2674.

64 FALLEN LEAF LAKE TRAIL

2.0 mi / 1.0 hr   🏃1 ⛰9

near South Lake Tahoe

BEST (

Fallen Leaf Lake, at 6,400 feet in elevation, is the second-largest lake in the Tahoe Basin, and some say it's the prettiest. Too bad most of its shore-front lands are privately owned. But luckily, this path allows you access to the part that is public. The short, mostly flat trail leads from the trailhead to the lake and then along its northern edge to the dam, which you can walk across. Much of the trail hugs the lake's shoreline, so you can look out across the blue water and feel that sense of peace that comes from the sight of deep, sapphire waters. You also get excellent views of Glen Alpine Canyon and Mount Tallac. In the fall, the shoreline of Fallen Leaf Lake is one of the best spots near Tahoe to admire the quaking aspens turning gold. Campers staying at Fallen Leaf Lake Campground can access this trail from their tents.

User Groups: Hikers, dogs, horses, and mountain bikes. No wheelchair facilities.

Permits: No permits are required. Parking and access are free.

Maps: For a map, ask the U.S. Forest Service for Lake Tahoe Basin Management Unit. A Lake Tahoe map is available for a fee from Tom Harrison Maps. For a topographic map, ask the USGS for Emerald Bay.

Directions: From South Lake Tahoe, take Highway 89 north and drive 2.9 miles to Fallen Leaf Lake Road. Turn left and drive 0.8 mile to the Fallen Leaf Lake dirt parking area on the right. It is not signed.

Contact: Lake Tahoe Basin Management Unit, 35 College Drive, South Lake Tahoe, CA 96150, 530/543-2600, www.fs.fed.us/r5—

click on Forest Offices; Visitors Center (open only in summer), 530/543-2674.

65 ANGORA LAKES TRAIL

1.0 mi / 0.5 hr   🏃1 ⛰8

at Angora Lake near South Lake Tahoe in Tahoe National Forest

BEST (

Upper Angora Lake is a sight to behold. The little lake is a pristine jewel back by a high granite wall. From the parking lot, hike uphill on the signed dirt road, and in 15 minutes, you'll be looking at Lower Angora Lake off to the left, which has a few cabins on its far side. Continue beyond its edge another 0.25 mile and, voilà, you reach the upper lake and Angora Lakes Resort, built in 1917. Although the resort cabins are always rented way in advance, day users can buy a lemonade and sit at a picnic table to watch the action, or take part in it, at the small, picturesque lake. Action? What action? Rowboats can be rented for a few bucks for a romantic cruise about the little lake. In mid-summer, toddlers wade around at the shallow beach area, and plenty of folks just plunk themselves down along the shoreline to stare at the bowl-shaped, glacial cirque lake. It has a high granite wall on its far side, where in early summer a waterfall of snowmelt flows down to the lake. The Angora Lakes are extremely popular with children's day camps and groups, and on some days, the little ones outnumber the old folks.

User Groups: Hikers, dogs, horses, and mountain bikes. No wheelchair facilities.

Permits: No permits are required. Parking is $5.

Maps: For a map, ask the U.S. Forest Service for Lake Tahoe Basin Management Unit. A Lake Tahoe map is available for a fee from Tom Harrison Maps. For a topographic map, ask the USGS for Echo Lake.

Directions: From South Lake Tahoe, take Highway 89 north and drive 2.9 miles to Fallen Leaf Lake Road. Turn left and drive two miles to a fork. Turn left and drive 0.5

mile to Forest Road 12N14. Bear right on Forest Service Road 12N14 and drive 2.3 miles (great views to the right) to the road's end and the trailhead.

Contact: Lake Tahoe Basin Management Unit, 35 College Drive, South Lake Tahoe, CA 96150, 530/543-2600, www.fs.fed.us/r5—click on Forest Offices; Visitors Center, (open only in summer), 530/543-2674.

66 ROCKBOUND PASS AND LAKE DORIS
12.0 mi / 6.0 hr-2.0 days 🏃3 ⛰9

in the Desolation Wilderness

To make the epic trip to 8,650-foot Rockbound Pass, follow the trail notes for the route to Gertrude and Tyler Lakes (see next listing) for the first 1.9 miles. Bear left to stay on Rockbound Pass Trail and hike through mixed conifers to get your first glimpse of Rockbound Pass at 2.5 miles, a distant notch in the mountains to the north. To reach it, you must descend a bit and cross the Jones Fork of Silver Creek, then parallel the stream on its course from Maud Lake. You're traveling in very rocky terrain now. The trail is even blasted out of granite in places. You'll reach the western shores of 7,700-foot Maud Lake at 4.5 miles. Many backpackers make camp here, while day hikers continue the ascent to the pass. It's not much farther; after a steady climb, you gain its wide summit at 5.9 miles. The views of Desolation Wilderness open wide, including views back at Maud Lake and ahead to Lake Doris, but the howling wind often prevents hikers from staying long. If that's the case, descend 0.5 mile to Lake Doris, just to the left of the trail, where you can make camp, or if you're day hiking, just hang out and rest. The total elevation gain on this trip is 1,700 feet, plus a short descent to Lake Doris.

User Groups: Hikers, dogs, and horses. No mountain bikes. No wheelchair facilities.

Permits: Permits are required year-round for both day and overnight use. Day hikers may obtain a free permit from a ranger station or may self-issue at most major trailheads. Backpackers camping in Desolation Wilderness are subject to trailhead quotas. There is a $5 reservation fee, plus $5 per person for one night, $10 per person for two or more nights up to 14 days (nonrefundable). Children ages 12 and under are free. Golden Passes do not apply to personal-use permits. For groups, the cost of a single permit will not exceed $100.

Directions: From Placerville, take Highway 50 east for 40 miles to Kyburz and continue five miles to the signed turnoff for Wrights Lake on the north side of the highway (about 15 miles west of South Lake Tahoe). Turn left (north) on Wrights Lake Road and drive eight miles to Wrights Lake Visitors Center. Continue straight for 0.5 mile to the Rockbound trailhead (on the way to Dark Lake).

Contact: Eldorado National Forest, Pacific Ranger District, 7887 Highway 50, Pollock Pines, CA 95726, 530/644-2349, www.fs.fed.us/r5—click on Forest Offices.

67 GERTRUDE AND TYLER LAKES
9.0 mi / 5.0 hr or 2.0 days 🏃4 ⛰9

in the Desolation Wilderness

There's a ton of stellar hiking to be accomplished in the Wrights Lake area. The trip to Gertrude and Tyler Lakes stands out. It provides great scenery, a good workout, and a chance to practice your cross-country skills on the way to Tyler Lake. A clearly defined trail leads to pretty Gertrude Lake. But Tyler Lake, higher and lovelier, is found only by those who forge their own way. That makes for a fun little adventure if you desire.

Begin on Rockbound Pass Trail, passing pastoral Beauty Lake 0.5 mile out and continuing on a remarkably easy path until you see a sign for Tyler Lake at 1.9 miles. There,

HIKING

bear right and prepare to work a lot harder for the rest of the hike. One memorable 0.5-mile stretch goes straight uphill and will cause you to question your sanity. Luckily the worst part doesn't last long, and the views of the spectacular peaks of the Crystal Range will distract you. At 3.5 miles you'll reach a hard-to-spot left spur trail (100 yards long) leading to the grave of William Tyler, a rancher who died here in a blizzard in the 1920s. A half mile beyond this cutoff is Gertrude Lake, at 8,000 feet. A nearly invisible right fork just past the grave cutoff is the start of an unmaintained trail to Tyler Lake, which lies 400 feet higher than Gertrude Lake. If you miss the use trail turnoff, watch for occasional rock cairns and keep an eye on your trail map. Tyler Lake lies 0.5 mile southeast of Gertrude Lake.

Of the two lakes, Tyler is more beautiful, set in a granite basin with a few sparse pines on its shores. Because it's slightly difficult to locate, you have an excellent chance at solitude at Tyler Lake, even on summer weekends.

User Groups: Hikers, dogs, and horses. No mountain bikes. No wheelchair facilities.

Permits: Permits are required year-round for both day and overnight use. Day hikers may obtain a free permit from a ranger station or may self-issue at most major trailheads. Backpackers camping in Desolation Wilderness are subject to trailhead quotas. There is a $5 reservation fee, plus $5 per person for one night, $10 per person for two or more nights up to 14 days (nonrefundable). Children ages 12 and under are free. Golden Passes do not apply to personal-use permits. For groups, the cost of a single permit will not exceed $100.

Maps: For a map, ask the U.S. Forest Service for Desolation Wilderness or Eldorado National Forest. A Lake Tahoe or Desolation Wilderness map is also available from Tom Harrison Maps. For topographic maps, ask the USGS for Pyramid Peak and Rockbound Valley.

Directions: From Placerville, take Highway 50 east for 40 miles to Kyburz and continue five miles to the signed turnoff for Wrights Lake (about 15 miles west of South Lake Tahoe). Turn left (north) on Wrights Lake Road and drive eight miles to Wrights Lake Visitors Center. Continue straight past the visitors center for 0.5 mile to the Rockbound trailhead (on the way to Dark Lake).

Contact: Eldorado National Forest, Pacific Ranger District, 7887 Highway 50, Pollock Pines, CA 95726, 530/644-2349, www.fs.fed .us/r5—click on Forest Offices; Lake Tahoe Basin Management Unit, 35 College Drive, South Lake Tahoe, CA 96150, 530/543-2600, www.fs.fed.us/r5—click on Forest Offices; Visitors Center (open only in summer), 530/543-2674.

68 TWIN AND ISLAND LAKES

6.4 mi / 4.0 hr or 2.0 days   🏃3   ⛺10

in the Desolation Wilderness

Of all the hiking possibilities in the Wrights Lake area, this trip is hands-down the most scenic. It is crowned by the most striking views in the entire Desolation Wilderness and miles of solid granite under your feet as you walk. The trail is extremely well marked, and its moderate grade is suitable for all types of hikers. The first 1.2 miles from the Twin Lakes trailhead have only a gentle climb to the intersection with the trail to Grouse, Hemlock, and Smith Lakes. Bear left for Twin Lakes and climb up over granite until 0.75 mile later you crest a ridge and start to descend. The vistas of jagged Crystal Range peaks to the northeast make an awesome backdrop. At 2.5 miles, you'll reach the dam at Lower Twin Lake. Cross it and continue hiking along the lake's northwest shore to tiny Boomerang Lake, at three miles. The lake is shaped like its name and is shallow enough to provide warm water for swimming. Another 0.25 mile on the trail brings you to the south end of Island Lake, where the vistas of the Crystal Range are the best of the trip, and where most hikers burn a heck of a lot of film. If you ever wanted to sell somebody on the beauty of the Northern Sierra, this trail would be the place to do it.

The only downer on the trip to Twin and Island Lakes is the sheer number of people who make this journey every day during the summer months. Of course, when you see the lakes, you'll know why they are so darn popular.

User Groups: Hikers, dogs, and horses. No mountain bikes. No wheelchair facilities.

Permits: Permits are required year-round for both day and overnight use. Day hikers may obtain a free permit from a ranger station or may self-issue at most major trailheads. Backpackers camping in Desolation Wilderness are subject to trailhead quotas. There is a $5 reservation fee, plus $5 per person for one night, $10 per person for two or more nights up to 14 days (nonrefundable). Children ages 12 and under are free. Golden Passes do not apply to personal-use permits. For groups, the cost of a single permit will not exceed $100.

Maps: For a map, ask the U.S. Forest Service for Eldorado National Forest or Desolation Wilderness. A Lake Tahoe or Desolation Wilderness map is also available for a fee from Tom Harrison Maps. For a topographic map, ask the USGS for Pyramid Peak.

Directions: From Placerville, take Highway 50 east for 40 miles to Kyburz and continue five miles to the signed turnoff for Wrights Lake (about 15 miles west of South Lake Tahoe). Turn left (north) on Wrights Lake Road and drive eight miles to Wrights Lake Visitors Center. Turn right and continue one mile beyond the campground to the end of the road and the Twin Lakes trailhead.

Contact: Eldorado National Forest, Pacific Ranger District, 7887 Highway 50, Pollock Pines, CA 95726, 530/644-2349, www.fs.fed .us/r5—click on Forest Offices; Lake Tahoe Basin Management Unit, 35 College Drive, South Lake Tahoe, CA 96150, 530/543-2600, www.fs.fed.us/r5—click on Forest Offices; Visitors Center (open only in summer), 530/543-2674.

69 GROUSE, HEMLOCK, AND SMITH LAKES

6.0 mi / 3.0 hr or 2.0 days 🏃4 ⛰10

in the Desolation Wilderness

The Crystal Basin area is a magical place on the western edge of the Desolation Wilderness. This is where the high peaks of the Crystal Range overlook the basin and its multitude of lakes. Several excellent day hikes and backpacking trips are possible in this area, most of which begin from popular Wrights Lake Campground. Of those, the trip to Grouse, Hemlock, and Smith Lakes is a favorite, despite the relentless climb required to reach all three lakes. From the parking area, Twin Lakes Trail winds past a meadow and then enters a pine and fir forest interspersed with stretches of hard granite. At a trail junction 1.2 miles out, head right for Grouse, Hemlock, and Smith Lakes. Small and pretty Grouse Lake is a one-mile, heart-pumping climb away, with many fine glances back at Wrights Lake and Icehouse Reservoir as you ascend. Many backpackers camp at Grouse Lake; look for wood posts that indicate designated campsites, and note that camping within 500 feet of Grouse Lake and its tributaries is prohibited. More hardy types and day hikers should head for Hemlock and Smith Lakes, farther uphill. The lakes get progressively prettier as you go, but the ascent gets steeper, too. Tiny Hemlock Lake is only 0.5 mile from Grouse Lake, and it boasts a spectacular rock slide on one shoreline and many scrawny hemlock trees on the other. Smith Lake lies another 0.5 mile beyond, way up high near tree line, at 8,700 feet, and it's a stunner.

User Groups: Hikers, dogs, and horses. No mountain bikes. No wheelchair facilities.

Permits: Permits are required year-round for both day and overnight use. Day hikers may obtain a free permit from a ranger station or may self-issue at most major trailheads. Backpackers camping in Desolation Wilderness are subject to trailhead quotas. There is a $5

HIKING

HIKING

reservation fee, plus $5 per person for one night, $10 per person for two or more nights up to 14 days (nonrefundable). Children ages 12 and under are free. Golden Passes do not apply to personal-use permits. For groups, the cost of a single permit will not exceed $100.
Maps: For a map, ask the U.S. Forest Service for Eldorado National Forest or Desolation Wilderness. A Lake Tahoe or Desolation Wilderness map is also available for a fee from Tom Harrison Maps. For a topographic map, ask the USGS for Pyramid Peak.

Directions: From Placerville, take Highway 50 east for 40 miles to Kyburz and continue five miles to the signed turnoff for Wrights Lake (about 15 miles west of South Lake Tahoe). Turn left (north) on Wrights Lake Road and drive eight miles to Wrights Lake Visitors Center. Turn right and continue one mile beyond the campground to the end of the road and the Twin Lakes trailhead.

Contact: Eldorado National Forest, Pacific Ranger District, 7887 Highway 50, Pollock Pines, CA 95726, 530/644-2349, www.fs.fed .us/r5—click on Forest Offices; Lake Tahoe Basin Management Unit, 35 College Drive, South Lake Tahoe, CA 96150, 530/543-2600, www.fs.fed.us/r5—click on Forest Offices; Visitors Center (open only in summer), 530/543-2674.

🔟 LYONS CREEK TRAIL
9.0 mi / 4.5 hr or 2.0 days 🏃3 ⛰9

In the Desolation Wilderness

This may be the "easiest" hike in the entire Wrights Lake area. That is because is requires "only" a 1,700-foot elevation gain to visit two beautiful lakes. Because this trailhead is a few miles distant from popular Wrights Lake Campground, it gets far fewer visitors than the trails that start right out of camp. The trip's total mileage is long, but the grade is mellow, except for the final 0.5 mile to Lyons Lake.

The trail keeps to the south side of Lyons Creek for four solid miles, passing through woods and meadows, then crosses the stream and reaches a junction 0.1 mile farther on. Lyons Lake is to the left and steeply uphill; Lake Sylvia is 0.5 mile to the right. Take your pick, or better yet, go see both. Lake Sylvia is shadowed by Pyramid Peak and has good campsites along its shoreline. Lyons Lake requires a nasty 450-foot climb in 0.5 mile, but its superior scenery makes it well worth the effort.

If you're fond of walking along coursing waterways, following the gurgle and babble of a creek as you hike, you'll love this hike. Wildflowers proliferate in early summer, and views of Pyramid Peak (just shy of 10,000 feet in elevation) inspire you as you gently ascend.

User Groups: Hikers, dogs, and horses. No mountain bikes. No wheelchair facilities.

Permits: Permits are required year-round for both day and overnight use. Day hikers may obtain a free permit from a ranger station or may self-issue at most major trailheads. Backpackers camping in Desolation Wilderness are subject to trailhead quotas. There is a $5 reservation fee, plus $5 per person for one night, $10 per person for two or more nights up to 14 days (nonrefundable). Children ages 12 and under are free. Golden Passes do not apply to personal-use permits. For groups, the cost of a single permit will not exceed $100.
Maps: For a map, ask the U.S. Forest Service for Eldorado National Forest or Desolation Wilderness. A Lake Tahoe or Desolation Wilderness map is also available for a fee from Tom Harrison Maps. For a topographic map, ask the USGS for Pyramid Peak.
Directions: From Placerville, take Highway 50 east for 40 miles to Kyburz and continue five miles to the signed turnoff for Wrights Lake (about 15 miles west of South Lake Tahoe). Turn left (north) on Wrights Lake Road and drive four miles to the signed spur for the Lyons Creek Trail. Turn right and drive a short distance to the trailhead.

Contact: Eldorado National Forest, Pacific Ranger District, 7887 Highway 50, Pollock Pines, CA 95726, 530/644-2349, www.fs.fed .us/r5—click on Forest Offices; Lake Tahoe Basin Management Unit, 35 College Drive, South Lake Tahoe, CA 96150, 530/543-2600, www.fs.fed.us/r5—click on Forest Offices; Visitors Center (open only in summer), 530/543-2674.

71 HORSETAIL FALLS VISTA
2.0 mi / 1.0 hr   🏃1 ⛰9

in Eldorado National Forest
near South Lake Tahoe

Horsetail Falls is the well-known waterfall that takes your breath away as you're driving west along U.S. 50. Approximately 15,000 people each summer glimpse the falls from their cars, then pull over at the giant parking lot by the trailhead and start hiking to get closer to it. Routed past a gorgeous stretch of Pyramid Creek called the Cascades, the trail stays outside of the wilderness boundary and provides a safe and easy alternative for casual visitors. Although the trail doesn't go all the way to the base of Horsetail Falls, it provides many excellent views of it, as well as of Pyramid Creek's glacier-carved canyon.

The trail has been a source of controversy because the waterfall is located within the Desolation Wilderness boundary on a rough but serviceable route, but the first mile of trail is outside the wilderness boundary and is easily accessible from the highway. That first easy mile has encouraged many inexperienced visitors to try to hike to the falls, resulting in numerous accidents and even deaths in the wilderness area, where the trail dissipates and follows stream banks that are rough and slippery. The Forest Service has carried out the wilderness mandate by not making mechanical alterations to the trail, such as building bridges or blasting an obvious path into the granite.

Instead, to decrease the frequent injuries, the 1.5-mile Pyramid Creek Loop Trail was built in 1999. Made specifically for day users who just want to see Horsetail Falls and spectacular, granite-lined Pyramid Creek, the Pyramid Creek Loop takes off from the main trail about 0.5 mile in. This was a sensible solution to a difficult problem. The trail is a winner.

User Groups: Hikers and dogs. No horses or mountain bikes. No wheelchair facilities.

Permits: No permits are required if you stay out of the wilderness boundary. Parking is $3 per vehicle.

Maps: For a map, ask the U.S. Forest Service for Eldorado National Forest. A Lake Tahoe map is available for a fee from Tom Harrison Maps. For a topographic map, ask the USGS for Echo Lake.

Directions: From Placerville, take Highway 50 east to Strawberry (about 20 miles from South Lake Tahoe) and continue about three miles to Twin Bridges and a large pullout on the north side of the highway (.5 mile west of the turnoff for Camp Sacramento). Park in the designated parking lot for the signed trailhead.

Contact: Eldorado National Forest, Pacific Ranger District, 7887 Highway 50, Pollock Pines, CA 95726, 530/644-2349, www.fs.fed .us/r5—click on Forest Offices.

72 RALSTON PEAK
8.0 mi / 5.0 hr   🏃4 ⛰10

in the Desolation Wilderness
near South Lake Tahoe

The route to Ralston Peak has a little of everything: dense forest, open manzanita-covered slopes, meadows, and granite ridges. It also has lots of one thing: elevation gain. From trailhead to summit, you ascend from 6,400 to 9,240 feet over the course of four miles.

Begin by walking northward up the paved road from the east side of the parking area for 200 yards. Look for the trail leading off on the left. Climb upward through nonstop trees and nonstop switchbacks for a mile; then enter a more open area as you pass the wilderness boundary sign at 1.5 miles. The views start to widen. Your lungs request a lunch break, but they don't get one until 2.5 miles up, when you finally gain the ridge. A half mile later, the break is over, and you climb again, this time to another ridge at 3.5 miles, covered in meadow grasses and wildflowers. Part ways with the main trail and look for a trail to your right leading to the top of Ralston Peak, 0.5 mile away. Scramble up over jumbled rock to gain the 9,235-foot summit, and take in the view of Lake Tahoe, Fallen Leaf Lake, Carson Pass, Echo Lakes, and below you (to the north), Ralston Lake. This is simply a spectacular lookout. To get it, you may also find that your butt gets kicked.

User Groups: Hikers and dogs. No horses or mountain bikes. No wheelchair facilities.

Permits: Permits are required year-round for both day and overnight use. Day hikers may obtain a free permit from a ranger station or may self-issue at most major trailheads. Backpackers camping in Desolation Wilderness are subject to trailhead quotas. There is a $5 reservation fee, plus $5 per person for one night, $10 per person for two or more nights up to 14 days (nonrefundable). Children ages 12 and under are free. Golden Passes do not apply to personal-use permits. For groups, the cost of a single permit will not exceed $100.

Maps: For a map, ask the U.S. Forest Service for Eldorado National Forest or Desolation Wilderness. A Lake Tahoe or Desolation Wilderness map is also available for a fee from Tom Harrison Maps. For a topographic map, ask the USGS for Echo Lake.

Directions: From Placerville, take Highway 50 east to Twin Bridges and continue 1.5 miles to Camp Sacramento and the turnoff. There is a parking area off the north side of U.S. 50 and a sign for Ralston Trail to Lake of the Woods.

From South Lake Tahoe, take Highway 89 south for five miles to Highway 50. Turn right (west) on U.S. 50 and drive about 14 miles to the turnoff for Camp Sacramento (if you reach Twin Bridges, you've gone 1.5 miles too far west).

Contact: Eldorado National Forest, Pacific Ranger District, 7887 Highway 50, Pollock Pines, CA 95726, 530/644-2349, www.fs.fed .us/r5—click on Forest Offices; Lake Tahoe Basin Management Unit, 35 College Drive, South Lake Tahoe, CA 96150, 530/543-2600, www.fs.fed.us/r5—click on Forest Offices; Visitors Center (open only in summer), 530/543-2674.

73 BOAT TAXI TO LAKE ALOHA
6.0-12.0 mi / 3.5-6.0 hr ㊟3 △10

in the Desolation Wilderness

This is a sensational trip. It starts with a boat taxi across the two Echo Lakes and before getting dropped off at the trailhead for the Pacific Crest Trail. Then it's an easy climb to great views with a series of spur trails to beautiful alpine lakes in Desolation Wilderness, crowned by Lake Aloha in Desolation Valley.

From the hiker's parking lot, walk 0.25 mile downhill to the resort and the boat launch area, at the edge of Echo Lake. The boat taxi leaves at frequent intervals (or whenever more than two people show up) from 8 A.M. to 6 P.M. daily all summer. The trip costs $9.50 each way and is well worth it to get you to the border of the Desolation Wilderness. The boat carries hikers two miles to the far end of Upper and Lower Echo Lakes, passing many lovely lakeside cottages.

From the boat taxi drop-off point, gain the main trail (Pacific Crest Trail) and head to your left. The 3.5-mile hike to the eastern edge of Lake Aloha starts with a steady climb up to a ridge. Be sure to stop and turn around to enjoy the stunning lake view. After topping the ridge, the hike is an easy saunter. You'll pass several signed junctions with numerous trails along the way, all of which lead to various lakes in very short distances. Your best bet is to stay on the main path for Lake Aloha, then take some of the cutoffs to neighboring lakes on your way back. When you reach Lake Aloha's shore, hike along its beautiful north side for a distance, admiring the rocky coves and islands of the giant, shallow lake. At one time, Lake Aloha was several small lakes. They were dammed with a unique rock wall to create this huge body of water. The effect is a bit surreal, although beautiful. The lake's elevation is 8,116 feet.

On the trip back, take one or more of the signed trail junctions and visit Lake of the Woods, Lake Lucille, Lake Margery, Tamarack Lake, or Ralston Lake—all less than one mile off Lake Aloha Trail. Tamarack Lake is the best for scenery; Lake of the Woods is the best for fishing.

On the return trip, some bypass the boat taxi and continue on the Pacific Crest Trail back to the parking area. That will add 2.5 miles to your trip. The trail rises well above the lake, eventually passing a series of vacation homes.

User Groups: Hikers and dogs (not advised because sharp rocks can bruise their foot pads). No horses or mountain bikes. No wheelchair facilities.

Permits: Boat taxi (not required) is $9.50 per hiker one-way, $3.50 for dogs. Permits are required year-round for both day and overnight use. Day hikers may obtain a free permit from a ranger station or may self-issue at most major trailheads. Backpackers camping in Desolation Wilderness are subject to trailhead quotas. There is a $5 reservation fee, plus $5 per person for one night, $10 per person for two or more nights up to 14 days (nonrefundable). Children ages 12 and under are free. Golden Passes do not apply to personal-use permits. For groups, the cost of a single permit will not exceed $100.

Maps: For a map, ask the U.S. Forest Service for Desolation Wilderness. A Lake Tahoe or Desolation Wilderness map is also available for a fee from Tom Harrison Maps. For a topographic map, ask the USGS for Echo Lake.

Directions: From Placerville, take Highway 50 east toward Tahoe and Echo summit to Sierra at Tahoe Ski Resort and then continue 1.8 miles to Johnson Pass Road and a signed turnoff (brown sign) for Berkeley Camp/Echo Lake (one mile west of Echo Summit). Turn left and drive 0.5 mile to Echo Lakes Road. Turn left and drive one mile to a series of parking lots located 0.25 mile before the road ends at Echo Lakes Resort. Hikers not staying at the resort must park in one of the upper lots or alongside the road, not in the main lower lot by the resort, and walk down to the marina, boat taxi, or trailhead.

From South Lake Tahoe: Take Highway 89 south for five miles to U.S. 50. Turn right (west) on U.S. 50 and drive 5.5 miles to the signed turnoff for Echo Lakes on the right (one mile west of Echo Summit.) Turn right and drive 0.5 mile to Echo Lakes Road. Turn left and drive one mile to a series of parking lots located 0.25 mile before the road ends at Echo Lakes Resort.

Contact: Echo Lakes Chalet, 530/659-7207, www.echochalet.com; Eldorado National Forest, Pacific Ranger District, 7887 Highway 50, Pollock Pines, CA 95726, 530/644-2349, www.fs.fed.us/r5—click on Forest Offices; Lake Tahoe Basin Management Unit, 35 College Drive, South Lake Tahoe, CA 96150, 530/543-2600, www.fs.fed.us/r5—click on Forest Offices; Visitors Center (open only in summer), 530/543-2674.

🔲 ECHO LAKES RESORT TO BARKER PASS (PCT)

32.3 mi one-way / 3.0 days   👫4   ⛰9

from Echo Lake near U.S. 50 south of Lake Tahoe to Forest Road 3 near Barker Pass northwest of Emerald Bay

The Desolation Wilderness (and the neighboring Granite Chief Wilderness) are filled with sculpted granite domes and hundreds of gemlike lakes. All is pristine, yet access is also quite easy, making this the most heavily used section of the PCT all summer long. The trip starts at Echo Lake (elevation 7,400 feet), climbs through pines past Upper Echo Lake, and then continues up and north toward Triangle Lake, one of dozens of lakes you pass on your northward route. They come and go—Lake Margery, Lake Aloha, and then Heather, Susie, and Gilmore Lakes, and finally Dicks Lake (at 9,380 feet). There are so many, in fact, that you can plan on a perfect campsite near a lake every night, providing you don't mind the company of other hikers drawn by classic beauty. The views are dramatic as well, across miles and miles of the glacial-carved granite, all of it marvelous high Sierra landscape. As you continue, you'll discover Upper and Middle Velma Lakes, both very pretty and with good fishing. The trail skirts the ridgeline, keeping the higher knobs to the east as it gradually descends toward Richardson Lake, just beyond the Desolation Wilderness boundary—ready now to enter the Granite Chief Wilderness.

To continue north on the PCT, see the *Barker Pass to Donner Pass (PCT)* hike in this chapter. If you are walking this trail in reverse, see the *Carson Pass to Echo Lakes Resort (PCT)* hike in this chapter.

User Groups: Hikers, dogs, and horses. No mountain bikes. No wheelchair facilities.

Permits: A backcountry permit is required for traveling through various wilderness and special-use areas the trail traverses. In addition, a campfire permit is required for the use of portable camp stoves or the building of campfires where allowed. To make it simple, you can contact the national forest, Bureau of Land Management (BLM), or national park office at your point of entry for a combined permit that is good for traveling through multiple-permit areas during your dates of travel.

Maps: For topographic maps, ask the USGS for Echo Lake, Emerald Bay, and Rockbound Valley.

Directions: From Placerville, take Highway 50 east toward Tahoe and Echo summit to

Sierra at Tahoe Ski Resort and then continue 1.8 miles to Johnson Pass Road and a signed turnoff (brown sign) for Berkeley Camp/Echo Lakes (one mile west of Echo Summit). Turn left and drive 0.5 mile to Echo Lakes Road. Turn left and drive one mile to a series of parking lots located 0.25 mile before the road ends at Echo Lakes Resort. Hikers not staying at the resort must park in one of the upper lots or alongside the road, not in the main lower lot by the resort, and walk down to the marina, boat taxi, or trailhead.

From South Lake Tahoe: Take Highway 89 south for five miles to U.S. 50. Turn right (west) on U.S. 50 and drive 5.5 miles to the signed turnoff for Echo Lakes on the right (one mile west of Echo Summit.) Turn right and drive 0.5 mile to Echo Lakes Road. Turn left and drive one mile to a series of parking lots located 0.25 mile before the road ends at Echo Lakes Resort.

To reach the Barker Pass trailhead, from Tahoe Pines on Highway 89, head north for 0.5 mile to the Kaspian Picnic Grounds and then bear left (west) for seven miles on Forest Service Road 15N03.

Contact: Echo Lakes Chalet, 530/659-7207, www.echochalet.com; Lake Tahoe Basin Management Unit, 35 College Drive, South Lake Tahoe, CA 96150, 530/543-2600, www.fs.fed .us/r5—click on Forest Offices; Visitors Center (open only in summer), 530/543-2674.

75 DARDANELLES LAKE AND ROUND LAKE
7.6 mi / 4.5 hr   🚶3 ⛰9

near Carson Pass

Dardanelles Lake (elevation 7,740 feet) is striking and gorgeous, set in a pocket with a granite backdrop. The route to Dardanelles Lake and Round Lake, along the Tahoe Rim Trail, starts out steep but gets easier as it goes. It enters "Meiss Country," that large and wonderful roadless area south of Lake Tahoe, where the forces that shaped the land were ice (glaciers) and fire (volcanic action). Both have made their presence clearly visible.

From the parking lot, the trail heads south, crosses Highway 89 in about 100 yards, then makes an initial climb through fir and pine forest to Big Meadow. The meadow makes lovely, level walking for 0.25 mile; then it's back into the trees. Follow the trail signs for Round Lake until you complete a steep, short descent at two miles out. At the bottom of the hill, turn sharply right on Meiss Meadow Trail toward Christmas Valley. Walk less than 0.25 mile, then turn left and cross a creek for the final 1.2 miles to Dardanelles Lake. It's good for swimming, fishing, and picnicking. If you time your trip for autumn, you'll be treated to a marvelous color display from the aspens and alders that grow along this trail's many streams.

On your return, retrace your steps to the junction at the bottom of the hill, then hike 0.75 mile in the opposite direction to visit Round Lake. Although not quite as scenic as Dardanelles Lake, Round Lake provides a stark, fascinating contrast to its neighbor: It is surrounded by volcanic rock formations, not granite cliffs.

Note that this trail is open to mountain bikers. On weekdays you might not see a single bike, but on weekends you'll see plenty.

User Groups: Hikers, dogs, horses, and mountain bikes. No wheelchair facilities.

Permits: No permits are required. Parking and access are free.

Maps: For a map, ask the U.S. Forest Service for Lake Tahoe Basin Management Unit. A Lake Tahoe map is available for a fee from Tom Harrison Maps. For a topographic map, ask the USGS for Echo Lake.

Directions: From South Lake Tahoe, take Highway 89 south for five miles to Meyers and the junction with Highway 89, and then continue south on Highway 89 for five more miles to the Big Meadow trailhead parking area on the northwest side of the road. Turn left off the highway, then bear left and park near the restrooms. The trail begins from the south side of the parking lot loop and crosses Highway 89 in about 100 yards.

Contact: Lake Tahoe Basin Management Unit, 35 College Drive, South Lake Tahoe, CA 96150, 530/543-2600, www.fs.fed.us/r5—click on Forest Offices; Visitors Center (open only in summer), 530/543-2674.

76 LAKE MARGARET
4.6 mi / 3.0 hr

near Carson Pass and Kirkwood Lake

BEST

Can you imagine a hike to an alpine lake with only a 500-foot elevation gain? It might seem too good to be true, but here you are. If you need an easy-trail fix, Lake Margaret should do the trick.

The trail undulates gently, never gaining or losing more than a couple hundred feet. The first stretch is actually downhill. Then the path climbs gently over a small ridge and then descends again over duck-marked granite slabs. You'll cross branches of Caples Creek twice in the first mile. At 1.5 miles, the trail passes by a couple of tiny ponds. At two miles out, after crossing another creek, you'll find yourself in a lovely grove of aspens and knee-high wildflowers. At 2.3 miles, after about an hour of walking and only a minor expenditure of energy, you'll reach the granite shoreline of Lake Margaret. Swimming is excellent. A few tiny islands and many shoreline boulders make fine sunbathing spots. Figure on staying awhile. The lake's elevation is 7,500 feet.

Note that although most of the trails in the Carson Pass area are famous for wildflowers, the proximity of several small streams makes the bloom especially showy on this path. The peak wildflower season is from mid-June to mid-August.

User Groups: Hikers, leashed dogs, horses, and mountain bikes. No wheelchair facilities.

Permits: No permits are required. Parking and access are free.

HIKING

Maps: For a map, ask the U.S. Forest Service for Eldorado National Forest or Mokelumne Wilderness. For a topographic map, ask the USGS for Caples Lake.

Directions: From South Lake Tahoe, take Highway 89 south for five miles to Meyers and the junction with Highway 89, and then continue south on Highway 89 for 11 miles to Highway 88. Turn west on Highway 88 and drive 14.5 miles to the Lake Margaret sign, on the north side of the road (5.5 miles west of Carson Pass Summit, and 5.5 miles east of Silver Lake.) Turn north and park at the trailhead parking area.

Contact: Eldorado National Forest, Amador Ranger District, 26820 Silver Drive, Pioneer, CA 95666, 209/295-4251, www.fs.fed.us/r5—click on Forest Offices.

77 EMIGRANT LAKE
8.0 mi / 4.0 hr or 2.0 days 🏃2 ⛰9

in the Mokelumne Wilderness
near Caples Lake

The trailhead at Caples Lake is often jam-packed with backpackers, so do yourself a favor: visit here midweek or in the off-season, or make your trip a day hike instead of an overnight. Why is this trail so popular? It's wonderfully scenic and surprisingly easy.

The trail leads from the spillway at Caples Lake up and along the lake's south side, following an old emigrant route. The first two miles are right along the lake's edge, climbing gently above the shoreline, always in the shade of big conifers. If you enjoy hiking near water, you'll love this pathway. More climbing alongside Emigrant Creek leads hikers to a stream crossing at 3.5 miles, followed by another crossing. A few switchbacks carry you up to Emigrant Lake, a beautiful cirque lake set at 8,600 feet, with many fine sunbathing rocks. Covered Wagon Peak and Thimble Peak, at 9,500 feet, rise above the scene. The trail's total elevation gain is less than 1,000

feet, making this a surprisingly easy day hike, even with its eight-mile distance. But know before you go: Most of the trail's ascent is packed into the last 1.8 miles, which will leave you breathing hard. Note that no campfires are permitted above 8,000 feet.

User Groups: Hikers, leashed dogs, and horses. No mountain bikes. No wheelchair facilities.

Permits: No day-hiking permits are required. A free wilderness permit is required for overnight stays; it is available from the Amador Ranger Station, the Carson Pass Information Station, or the Eldorado Information Center. Maximum group size for day use is 12. Maximum group size for overnight use is eight. No self-registration is available at the trailhead.

Maps: For a map, ask the U.S. Forest Service for Eldorado National Forest or Desolation Wilderness. For a topographic map, ask the USGS for Caples Lake.

Directions: From South Lake Tahoe, take Highway 89 south for five miles to Meyers and the junction with Highway 89, and then continue south on Highway 89 for 11 miles to Highway 88. Turn west on Highway 88 and drive 14 miles (five miles west of Carson Pass) to the west side of Caples Lake and the trailhead parking area.

Contact: Eldorado National Forest, Amador Ranger District, 26820 Silver Drive, Pioneer, CA 95666, 209/295-4251, www.fs.fed.us/r5—click on Forest Offices.

78 MINKALO TRAIL
7.0 mi / 3.5 hr 🏃2 ⛰8

near Silver Lake

Since Silver Lake has a fair number of rental cabins and private homes on its shore, it appears less wild than nearby Caples Lake. Still, the big blue lake, at 7,300 feet in elevation, is beautiful, and if you want to hike near it, the Minkalo Trail is your best bet. The trail leads to Granite Lake in one mile and to Plasse's

Resort, on the south side of the lake, in three miles. Why not hike to both, then buy a pizza or a Power Bar at Plasse's Resort Trading Post to fuel up for the hike back to the Minkalo trailhead?

The trail starts out rocky and stays that way for the first 0.25 mile. Cross a bridge over Squaw Creek to a right fork that leads to Plasse's Resort. Take the left fork first, heading to Granite Lake, which you'll reach in about 20 minutes after a moderate climb. It's a pretty lake and good for swimming. After you've visited, return to the trail junction and hike southward, soon coming close to the edge of Silver Lake and staying in its proximity. You'll have many pretty lake views from here on out, including long looks at Treasure Island, Silver Lake's large island. It takes about an hour to reach the campground at Plasse's, an excellent place for horse lovers (and pizza lovers).

User Groups: Hikers, leashed dogs, horses, and mountain bikes. No wheelchair facilities.

Permits: No permits are required. Parking and access are free.

Maps: For a map, ask the U.S. Forest Service for Eldorado National Forest, or Desolation Wilderness. For a topographic map, ask the USGS for Caples Lake.

Directions: From South Lake Tahoe, take Highway 89 south for five miles to Meyers and the junction with Highway 89, and then continue south on Highway 89 for 11 miles to Highway 88. Turn right (west) on Highway 88 and drive 15.5 miles (10.8 miles west of Carson Pass) to the turnoff for Kit Carson Lodge on the north side of the road. Turn north and drive past Kit Carson Lodge, go left at the first fork, and go right at the second fork, to the parking for Minkalo Trail. (It's a total of 1.4 miles from Highway 88.) Walk back down the road for about 40 yards to find the trailhead.

Contact: Eldorado National Forest, Amador Ranger District, 26820 Silver Drive, Pioneer, CA 95666, 209/295-4251, www.fs.fed.us/ r5—click on Forest Offices.

79 OSBORNE HILL
2.6 mi / 1.5 hr

on Highway 4 near Lake Alpine

We like the way Lake Alpine looks from close up on Lakeshore Trail, but then again, we like the way Lake Alpine looks from far up on Osborne Hill, also known as Osborne Point. A short, healthy climb brings you to the point, from which you can look down at the lake and beyond into the Carson-Iceberg Wilderness. The trail ends there but connects to Emigrant West Trail if you wish to hike farther. If you're itching for winter to be over so you can go hiking, you'll be happy to know that Highway 4 is always open as far east as Silvertip Campground, but not always farther. Thus if the snow is dwindling, you'll have access to this trailhead often long before you can access the others near Lake Alpine.

User Groups: Hikers, dogs, horses, and mountain bikes. No wheelchair facilities.

Permits: No permits are required. Parking and access are free.

Maps: For a map, ask the U.S. Forest Service for Stanislaus National Forest. For a topographic map, ask the USGS for Tamarack.

Directions: From Angels Camp, take Highway 4 east for 40 miles to Bear Valley. Set your odometer at Bear Valley and drive east on Highway 4 for three miles to the Osborne Ridge trailhead (just east of Silvertip Campground). Take the trail that leads from the south side of the road.

Contact: Stanislaus National Forest, Calaveras Ranger District, P.O. Box 500, Hathaway Pines, CA 95233, 209/795-1381, www.fs.fed .us/r5—click on Forest Offices.

HIKING

80 LAKESHORE TRAIL AND INSPIRATION POINT

4.0 mi / 2.0 hr

on Highway 4 near Lake Alpine

It's hard to say which trail is better, Lakeshore Trail or Inspiration Point Trail. To solve the dilemma, hike both of them together. The trip starts with a short walk down a dirt road; then turn right onto a single track. After 10 minutes of hiking through a thick lodgepole pine forest peppered with tiny pinecones, you're at the edge of Lake Alpine, elevation 7,350 feet. Follow the trail to your left, and in another 10 minutes, you reach a left fork for Inspiration Point (Lakeshore Trail continues straight). You'll want to head out and back on both trails; it makes no difference which one you take first.

The Lakeshore Trail is flat and stays within 100 feet of the water's edge, offering many pretty lake vistas. Eventually the trail meets up with Slick Rock, a four-wheel-drive road, but there's no need to go that far. Just walk a mile or so to the dam, and then turn around and head back. The Inspiration Point Trail, on the other hand, is more of a workout: a steep one-mile climb to the summit at Inspiration Point, from which you can see for miles. Pick a clear day, and you'll be pointing out Lake Alpine, Elephant Rock, the Dardanelles, and Spicer Meadow Reservoir.

User Groups: Hikers, dogs, and horses. No mountain bikes. No wheelchair facilities.

Permits: No permits are required. Parking and access are free.

Maps: For a national forest map, ask for Stanislaus National Forest. For a topographic map, ask the USGS for Spicer Meadow Reservoir.

Directions: From Angels Camp, take Highway 4 east for 40 miles to Bear Valley. Set your odometer at Bear Valley and drive east on Highway 4 for 4.3 miles to the Lake Alpine East Shore trailhead turnoff, on the right. Turn right, drive 0.25 mile, and turn right again and drive 0.1 mile past Pine Marten Campground to the signed parking area and the trailhead.

Contact: Stanislaus National Forest, Calaveras Ranger District, P.O. Box 500, Hathaway Pines, CA 95233, 209/795-1381, www.fs.fed .us/r5—click on Forest Offices.

81 DUCK LAKE

3.0 mi / 1.5 hr

in the Carson-Iceberg Wilderness off Highway 4 near Lake Alpine

The trailhead at Silver Valley Campground is the start of the route to Duck Lake, and it's also one of the busiest trailheads into the Carson-Iceberg Wilderness. The trip to Duck Lake is a perfect easy hike for families or people just in the mood for a stroll, and the more ambitious can continue past the lake on an eight-mile round-trip to Rock Lake. It's only one mile to reach Duck Lake, but once you're there, you'll want to walk the loop trail around its perimeter, adding another mile to your trip. The area is the site of a historic cow camp, where animals have grazed since the late 19th century. You can examine the remains of a couple of early-20th-century cowboy cabins.

User Groups: Hikers, dogs, and horses. No mountain bikes. No wheelchair facilities.

Permits: No day-use permits are required. Parking and access are free.

Maps: For a map, ask the U.S. Forest Service for Stanislaus National Forest or Carson-Iceberg Wilderness. For a topographic map, ask the USGS for Spicer Meadow Reservoir.

Directions: From Angels Camp, take Highway 4 east for 40 miles to Bear Valley. Set your odometer at Bear Valley and drive east on Highway 4 for 4.3 miles to the Lake Alpine East Shore trailhead turnoff on the right. Turn right and continue straight to Silver Valley Campground and the Silver Valley trailhead.

Contact: Stanislaus National Forest, Calaveras Ranger District, P.O. Box 500, Hathaway Pines, CA 95233, 209/795-1381, www.fs.fed .us/r5—click on Forest Offices.

82 WOODCHUCK BASIN TO WHEELER LAKE

6.4 mi / 3.5 hr   🏃3   ⛰8

in the Mokelumne Wilderness off Highway 4 near Lake Alpine

This trail is located only a mile from the campgrounds at Lake Alpine. So you might think that the Woodchuck Basin trailhead (elevation 7,800 feet) should have a parking lot full of cars. But it rarely does. The trail leads into the Mokelumne Wilderness, and after climbing uphill on it for 1.7 forested miles, you reach a junction where you can go left for Underwood Valley or right for tiny Wheeler Lake. Bear right, pass a Mokelumne Wilderness sign, and in moments, you are heading for a 1.5-mile steep descent to Wheeler Lake. Think it over before you go, because you'll need to regain those 1,000 feet on the way home. But if you're willing to take the plunge, you're treated to a picturesque, tree- and granite-lined lake, where you can pass the afternoon with little fear that you'll be bugged by a busload of other hikers. Dog owners should note that Tuolumne County has a leash law that is strictly enforced.

User Groups: Hikers, leashed dogs, and horses. No mountain bikes. No wheelchair facilities.

Permits: No permits are required. Parking and access are free.

Maps: For a map, ask the U.S. Forest Service for Stanislaus National Forest or Mokelumne Wilderness. For a topographic map, ask the USGS for Spicer Meadow Reservoir.

Directions: From Angels Camp, take Highway 4 east for 40 miles to Bear Valley. Set your odometer at Bear Valley and drive east on Highway 4 for 5.5 miles to the Woodchuck Basin trailhead on the left. Turn left and drive 0.25 mile to the parking area.

Contact: Stanislaus National Forest, Calaveras Ranger District, P.O. Box 500, Hathaway Pines, CA 95233, 209/795-1381, www.fs.fed.us/r5—click on Forest Offices.

83 NORTH GROVE LOOP

1.0 mi / 0.5 hr   🏃1   ⛰7

northeast of Arnold on Highway 4

Even though there are 150 giant sequoias at Calaveras Big Trees State Park, the highlight is actually the one known as The Big Stump. Well, the state park gets a lot of visitors, and this is the most popular walk here, so you can expect other people—lots of 'em—on weekends. The easy trail is routed among the giant sequoias, and the sweet fragrance of the massive trees fills the air. You will never forget that scent. These trees, of course, are known not for their height but for their tremendous diameter: It can take a few dozen people, linking hands, to encircle one. This trip is actually best in winter after fresh snowfall, when your footsteps are the only signs of life, and it feels like you are in a time machine.

Now about that stump: Back in the day, a gent wanted to prove how big the trees were to folks on the East Coast, so naturally, he cut the biggest one down, collected the bark and wasted the wood, then took it by railroad to the World's Fair and re-assembled it to prove how big it was. Except everybody thought it was a hoax, and then shortly thereafter, the bark collection was burned in a fire. Surprised the guy didn't shoot a Bigfoot while he was at it? The giant stump has been used for just about everything, including a dance floor. According to projections, if it had been allowed to grow, it would be bigger than the General Sherman Tree in Sequoia National Park, the largest living thing by volume on the planet.

User Groups: Hikers and wheelchairs. No dogs, horses, or mountain bikes.

Permits: No permits are required. A state park entrance fee of $6 is charged each vehicle.

Maps: A brochure and trail map is available for a fee at Calaveras Big Trees State Park at the address below. For a topographic map, ask the USGS for Dorrington.

Directions: From Angels Camp, take Highway

4 east for 23 miles to Arnold, and then continue for four miles to the park entrance. The trailhead is adjacent to the park entrance.

Contact: Calaveras Big Trees State Park, P.O. Box 120, Arnold, CA 95223, 209/795-2334; Columbia State Park, 209/532-0150, www .parks.ca.gov—click on Find A Park.

84 SOUTH GROVE LOOP
5.0 mi / 3.0 hr 🥾2 ⛺8

northeast of Arnold on Highway 4

The two largest sequoias in Calaveras Big Trees State Park are found on a spur trail of this hike, and that makes it a must-do for visitors. But so many tourists are content to just walk the little trail at the North Grove, look at the giant stump, and then hit the road. Why rush? As long as you're at the park, take the South Grove Loop. The loop itself is 3.5 miles long, but the highlight is a spur trail that branches off 0.75 mile to the Agassiz Tree and the Palace Hotel Tree, two monster-sized specimens. For a great photograph, have someone take a picture of you standing at the base of one of these trees; you will look like a Lilliputian from *Gulliver's Travels*.

User Groups: Hikers only. No dogs, horses, or mountain bikes. No wheelchair facilities.

Permits: No permits are required. A state park entrance fee of $6 is charged each vehicle.

Maps: A brochure and trail map is available for a fee at Calaveras Big Trees State Park at the address below. For a topographic map, ask the USGS for Boards Crossing.

Directions: From Angels Camp, take Highway 4 east for 23 miles to Arnold, and then continue for four miles to the park entrance. Turn right into the park entrance, then drive down the parkway for nine miles to the trailhead, on the right. Note: The road is closed in winter.

Contact: Calaveras Big Trees State Park, P.O. Box 120, Arnold, CA 95223, 209/795-2334; Columbia State Park, 209/532-0150, www .parks.ca.gov—click on Find A Park.

85 CARSON PASS TO ECHO LAKES RESORT (PCT)
15.8 mi one-way / 1.0-2.0 days 🥾4 ⛺10

from Carson Pass at Highway 88 north to Echo Lake near U.S. 50, just south of Lake Tahoe

BEST ◖

When you've hiked on the Pacific Crest Trail for weeks, the first glimpse of Lake Tahoe in the distance can seem like a privileged view into heaven. That view is just a few miles from Ebbetts Pass. You start by hiking over a short mountain rim (nice view to the west of Caples Lake) and then you drop into the headwaters of the Truckee River. As you look northward after making the rim, Lake Tahoe suddenly comes into view. It's like having a divine vision. And finally there is water available from several small creeks as you walk into the Truckee headwaters. At the same time, you will be greeted by a high meadow surrounded by a light forest. All seems right with the world again. With Echo Lakes Resort within one day's hiking time, you will be amazed at how inspired you can get on this section of trail. It's very pretty, weaving through lush canyons and along creeks, eventually reaching beautiful and tiny Showers Lake. Here the trail seems to drop off to never-never land, descending very quickly and steeply in the march toward Tahoe. Contentment reigns. When you reach Little Norway, however, reality sets in. Cars are everywhere. The trail suddenly grinds down amid cabins and vacation property. There's one last hill to climb, and then the PCT drops quickly to the parking lot for Echo Lakes.

Almost nobody hiking the PCT immediately heads north into the Desolation Wilderness from here. Virtually everyone stops for at least a day to get cleaned up, resupplied, and fed by something other than a Power Bar. But after a day, the trail calls again. If you hear it, well, you just have to answer it.

To continue north on the PCT, see the *Echo Lakes Resort to Barker Pass (PCT)* hike in this chapter. If you are walking this trail in reverse, see the *Blue Lakes Road to Carson Pass (PCT)* hike in this chapter.

User Groups: Hikers, dogs, and horses. No mountain bikes. No wheelchair facilities.

Permits: A backcountry permit is required for traveling through various wilderness and special-use areas that the trail traverses. In addition, a campfire permit is required for the use of portable camp stoves or the building of campfires where permitted. To make it simple, you can contact the national forest, Bureau of Land Management (BLM), or national park office at your point of entry for a combined permit that is good for traveling through multiple-permit areas during your dates of travel.

Maps: For national forest maps, ask for Lake Tahoe Basin Management Unit, Tahoe National Forest, Eldorado National Forest, and Stanislaus National Forest. For topographic maps, ask the USGS for Carson Pass, Caples Lake, and Echo Lake.

Directions: To reach the Carson Pass trailhead: From South Lake Tahoe, take Highway 89 south for five miles to Meyers and the junction with Highway 89, and then continue south on Highway 89 for 11 miles to Highway 88. Turn right (west) on Highway 88 and drive 10 miles to Carson Pass.

For the Echo Lakes Resort trailhead: From South Lake Tahoe, take Highway 89 south for five miles to U.S. 50. Turn right (west) on U.S. 50 and drive 5.5 miles to the signed turnoff for Echo Lakes on the right (one mile west of Echo Summit.) Turn right and drive 0.5 mile to Echo Lakes Road. Turn left and drive one mile to a series of parking lots located 0.25 mile before the road ends at Echo Lakes Resort. Hikers not staying at the resort must park in one of the upper lots or alongside the road, not in the main lower lot by the resort, and walk down to the marina, boat taxi, or trailhead.

Contact: Eldorado National Forest, Amador Ranger District, 26820 Silver Drive, Pioneer, CA 95666, 209/295-4251, www.fs.fed .us/r5—click on Forest Offices; Lake Tahoe Basin Management Unit, 35 College Drive, South Lake Tahoe, CA 96150, 530/543-2600, www.fs.fed.us/r5—click on Forest Offices; Visitors Center (open only in summer), 530/543-2674.

86 SHOWERS LAKE
10.0 mi / 6.0 hr

near Caples Lake

Here's a day hike on the Pacific Crest Trail into the land of Meiss Country, that is, the headwaters for the Upper Truckee River and the home of the endangered Lahontan cutthroat trout.

For the trip to Showers Lake, head uphill from the trailhead on the PCT, climbing through Meiss Pass and then dropping into a huge valley basin. Views along the way include Mount Round Top, Elephant Back, and Red Lake Peak, expanding to include far-off Lake Tahoe, to the north. It's 2.9 miles to a fork with the Tahoe Rim Trail (TRT), just beyond a crossing of Upper Truckee River, which is little more than a stream here. While stopping to pump a canteen's worth of water here, we've had hummingbirds come up and eye us from a foot away.

The right fork leads 2.2 miles to Round Lake, Meiss Country's largest lake and a popular destination, but stay left on the PCT and TRT, and cross the river again on your way to Showers Lake, 2.1 miles farther. The last half mile of trail is a 350-foot descent to Showers Lake, with 9,590-foot Little Round Top poking up above it to the west. The trail leads along the east side of the lake, where campsites can be found. The lake is set at 8,790 feet and is the highest lake in the Upper Truckee River Basin. It's very pretty.

This trip is popular with the horsy set. A separate trail leads to Showers Lake from Schneider Camp, a large horse camp, so weekends bring a fair amount of horse traffic. Also note that the trip begins in Eldorado National Forest, but two-thirds of the trail is within jurisdiction of the Lake Tahoe Basin Management Unit.

Although Meiss Country is not designated wilderness, it might as well be, because there are no roads cutting into it, and all is peaceful and serene. The Pacific Crest Trail and a completed stretch of Tahoe Rim Trail are the main routes through Meiss Country. Note that no bikes are permitted on the PCT, but we've seen plenty of tire tread here.

User Groups: Hikers, leashed dogs, and horses. No mountain bikes. No wheelchair facilities.

Permits: No permits are required. A $3 parking fee is charged per vehicle.

Maps: For a map, ask the U.S. Forest Service for Eldorado National Forest or Mokelumne Wilderness. For topographic maps, ask the USGS for Caples Lake and Carson Pass.

Directions: From South Lake Tahoe, take Highway 89 south for five miles to Meyers and the junction with Highway 89, and then continue south on Highway 89 for 11 miles to Highway 88. Turn west on Highway 88 and drive 10 miles to Carson Pass Summit. The parking area and Meiss trailhead are on the right (north), across the highway from (and slightly west of) the Carson Pass Information Station.

Contact: Eldorado National Forest, Amador Ranger District, 26820 Silver Drive, Pioneer, CA 95666, 209/295-4251 www.fs.fed.us/r5—click on Forest Offices.

87 WINNEMUCCA LAKE FROM WOODS LAKE

3.0 mi / 1.5 hr 🚶2 ⛰️10

in the Mokelumne Wilderness
near Carson Pass

BEST (

Woods Lake is a little magical spot where you can drive right up, walk a few feet to the water's edge, and plunk in your fishing line. It's also the trailhead for numerous great hikes into the Mokelumne Wilderness, including this easy trip to deep blue Winnemucca Lake, set at the base of fantastic-looking Mount Round Top (elevation 10,381 feet).

After setting off down the trail, in a mile you will pass by the remains of an arrastra, a device used for crushing gold or silver ore, evidence

of this area's mining past. Continue walking through big conifers until you come out to a glacial moraine, where your view of Mount Round Top, a huge old volcanic vent, opens wide. Snow-capped most of summer in most years, imposing Round Top is a stunning sight. So are the early summer wildflowers that bloom in profusion on the open slopes surrounding the path. In 1.5 miles of gentle to moderate climbing, you reach the edge of Winnemucca Lake, right at the foot of Mount Round Top, a gorgeous circle of blue. Although there are several options for hiking farther from here (see next listing), for many people, this destination is perfect enough.

The peak season for wildflowers is mid-June to mid-August, at its very best in mid-to-late July. If you hiked this trail in years past, you may remember that it once started by crossing a footbridge. That is no longer true.

The land here has been formed by volcanic action, so as you walk, you constantly have to remind yourself that you aren't at Mount Lassen or Mount Shasta, you're just south of Tahoe in Carson Pass. The beauty attracts a ton of people, often 200 to 300 on summer weekends.

User Groups: Hikers, leashed dogs, and horses. No mountain bikes. No wheelchair facilities.

Permits: A free wilderness permit is required for overnight stays; it is available from the Amador Ranger Station, the Carson Pass Information Station, or the Eldorado Information Center. A parking fee of $3 is charged, good for overnight use.

Maps: For a map, ask the U.S. Forest Service for Mokelumne Wilderness or Eldorado National Forest. For topographic maps, ask the USGS for Caples Lake and Carson Pass.

Directions: From South Lake Tahoe, take Highway 89 south for five miles to Meyers and the junction with Highway 89, and then continue south on 89 for 11 miles to Highway 88. Turn right (west) on Highway 88 and drive 12 miles to the Woods Lake Campground turnoff, on the south side of the road (1.5 miles west of Carson Pass Summit). Turn left and drive one mile to the trailhead parking area (.5 mile before reaching Woods Lake).

Contact: Eldorado National Forest, Amador Ranger District, 26820 Silver Drive, Pioneer, CA 95666, 209/295-4251, www.fs.fed.us/r5—click on Forest Offices.

88 ROUND TOP SUMMIT AND WINNEMUCCA LAKE LOOP

6.6 mi / 4.0 hr   🏃4 ⛰10

in the Mokelumne Wilderness
near Carson Pass

If you want all the scenic beauty of Winnemucca Lake Trail, but you also want a longer walk and a little more solitude, try this loop trip instead. Note that although the loop trail itself is a relatively easy hike, adding on a side trip to the summit of Mount Round Top gives this hike a difficulty rating of a resounding 4. There is no real trail to Round Top's summit, and the most obvious use trail goes straight uphill at a punishing grade.

The path is the same route as Winnemucca Lake Trail for the first 1.5 miles to Winnemucca's edge, but then you bear right and cross the stream on the west side of the lake. From there, it's one mile uphill to Round Top Lake, steep enough to get you puffing. The gorgeous volcanic scenery makes it all worthwhile. Round Top Lake is set below The Sisters, two peaks that are both over 10,000 feet high. You also have views of Mount Round Top and Fourth of July Peak. It's incredibly dramatic. From the eastern edge of Round Top Lake, you'll see an obvious path heading up the side of Mount Round Top. If you like a little challenge and you're surefooted, go for it. The grade is brutal, but when you reach the top after a final rocky scramble, you have a stunning view of The Dardanelles, Lake Tahoe, Caples Lake, Woods Lake, Round Top Lake, Winnemucca Lake, and Frog Lake. Perhaps most impressive is deep Summit City Canyon, 3,000 feet below the south side of Round Top. At 10,380 feet, Mount Round Top is the highest peak in the Carson Pass area and is the finest place for a bird's-eye view. The summit is more like a

knife-thin, rocky ridge, so watch your footing. This is not a place for children or inexperienced hikers.

After your summit visit, return downhill to Round Top Lake to finish out your loop. Follow the lake's outlet creek on Lost Cabin Mine Trail for two miles back to Woods Lake Campground; then wind your way through the camp back to the Woods Lake Picnic Area, where you left your car.

User Groups: Hikers, leashed dogs, and horses. No mountain bikes. No wheelchair facilities.

Permits: A free wilderness permit is required for overnight stays; it is available from the Amador Ranger Station, the Carson Pass Information Station, or the Eldorado Information Center.

Maps: For a map, ask the U.S. Forest Service for Mokelumne Wilderness or Eldorado National Forest. For topographic maps, ask the USGS for Caples Lake and Carson Pass.

Directions: From South Lake Tahoe, take Highway 89 south for five miles to Meyers and the junction with Highway 89, and then continue south on Highway 89 for 11 miles to Highway 88. Turn right (west) on Highway 88 and drive 12 miles to the Woods Lake Campground turnoff, on the south side of the road (1.5 miles west of Carson Pass Summit). Turn left and drive 1.5 miles to the trailhead parking area, by the picnic area at Woods Lake.

Contact: Eldorado National Forest, Amador Ranger District, 26820 Silver Drive, Pioneer, CA 95666, 209/295-4251, www.fs.fed.us/r5—click on Forest Offices.

89 FOURTH OF JULY LAKE

8.8 mi / 4.5 hr or 2.0 days 🏃4 ⛰9

in the Mokelumne Wilderness
near Caples Lake

The biggest problem in a trip to Fourth of July Lake is the high number of people. Carson Pass is a stellar trailhead, and with several lakes and Mount Round Top so close, there can be 200 to 300 hikers on summer weekends. So timing becomes key, along with deciding which way to go. There are so many ways from so many trailheads, including ones at Carson Pass and Upper Blue Lake.

The shortest and most direct route is from Woods Lake trailhead, located 0.5 mile before the Woods Lake Campground and picnic area. This includes a nice stopover at Round Top Lake, two miles in. You pass some old mining cabins before you enter the wilderness boundary. Pass the eastern flank of 9,000-foot Black Butte, an old volcanic vent that is similar in appearance to Mount Round Top a few miles to the east. In less than an hour, you arrive at Round Top Lake, a worthy destination in itself and a good spot for a snack break beneath the sturdy shoulders of the two peaks of The Sisters. It's only two more miles to Fourth of July Lake, but they are steep and downhill, which means you must climb back out on the way home. This is actually good news: It means you will leave the majority of the crowds behind. Most people give up at Fourth of July Saddle, a rocky overlook that sits 1,000 feet above the lake. In addition to the tough grade, the route is often dusty. At the lake, fishing is good for brook trout, and many campsites can be found near its edge. Late in the summer, a sandy beach gets exposed, perfect for swimmers.

User Groups: Hikers, leashed dogs, and horses. No mountain bikes. No wheelchair facilities.

Permits: A free wilderness permit is required for overnight stays; it is available from the Amador Ranger Station, the Carson Pass Information Station, or the Eldorado Information Center.

Maps: For a map, ask the U.S. Forest Service for Eldorado National Forest or Mokelumne Wilderness. For a topographic map, ask the USGS for Caples Lake.

Directions: From South Lake Tahoe, take Highway 89 south for five miles to Meyers and the junction with Highway 89, and then continue south on Highway 89 for 11 miles to Highway 88. Turn right (west) on Highway 88 and drive 12 miles to the Woods Lake Campground turnoff, on the south side of the road (1.5 miles west of Carson Pass Summit). Turn

left and drive one mile to the trailhead (.5 mile before the campground and picnic area).

Contact: Eldorado National Forest, Amador Ranger District, 26820 Silver Drive, Pioneer, CA 95666, 209/295-4251, www.fs.fed.us/r5—click on Forest Offices.

90 FROG LAKE

1.8 mi / 1.0 hr

in the Mokelumne Wilderness
near Carson Pass

Any hiking trip from the Carson Pass trailhead is going to be packed with people. So it is here, with 200-plus people out on weekends. That known, this trail is educational and beautiful. The short walk to Frog Lake is suitable even for small children, and if you're more ambitious, you can continue another 1.5 miles to beautiful Winnemucca Lake. At Frog Lake, you are provided with a fascinating look at Elephant Back (elevation 9,585 feet), which looks exactly like its name. It's a lava dome, a round mass of solid lava. The lake is a beautiful turquoise color, perfect for picnicking, although because the area is rather open and exposed, the wind sometimes blows with ferocity.

Plenty of people take this walk in early summer to see the wildflowers, especially lupine and Indian paintbrush, from mid-June to mid-August (best in late July). A huge patch of wild iris also blooms alongside Frog Lake. It's a sight to behold. There are many other species of wildflowers here. An identification sheet is posted at the billboard near the trailhead and at the visitors center.

At the visitors center, you can learn about Kit Carson, the great explorer for whom this pass was named, and you can learn about the geologic forces that shaped this region, which is called the Round Top Geologic Area. Evidence of both glacial and volcanic action can be seen with every step you take.

User Groups: Hikers, leashed dogs, and horses. No mountain bikes. No wheelchair facilities.

Permits: A free wilderness permit is required for overnight stays between April 1 and November 30; it is available from the Amador Ranger Station, the Carson Pass Information Station, or the Eldorado Information Center. A $3 parking fee is charged per vehicle.

Maps: For a map, ask the U.S. Forest Service for Eldorado National Forest or Mokelumne Wilderness. For a topographic map, ask the USGS for Carson Pass.

Directions: From South Lake Tahoe, take Highway 89 south for five miles to Meyers and the junction with Highway 89, and then continue south on Highway 89 for 11 miles to Highway 88. Turn right (west) on Highway 88 and drive 10 miles to Carson Pass Summit. The parking area and trailhead are on the left, by the Carson Pass Information Station.

Contact: Eldorado National Forest, Amador Ranger District, 26820 Silver Drive, Pioneer, CA 95666, 209/295-4251, www.fs.fed.us/r5—click on Forest Offices.

91 RAYMOND LAKE
11.0 mi / 1.0-2.0 days   🥾3 ⛺9

in the Mokelumne Wilderness near Blue Lakes

Raymond Lake is a popular weekend trip despite the 3,000-foot climb. The pretty campsites at the little lake are used by PCT hikers and weekenders making this a two-day in-and-outer. That is, about five miles in and about five miles out, and that's why it works, especially for couples or young families new to backpacking. The lake is about 10 acres in size and is set at 9,000 feet, with several small campsites sprinkled near the lake. The trail starts near Wet Meadows Reservoir and heads east from the access road on the Pacific Crest Trail. Keep following the PCT for 4.5 miles, then turn right on Raymond Lake Trail. Most of this 4.5-mile stretch is a moderate ascent. The final stretch is only a mile but is a butt-kicker, mostly because you're already getting tired when you begin it. The lake is set below 10,000-foot Raymond Peak, an alpine peak.

User Groups: Hikers, dogs, and horses. No mountain bikes. No wheelchair facilities.

Permits: A free wilderness permit is required for overnight stays; it is available on the wilderness bulletin board at the trailhead, from the ranger station in Markleeville, the Carson Pass Information Station, or the Carson Ranger district in Carson City. Groups are limited to 12, and no campfires are permitted above 8,000 feet.

Maps: For a map, ask the U.S. Forest Service for Humboldt-Toiyabe National Forest, Carson District. For topographic maps, ask the USGS for Pacific Valley and Ebbetts Pass.

Directions: From South Lake Tahoe, take Highway 89 south for five miles to Meyers and the junction with Highway 89, and then continue south on Highway 89 for 11 miles to Highway 88. Turn right (west) on Highway 88 and drive 2.5 miles to the Blue Lakes turnoff, on the south side of the road. Turn south and drive 11 miles to the left turnoff for Tamarack Lake and Wet Meadows. Bear left and drive three miles to the left turnoff for Lower Sunset Lake. Turn left and drive a short distance to the trailhead.

Contact: Humboldt-Toiyabe National Forest, 1200 Franklin Way, Sparks, NV 89431, 775/331-6444, www.fs.fed.us/htnf.

92 GRANITE LAKE
4.0 mi / 2.0 hr   🥾1 ⛺9

in the Mokelumne Wilderness near Blue Lakes

Campers at Middle Creek Campground can set out from their tents on this trail to Granite Lake. But everyone else must begin by the dam at Upper Blue Lake and follow a well-signed but meandering route to enter the Mokelumne Wilderness, one mile in. Only one mile beyond the wilderness boundary lies Granite Lake, requiring a total 550-foot climb over well-graded trail. You'll barely notice you're climbing; this is a very easy pathway. A quarter mile past the boundary sign, you'll see a large pond, but don't mistake that for Granite Lake, which is another 20 minutes farther on the trail. The granite basin it's set in and the granite that lines its shores are a dead giveaway that you've made it to the proper destination. Hope you brought your swimsuit for the deep, chilly waters. If you want to hike farther, Grouse Lake is another four miles beyond.

Side note: Don't be concerned if there are lots of cars in the dam parking lot. Most of them belong to anglers, not hikers.

User Groups: Hikers, leashed dogs, and horses. No mountain bikes. No wheelchair facilities.

Permits: A free wilderness permit is required for overnight; it is available from the Amador Ranger Station, the Carson Pass Information Station, or the Eldorado Information Center.

Maps: For a map, ask the U.S. Forest Service for Eldorado National Forest. For a topographic map, ask the USGS for Pacific Valley.

Directions: From South Lake Tahoe, take Highway 89 south for five miles to Meyers and the junction with Highway 89, and then continue south on Highway 89 for 11 miles to Highway 88. Turn right (west) on Highway 88 and drive 2.5 miles to the Blue Lakes turnoff, on the south side of the road. Turn south and drive 12 miles to the fork at Lower Blue Lake. Turn right and drive 1.5 miles to the dam by Upper Blue Lake, shortly past Middle Creek Campground; turn left into the parking area. The Grouse Lake Trail leads to Granite Lake from the west side of the parking area.

Contact: Eldorado National Forest, Amador Ranger District, 26820 Silver Drive, Pioneer, CA 95666, 209/295-4251, www.fs.fed.us/r5—click on Forest Offices.

93 HOT SPRINGS CREEK WATERFALL
3.0 mi / 1.5 hr   🏃1 ⛰8

in Grover Hot Springs State Park
near Markleeville

Even without a waterfall, this would be a great trail to walk. It leads through the giant Jeffrey pines of Hot Springs Valley, enclosed by rocky cliffs and 10,000-foot peaks. The route starts from just beyond the campgrounds in Grover Hot Springs State Park. From here, you hike on the Burnside Lake and Charity Valley Trails for 0.5 mile, then branch off on a left fork. The trail is well signed for the waterfall. Some people get a bit confused on the trail where you reach a jumbled pile of boulders, but the correct answer is simply to go up and over them. Hot Springs Canyon gradually narrows on its way to the falls, and when you near the creek's edge, you'll see many small trout swimming in its pools. The waterfall is about 50 feet high and is best seen from April to July. Technically it is outside of state parkland and in Toiyabe National Forest, so you'll see backpackers' campfire rings on the cliff above the falls. The trailhead elevation is 5,900 feet, and the waterfalls are set at 6,200 feet; hence, there's a 300-foot climb.

User Groups: Hikers and leashed dogs (not recommended). No horses or mountain bikes. No wheelchair facilities.

Permits: No permits are required. A day-use fee of $6 is charged per vehicle; there is a fee of $5 per person for use of the hot springs pool.

Maps: A map of Grover Hot Springs State Park is available for $0.25 at the entrance station. For a topographic map, ask the USGS for Markleeville.

Directions: From South Lake Tahoe, take Highway 89 south for five miles to Meyers and the junction with Highway 89, and then continue south on Highway 89 for 11 miles to Highway 88. Turn left on Highway 88/89 and drive 13 miles to Markleeville at Hot Springs Road. Turn right (west) on Hot Springs Road and drive 3.5 miles to the state park entrance. The signed trailhead is 0.25 mile beyond the entrance station and campground turnoffs, at a gated dirt road.

Contact: Grover Hot Springs State Park, P.O. Box 188, Markleeville, CA 96120, 530/694-2248 or 530/525-7232, www.parks.ca.gov—click on Find A Park.

94 BURNSIDE LAKE
8.4 mi / 5.0 hr   🏃3 ⛰9

in Humboldt-Toiyabe National Forest
near Markleeville

The Burnside Lake Trail leaves Grover Hot Springs State Park at 5,900 feet in elevation and climbs west to Burnside Lake, at 8,160 feet, a gain of 2,260 feet. The climb is spaced out over four miles, so it's a steady workout to the lake. Along the way, you pass tall and majestic sugar pines and rocky outcrops, with 10,023-foot Hawkins Peak and 9,417-foot Markleeville Peak towering over the scene. The lake is about 10 surface acres and is popular for trout fishing. Although you can start hiking on the trail from Hot Springs Road shortly before the state park entrance, it's best to start from the park's trailhead. Not only does it shave one mile off your trip, but also when you return from your hike, you can take a dip in the 102- to 104-degree hot springs and soothe those aching muscles. Although you may encounter some mountain bikers on the trail at first, they will soon branch off on their way to Charity Valley.

User Groups: Hikers, dogs, horses, and mountain bikes. No wheelchair facilities.

Permits: No permits are required. A day-use fee of $6 is charged per vehicle at Grover Hot Springs State Park. Parking and access are free if you park and begin the trail outside the park entrance.

Maps: For a map, ask the U.S. Forest Service for Humboldt-Toiyabe National Forest, Carson District. A map of Grover Hot Springs State Park is available for $0.25 at the entrance station. For a topographic map, ask the USGS for Markleeville.

Directions: From South Lake Tahoe, take Highway 89 south for five miles to Meyers and the junction with Highway 89, and then continue south on Highway 89 for 11 miles to Highway 88. Turn left on Highway 88/89 and drive 13 miles to Markleeville at Hot Springs Road. Turn right (west) on Hot Springs Road and drive 3.5 miles to the state park entrance.

The signed trailhead is 0.25 mile beyond the entrance station and campground turnoffs, at a gated dirt road. Another trailhead is located outside the state park on Hot Springs Road, 0.75 mile before the state park entrance, and is signed for Charity Valley.

Contact: Grover Hot Springs State Park, P.O. Box 188, Markleeville, CA 96120, 530/694-2248 or 530/525-7232, www.parks .ca.gov—click on Find A Park; Humboldt-Toiyabe National Forest, 1200 Franklin Way, Sparks, NV 89431, 775/331-6444, www .fs.fed.us/htnf.

95 BLUE LAKES ROAD TO CARSON PASS (PCT)
12.0 mi one-way / 1.0 day   🏃4 ⛰9

from Blue Lakes Road north to Carson Pass and Highway 88

Many hikers underestimate the climb over Elephant Back to reach Carson Pass. After all, on a map, it doesn't look like much, and from a distance, as you size it up, it looks easy enough. Wrong! It's a long, grueling pull. The trip out of Blue Lakes starts easily, with a dirt road often in view and adding a bit of early angst to the affair. As you go, you keep wondering when the climb will start. Well, eventually it does, and, alas, it takes a couple of hours—a long, steady march. After topping the Elephant Back, the route drops down to Carson Pass at a rest stop, where you'll likely meet humanity, but believe it or not, no water! Conserve yours if you plan to go onward, because it takes another hour of hiking before you'll reach the next trickle.

To continue north on the PCT, see the *Carson Pass to Echo Lakes Resort (PCT)* hike in this chapter. If you are walking this trail in reverse, see the *Ebbetts Pass to Blue Lakes Road (PCT)* hike in this chapter.

User Groups: Hikers, dogs, and horses. No mountain bikes. No wheelchair access.

Permits: A backcountry permit is required

for traveling through various wilderness and special-use areas that the trail traverses. In addition, a campfire permit is required for the use of portable camp stoves or the building of campfires where allowed. To make it simple, you can contact the national forest, Bureau of Land Management (BLM), or national park office at your point of entry for a combined permit that is good for traveling through multiple-permit areas during your dates of travel.

Maps: For a map, ask the U.S. Forest Service for Lake Tahoe Basin Management Unit, Tahoe National Forest, Eldorado National Forest, and Stanislaus National Forest. For topographic maps, ask the USGS for Pacific Valley and Carson Pass.

Directions: To reach the Blue Lakes Road trailhead from the Highway 88/89 junction at Hope Valley, go west on Highway 88 to Blue Lakes Road and turn left. Stay on Blue Lakes Road for 11 miles to the trailhead parking, just before reaching Blue Lakes. For the Carson Pass trailhead from the Highway 88/89 junction at Hope Valley, go west on Highway 88 to Carson Pass.

Contact: Eldorado National Forest, Amador Ranger District, 26820 Silver Drive, Pioneer, CA 95666, 209/295-4251, www.fs.fed.us/r5—click on Forest Offices.

96 KINNEY LAKES
5.0 mi / 2.5 hr   🥾2 ⛰8

in Humboldt-Toiyabe National Forest
near Ebbetts Pass

From the Ebbetts Pass trailhead, Kinney Lakes is an easy tromp north on the Pacific Crest Trail (it's quite a bit farther to head south from Ebbetts Pass to reach Noble Lake; see the *Noble Lake* listing in this chapter). You pass little Sherrold Lake on the way to large Upper Kinney Lake (which is actually a reservoir).

You start hiking at 8,700 feet at the pass, so even though this trail has an easy to moderate grade, your lungs are getting a workout. The trail leads through a landscape of big coni-

fers with little undergrowth, typical of the high country. When the trees thin out, your views open wide. Raymond Peak and Reynolds Peak rule the skyline. At 1.6 miles, you reach a signed junction for Upper and Lower Kinney Lakes, and you can take your pick as to which one to visit first. The Pacific Crest Trail leads directly to the upper lake, while the lower lake must be visited by following an eastward fork from the PCT. The upper lake, though smaller, is the prettier of the two.

User Groups: Hikers, dogs, and horses. No mountain bikes. No wheelchair facilities.

Permits: Wilderness permits are required for overnight use. No campfires are allowed above 8,000 feet. Parking and access are free.

Maps: For a map, ask the U.S. Forest Service for Humboldt-Toiyabe National Forest, Carson District. For a topographic map, ask the USGS for Ebbetts Pass.

Directions: From Angels Camp, drive east on Highway 4 for about 40 miles to Bear Valley. Set your odometer at Bear Valley, and drive 15 miles farther east on Highway 4 to Ebbetts Pass and the trailhead parking area. The trail is on the north side of the road. If you are coming from Markleeville, drive south on Highway 89/Highway 4 for 15 miles to Ebbetts Pass.

Contact: Humboldt-Toiyabe National Forest, 1200 Franklin Way, Sparks, NV 89431, 775/331-6444, www.fs.fed.us/htnf.

97 EBBETTS PASS TO BLUE LAKES ROAD (PCT)
12.0 mi one-way / 1.0 day   🥾3 ⛰8

from Highway 4 near Ebbetts Pass north to Blue Lakes Road just south of Carson Pass and Highway 88

As you leave Ebbetts Pass heading north, you'll cross a series of fantastic volcanic formations in the Mokelumne Wilderness. The country here may look stark from a distance, but it is loaded with tiny wildflowers. The trail is quite good; a lot of hikers make great time in this area. But the lack of available water can become a concern. Tank up whenever you get the chance, such as at Eagle Creek below Reynold Peak (9,690 feet). The Mokelumne Wilderness is a relative breeze, and you'll find yourself approaching civilization at a series of small lakes in Tahoe National Forest. The trail rises up a stark, wind-blown, sandy ridge, with excellent views of the Blue Lakes, but again, there is no water for several miles until you drop down near Lost Lake. You'll actually cross several roads on this stretch of trail, and maybe even see a car, a moment of irony for long-distance PCT hikers. To continue north on the PCT, see the *Blue Lakes Road to Carson Pass (PCT)* hike in this chapter.

User Groups: Hikers, dogs, and horses. No mountain bikes. No wheelchair facilities.

Permits: A backcountry permit is required for traveling through various wilderness and special-use areas that the trail traverses. In addition, a campfire permit is required for the use of portable camp stoves or the building of campfires (where permitted). To make it simple, you can contact the national forest, Bureau of Land Management (BLM), or national park office at your point of entry for a combined permit good for traveling through multiple-permit areas during your dates of travel.

Maps: For a map, ask the U.S. Forest Service for Lake Tahoe Basin Management Unit, Tahoe National Forest, Eldorado National Forest, and Stanislaus National Forest. For topographic maps, ask the USGS for Ebbetts Pass, Pacific Valley, and Carson Pass.

Directions: To reach the Ebbetts Pass trailhead from Angels Camp, head east on Highway 4 to Ebbetts Pass. To reach the Blue Lakes Road trailhead from the Highway 88/89 interchange at Hope Valley, head west on Highway 88 to Blue Lakes Road and turn left. Stay on Blue Lakes Road to the trailhead parking area, just before reaching Blue Lakes.

Contact: Eldorado National Forest, Amador Ranger District, 26820 Silver Drive, Pioneer, CA 95666, 209/295-4251, www.fs.fed.us/r5—click on Forest Offices.

98 NOBLE LAKE
9.0 mi / 4.5 hr 🚶2 ⛰8

in Humboldt-Toiyabe National Forest near Ebbetts Pass

Noble Lake lies just outside of the Carson-Iceberg Wilderness and is reachable by a steady climb on Noble Canyon Trail out of Silver Creek Campground, or by a shorter, gentler route from Ebbetts Pass. The latter is the best choice.

From Ebbetts Pass (elevation 8,700 feet), there's a 1,200-foot climb to the lake at 9,440 feet (which includes some descent as well). The lake is a fine spot for camping or just spending an afternoon. The scenery is classic high Sierra, big conifers, snowcapped peaks, hard granite, and lush meadows. A boulder field above the campsites is loaded with ground squirrels, and if you hike overnight here with a dog, they'll drive it crazy. This lake is excellent for swimming but poor for fishing. For camping, group size is limited to 15 people, and a 100-foot setback from the lake is required.

The lake route follows an access trail to the Pacific Crest Trail from the trailhead parking area. After 0.25 mile of climbing, you will join the PCT proper and head south, first climbing and then making a long descent into Noble Canyon. The trail from Silver Creek Campground joins your trail here, and some switchbacks follow. At three miles, you will cross Noble Creek and then climb again to a high meadow. Soon you can see Noble Lake; the main lake is to the right of the trail, but a smaller, unnamed lake is to the left, about 650 feet off the trail. Both have decent campsites and many good rocks to sit on and relax.

User Groups: Hikers, dogs, and horses. No mountain bikes. No wheelchair facilities.

Permits: No day-hiking permits are required. A free wilderness permit is available at the trailhead (self-issue). Parking and access are free.

Maps: For a map, ask the U.S. Forest Service for Humboldt-Toiyabe National Forest, Carson District. For a topographic map, ask the USGS for Ebbetts Pass.

Directions: From Angels Camp at the intersection of Highways 4 and 49, go east on Highway 4 for 40 miles to Bear Valley. Set your odometer at Bear Valley, and drive 15 miles farther east on Highway 4 to Ebbetts Pass and the trailhead parking area (located just east of Ebbetts Pass; do not park on Highway 4). The trailhead is on the south side of the road.

Contact: Humboldt-Toiyabe National Forest, 1200 Franklin Way, Sparks, NV 89431, 775/331-6444, www.fs.fed.us/htnf.

99 WOLF CREEK TRAIL
9.6 mi / 5.0 hr   🏃2 ⛰8

in the Carson-Iceberg Wilderness
near Markleeville

When the temperature heats up around Markleeville, you've got two choices: Head for the mineral springs at Grover Hot Springs State Park (the cool pool, not the hot pool), or take a hike on Wolf Creek Trail in the Carson-Iceberg Wilderness.

If you pick the latter, you're in for a fine time on this easy trail along Wolf Creek, starting at 6,480 feet in elevation. The trail is an old jeep road and is almost entirely shaded, and it meanders upstream and slightly uphill for a total of nine miles one-way. Most people do not hike the entire route, but rather take our suggested trip to Wolf Creek Falls. An ideal day hike is just to stroll along the creek for an hour or two, find a good spot along the stream to hang out for a while, then turn around and stroll back. Energetic types can hike 4.3 miles out to a fork for the steep Bull Canyon Trail to Bull Lake, then bear left and continue 0.5 mile beyond the fork to Wolf Creek Falls. The waterfall is found just off the trail to the left, about 50 yards beyond where the trail passes through a cattle fence. It's quite impressive early in the summer, as it thunders over a cliff of volcanic rock.

User Groups: Hikers, dogs, and horses. No mountain bikes. No wheelchair facilities.

Permits: A free wilderness permit is required

for overnight stays; it is available at the trailhead. Parking and access are free.

Maps: For a map, ask the U.S. Forest Service for Humboldt-Toiyabe National Forest, Carson District, and Carson-Iceberg Wilderness. For a topographic map, ask the USGS for Wolf Creek.

Directions: From South Lake Tahoe, take Highway 89 south for five miles to Meyers and the junction with Highway 89, and then continue south on Highway 89 for 11 miles to Highway 88. Turn left on Highway 88/89 and drive 13 miles to Markleeville. From Markleeville, continue south on Highway 89 for four miles to Monitor Pass Junction and Highway 4. Bear right (south) on Highway 4 and drive 2.5 miles to the signed turnoff for Wolf Creek, on the left. Turn left (south) and drive 4.9 miles to the trailhead, about 100 yards before the end of the road.

Contact: Humboldt-Toiyabe National Forest, 1200 Franklin Way, Sparks, NV 89431, 775/331-6444, www.fs.fed.us/htnf.

100 EAST CARSON RIVER TRAIL
4.0 mi / 2.0 hr   🏃2 ⛰8

in the Carson-Iceberg Wilderness
near Markleeville

The East Carson River Trail can be your salvation in spring when there's still too much snow around Ebbetts Pass. Trailhead elevation is only 6,240 feet at the north side of Wolf Creek Meadows (private property), which means it's snow-free before other nearby areas. Bear left at the trail junction just uphill from the trailhead and the sign noting Carson-Iceberg Wilderness (the right fork is the High Trail northern terminus). An interesting journey is 1.5 miles to Wolf Creek Lake (sometimes dry) and Railroad Canyon, the site of 19th-century logging operations. Although this trail continues onward and eventually meets up with the southern terminus of High Trail (and ends at the junction with Golden Canyon Trail), it is nearly impossible to make a loop trip out of the two trails, especially in early season. The High Trail reaches an elevation of nearly 8,000 feet and is often covered in snow early in the season. So just hike as far as you like, then head back the way you came.

User Groups: Hikers, dogs, and horses. No mountain bikes. No wheelchair facilities.

Permits: A free wilderness permit is required for overnight stays; it is available at the trailhead. Parking and access are free.

Maps: For a map, ask the U.S. Forest Service for Humboldt-Toiyabe National Forest, Carson District, and Carson-Iceberg Wilderness. For a topographic map, ask the USGS for Wolf Creek.

Directions: From South Lake Tahoe, take Highway 89 south for five miles to Meyers and the junction with Highway 89, and then continue south on Highway 89 for 11 miles to Highway 88. Turn left on Highway 88/89 and drive 13 miles to Markleeville. Continue south on Highway 89/Highway 4 for 7.5 miles to the signed turnoff for Wolf Creek on the left. Turn left (east) and drive 3.5 miles to the left turnoff signed for East Carson River Trail. Turn left and drive one mile to the road junction to Dixon Mine. Turn right and drive 0.25 mile to the trailhead.

Contact: Humboldt-Toiyabe National Forest, 1200 Franklin Way, Sparks, NV 89431, 775/331-6444, www.fs.fed.us/htnf.

101 HEISER LAKE
4.8 mi / 2.5 hr   🏃3 ⛰9

in the Carson-Iceberg Wilderness
near Ebbetts Pass

You know you're in for a good trip when the trailhead is located at a spot as pretty as the Mosquito Lakes, set at an elevation of 8,000 feet on Highway 4. The trail climbs and descends, then climbs and descends some more, mostly heading in a straight-line course due south to the lake. It's one of those trails where you've got to work equally hard traveling in both directions. At a junction with the trail from Bull Run Lake

two miles in, bear left and finish out the last 0.5 mile to Heiser Lake, set at 8,300 feet. The lake is granite bound, with a couple of tiny islands sticking out of its shallow waters. The tiny little lakes are popular with anglers from the nearby campgrounds, but this trail is popular with nature lovers, who set out on the short, moderate, day hike to Heiser Lake for a few hours of peace in the Carson-Iceberg Wilderness.

User Groups: Hikers, dogs, and horses. No mountain bikes. No wheelchair facilities.

Permits: No day-hiking permits are required. Parking and access are free.

Maps: For a map, ask the U.S. Forest Service for Stanislaus National Forest and Carson-Iceberg Wilderness. For topographic maps, ask the USGS for Pacific Valley and Spicer Meadow Reservoir.

Directions: From Angels Camp, take Highway 4 east for 40 miles to Bear Valley. Set your odometer at Bear Valley and drive 10 miles farther east on Highway 4 to the the Mosquito Lakes trailhead and Heiser Lake Trail. Park on the right (south) side of the road, across from the campground; there is only enough space for a few cars.

Contact: Stanislaus National Forest, Calaveras Ranger District, P.O. Box 500, Hathaway Pines, CA 95233, 209/795-1381, www.fs.fed .us/r5—click on Forest Offices.

102 BULL RUN LAKE
7.0 mi / 4.0 hr   🏃2 ⛰9

in the Carson-Iceberg Wilderness
near Ebbetts Pass

You might have to share the trail to Bull Run Lake with some horses. After all, their owners like the big parking lot at the trailhead, large enough for horse trailers. Maybe you should pack along a few extra apples or carrots, eh? Although longer than the nearby trail to Heiser Lake, this trip to Bull Run Lake is actually easier, because the trail is well graded, and the only really steep section is in the last 0.5 mile. The trailhead is set at 7,800 feet. The first 1.3 miles are almost level, traveling slightly downhill through a grassy meadow that is filled with wildflowers in the early summer and turns golden by September. After that, you start to climb, mostly through pine forest and over duck-lined stretches of granite. Watch for a trail junction at 2.2 miles, where you should turn right for Bull Run Lake (straight ahead is Heiser Lake). After a brief flat stretch, prepare for a final mile of climbing, with the last part being the most challenging. The lake is set at 8,300 feet and is a fine reward for your effort, set in a steep-walled granite bowl, with many smooth rock slabs to lie on. Note that the ambitious can add on a trip to Heiser Lake, which is two miles away from the junction. But with a steep up and down, it's better saved for backpackers or day hikers with an early start.

User Groups: Hikers, dogs, and horses. No mountain bikes. No wheelchair facilities.

Permits: No day-hiking permits are required. Parking and access are free.

Maps: For a map, ask the U.S. Forest Service for Stanislaus National Forest or Carson-Iceberg Wilderness. For topographic maps, ask the USGS for Pacific Valley and Spicer Meadow Reservoir.

Directions: From Angels Camp, take Highway 4 east for 40 miles to Bear Valley. Set your odometer at Bear Valley and drive 8.5 miles farther east on Highway 4 to the Stanislaus Meadow turnoff, on the right (Road 8N13). Turn right and drive a short distance to the trailhead parking area.

Contact: Stanislaus National Forest, Calaveras Ranger District, P.O. Box 500, Hathaway Pines, CA 95233, 209/795-1381, www.fs.fed .us/r5—click on Forest Offices.

103 CLARK FORK AND BOULDER LAKE

8.0 mi / 4.0 hr   🏃3   ⛰8

in the Carson-Iceberg Wilderness on Clark Fork Stanislaus River

From this trailhead at Iceberg Meadow, you immediately enter the Carson-Iceberg

Wilderness at the base of imposing Iceberg Peak. You will hike upstream on the northern edge of the Clark Fork Stanislaus River and enjoy wildflowers and a lovely mixed forest of white firs and Jeffrey pines. At the water's edge, the trees are leafier, including cottonwoods and aspens. The river pools are cold but useful for cooling off on a hot day. At 2.5 miles, you have a choice: Bear right (really straight) and continue along the Clark Fork, or turn left and hike steeply uphill along Boulder Creek. We suggest the left fork, following Boulder Creek for 1.5 miles uphill to tiny Boulder Lake. It's a good workout to a pretty destination. But hey, if you get tired, just cut the trip short and turn around when you reach Boulder Creek. Plenty of fishing holes and picnic spots can be found along the Clark Fork.

User Groups: Hikers, dogs, and horses. No mountain bikes. No wheelchair facilities.

Permits: A free wilderness permit is required for overnight stays and is available from the Summit Ranger Station. Parking and access are free.

Maps: For a map, ask the U.S. Forest Service for Stanislaus National Forest or Carson-Iceberg Wilderness. For a topographic map, ask the USGS for Donnell Lake.

Directions: From Sonora, take Highway 108 east for 46 miles to the left turnoff for Clark Fork Road (about 17 miles east of Strawberry). Turn left and follow Clark Fork Road for about seven miles to its end, at the Clark Fork trailhead at Iceberg Meadow.

Contact: Stanislaus National Forest, Summit Ranger District, 1 Pinecrest Lake Road, Pinecrest, CA 95364, 209/965-3434, www .fs.fed.us/r5—click on Forest Offices.

104 EAGLE MEADOW TO DARDANELLE

4.0 mi one-way / 2.0 hr   🏃2   ⛰8

near Dardanelle

BEST (

Your first order of business is to convince someone to drop you off at Eagle Meadow and pick you up at Dardanelle Resort. Then you can take this one-way trip, a scenic downhill stroll paralleling Eagle Creek. It's a trip for lovers of sub-alpine meadows, especially in the first mile. After it leaves the meadow, the trail enters a thick and lovely conifer forest, so you get a bit of shade along the path. The route gets a little steep in sections, so make sure your knees are in good enough shape for four miles of downhill before you make the trip.

User Groups: Hikers, leashed dogs, horses, and mountain bikes. No wheelchair facilities.

Permits: No permits are required. Parking and access are free.

Maps: For a map, ask the U.S. Forest Service for Stanislaus National Forest. For topographic maps, ask the USGS for Donnell Lake and Dardanelle.

Directions: From Sonora, take Highway 108 east for 41 miles to the turnoff for Niagara Creek Campground, on the right side of the highway (about 12 miles east of Strawberry). Turn right, then at 0.25 mile, turn right again on Forest Road 5N01 and continue on Forest Road 5N01 for seven miles to Eagle Meadow. This is the start of the one-way shuttle hike; the finish is at Dardanelle Resort on Highway 108, eight miles east of the Niagara Creek turnoff.

Contact: Stanislaus National Forest, Summit Ranger District, 1 Pinecrest Lake Road, Pinecrest, CA 95364, 209/965-3434, www .fs.fed.us/r5—click on Forest Offices.

105 TRAIL OF THE GARGOYLES
3.0 mi / 1.5 hr   👫1 ⛰8

near Strawberry and Pinecrest Lake
in Stanislaus National Forest

BEST (

It's hard to guess what's in store on the Trail of the Gargoyles. The trailhead is nondescript, but that quickly changes. The odd rock formations that line the trail are perched at the edge of a cliff at 7,400 feet in elevation. You walk just inches away from what appears to be the edge of the world, with only thin air between

you and the densely forested basin several hundred feet below. It's an easy and nearly flat trail, but if you have kids with you, keep a handhold on them at all times. By the way, the rock formations don't look much like gargoyles except for the fact that they are hanging off the edge of this abrupt abyss. The trailhead is in the middle of the 1.5-mile trail, which means you'll want to walk out and back in both directions. The trail on the north rim is slightly steeper.

User Groups: Hikers and leashed dogs. No horses or mountain bikes. No wheelchair facilities.

Permits: No permits are required. Parking and access are free.

Maps: For a map, ask the U.S. Forest Service for Stanislaus National Forest. For a topographic map, ask the USGS for Pinecrest.

Directions: From Sonora, take Highway 108 east for 32 miles to Strawberry, and then continue east 2.4 miles to Herring Creek Road (Forest Road 4N12). Turn right on Herring Creek Road and drive 6.7 miles to an often-unsigned turnoff on the left. Turn left and drive 0.2 mile to the trailhead.

Contact: Stanislaus National Forest, Summit Ranger District, 1 Pinecrest Lake Road, Pinecrest, CA 95364, 209/965-3434, www .fs.fed.us/r5—click on Forest Offices.

106 COLUMNS OF THE GIANTS
0.5 mi / 0.5 hr   👫1 ⛰8

near Dardanelle

This is the central Sierra's answer to Devils Postpile National Monument. Take it from us, it's no cheap imitation. The Columns of the Giants features remaining columns that are 30–40 feet in height and 3–4 feet in diameter. Although many are still standing tall or at least at an angle, others have shattered into thousands of pieces, creating a giant pile of rubble, at times just a jumbled heap of rocks. An interpretive trail sign explains that underneath this rock pile is evidence of the last small ice age in the Sierra, frozen remnants of ice fields that are replenished each year by winter snow and cold. The rock formations at the end of the Columns of the Giants geological trail were formed 150,000 years ago, when a series of volcanic eruptions occurred. The lava flow cooled rapidly, probably during cold weather, and cracked into narrow, hexagonal, basalt columns. This historical information gives you plenty to think about during your very short walk. Make sure you bring your camera.

User Groups: Hikers and leashed dogs. No horses or mountain bikes. No wheelchair facilities.

Permits: No permits are required. Parking and access are free.

Maps: For a map, ask the U.S. Forest Service for Stanislaus National Forest. For a topographic map, ask the USGS for Dardanelle.

Directions: From Sonora, take Highway 108 east for 50 miles to Pigeon Flat Campground (two miles east of Dardanelle) on the south side of the highway. If you're traveling west on Highway 108, the campground is 12.6 miles west of Sonora Pass. Park in the day-use parking lot just outside the camp.

Contact: Stanislaus National Forest, Summit Ranger District, 1 Pinecrest Lake Road, Pinecrest, CA 95364, 209/965-3434, www .fs.fed.us/r5—click on Forest Offices.

107 KENNEDY LAKE
14.8 mi / 2.0 days 🏃3 ⛰8

in the Emigrant Wilderness near Dardanelle

Follow the trail notes to Relief Reservoir (see next listing), but at 2.6 miles, take the left fork for Kennedy Lake. The trail climbs for another 1.6 miles, then goes flat for the final 3.2 miles to the lake. It's an easy two-day backpack trip, with low mileage and only a 1,200-foot elevation gain. Note that all the campsites are set downstream of the lake rather than along its shoreline.

If the number of cars in the Kennedy Meadows parking lot is scaring you, take heart. Many of them belong to people day hiking to fish at Relief Reservoir. If you have the time

and inclination for a longer trip to Kennedy Lake, you will leave a lot of your fellow hikers behind. Even so, don't expect solitude. You'll likely share the lake with other backpackers, horse packers, and grazing cows.

User Groups: Hikers, leashed dogs, and horses. No mountain bikes. No wheelchair facilities.

Permits: A free wilderness permit is required for overnight stays and is available from the Summit Ranger Station. Parking and access are free.

Maps: For a map, ask the U.S. Forest Service for Stanislaus National Forest or Emigrant Wilderness. For a topographic map, ask the USGS for Sonora Pass.

Directions: From Sonora, take Highway 108 east for 55 miles to the turnoff for Kennedy Meadows (six miles east of Dardanelle) on the south side of the highway. Turn right and drive one mile to the large parking area. If you're traveling west on Highway 108, the Kennedy Meadows turnoff is 9.1 miles west of Sonora Pass.

Contact: Stanislaus National Forest, Summit Ranger District, 1 Pinecrest Lake Road, Pinecrest, CA 95364, 209/965-3434, www .fs.fed.us/r5—click on Forest Offices.

108 RELIEF RESERVOIR
6.0 mi / 3.0 hr 🏃3 ⛰7

on the edge of the Emigrant Wilderness near Dardanelle

From the mammoth trailhead and parking lot at Kennedy Meadows, you can hike to Relief Reservoir (elevation 7,200 feet), do a little fishing, then hike back out. The route, called the Huckleberry Trail, leads along the Stanislaus River, enters the Emigrant Wilderness at one mile, then skirts its edge. Quickly you understand why this trip is so popular, the river canyon gets more and more beautiful as you head deeper into it. The trail had to be blasted into the steep and rocky hillside. Pass the left turnoff for roaring Kennedy Creek and Kennedy Lake at 2.6 miles, and then proceed straight for another 0.5 mile to an overlook of the reservoir. It's a steep drop down to the water's edge in the last 0.25 mile, which, of course, must be regained on the return trip.

The only downers are that pack animals have roughed up the trail, and the route is seriously overused. On weekends it seems you must constantly pull off the path to let horses and other hikers go by.

User Groups: Hikers, leashed dogs, and horses. No mountain bikes. No wheelchair facilities.

Permits: No day-use permits are required. Parking and access are free.

Maps: For a map, ask the U.S. Forest Service for Stanislaus National Forest or Emigrant Wilderness. For a topographic map, ask the USGS for Sonora Pass.

Directions: From Sonora, take Highway 108 east for 55 miles to the Kennedy Meadows turnoff (six miles east of Dardanelle) on the south side of the highway. Turn right and go one mile to the well-signed parking area. Day hikers can park 0.5 mile farther down the road, near Kennedy Meadows Resort. If you're traveling west on Highway 108, the Kennedy Meadows turnoff is 9.1 miles west of Sonora Pass.

Contact: Stanislaus National Forest, Summit Ranger District, 1 Pinecrest Lake Road, Pinecrest, CA 95364, 209/965-3434, www .fs.fed.us/r5—click on Forest Offices.

109 SARDINE FALLS
2.0 mi / 1.0 hr

near Sonora Pass

An easy hike through a high alpine meadow and culminating at a pretty waterfall is our idea of a fine way to spend an afternoon. The trip to Sardine Falls requires a little route finding, because there is no formal trail. But the going is easy since you can see the falls from the road and there are several overgrown jeep routes to follow.

From parking, head across the northwest side of the meadow. Look for a route that is signed Route Closed to Motorized Vehicles;

it's the most direct path. Cross Sardine Creek, which parallels Highway 108, and walk up the right side of larger McKay Creek. After climbing uphill over a rise, you'll hear and then see Sardine Falls, gracefully framed by a few sparse lodgepole pines.

User Groups: Hikers, leashed dogs, and horses. No mountain bikes. No wheelchair facilities.

Permits: No permits are required. Parking and access are free.

Maps: For a map, ask the U.S. Forest Service for Humboldt-Toiyabe National Forest, Bridgeport District. For a topographic map, ask the USGS for Pickel Meadow.

Directions: From the junction of U.S. 395 and Highway 108, take Highway 108 west and drive 12.5 miles (2.5 miles east of Sonora Pass) and park along the road in the gravel pullouts near the overgrown jeep roads on the northwest side of the meadow.

Contact: Humboldt-Toiyabe National Forest, Bridgeport Ranger District, HCR1 Box 1000, Bridgeport, CA 93517, 760/932-7070, www .fs.fed.us/htnf.

110 SONORA PASS TO EBBETTS PASS (PCT)
30.8 mi one-way / 3.0 days

from Highway 108 at Sonora Pass north to Highway 4 near Ebbetts Pass

While this section of the Pacific Crest Trail may not have the glamorous reputation of the stretch of trail in the southern Sierra, it's just as compelling for those of us who have hiked it. From Sonora Pass, you're forced to climb out for a good hour or two. Then you'll rise over Wolf Creek Gap (10,300 feet, the highest, most northern point on the PCT) and make the easy drop down the Carson Canyon. This is the start of the Carson-Iceberg Wilderness, a giant swath of land that is a rare, unpeopled paradise. The Sierra riparian zones here are lined with flowers, seemingly all kinds and all colors, often in luxuriant beds of greenness. The PCT climbs out of Carson Canyon around Boulder

Peak, then down and up two more canyons. All the while, you keep crossing creeks filled with natural gardens. You wind your way across and through these areas and eventually climb a ridge, then head down, steeply at times, to Ebbetts Pass. There's no water here. No problem. A short half-hour climb and you can be pumping water, and maybe setting up camp too, at little Sherrold Lake, not far from the edge of the Mokelumne Wilderness.

To continue north on the PCT, see the *Ebbetts Pass to Blue Lakes Road (PCT)* hike in this chapter.

User Groups: Hikers, dogs, and horses. No mountain bikes. No wheelchair facilities.

Permits: A wilderness permit is required for traveling through various wilderness and special-use areas the trail traverses. Contact the Stanislaus National Forest to obtain a permit that is good for the length of your trip.

Maps: For topographic maps, ask the USGS for Pickel Meadow, Disaster Peak, Dardanelles Cone, and Ebbetts Pass.

Directions: From Sonora, take Highway 108 east to Sonora Pass to the parking area and trailhead (south side of parking area).

Contact: Stanislaus National Forest, Summit Ranger District, 1 Pinecrest Lake Road, Pinecrest, CA 95364, 209/965-3434 or 209/532-3671 (for permits), www.fs.fed.us/r5—click on Forest Offices.

⑪ SECRET AND POORE LAKES
6.5 mi / 3.5 hr 🏃3 ⛰8

near Sonora Pass

This 6.5-mile loop trip begins at a footbridge over West Walker River at Leavitt Meadows Campground. After 0.25 mile, take the left fork for Secret Lake (this is no secret and you won't be alone here, most likely). Climb for nearly two miles through sage and Jeffrey pines, then descend 0.5 mile to Secret Lake. Much larger Poore Lake is visible over your left shoulder. Take a break at Secret Lake, then continue around the right side of the lake, hiking through sparse junipers and pines for 0.5 mile to the left turnoff for Poore Lake. Take the rougher 0.75-mile route to the large lake. If it's quiet, you can swim or fish for a few hours, then retrace your steps to the junction. From there, loop back to the campground on a lower trail that follows closer to the West Walker River through Leavitt Meadow. If Poore Lake turns out to be less than perfect, you can always hike beyond the return loop junction to little Roosevelt Lake.

Special Notes: No mountain bikes are permitted beyond Poore Lake, so that means Roosevelt Lake is free of them, at least in theory. In addition, there is no bridge available for off-road vehicles, so though this area was once an OHV spot, it is no longer. Finally, a nearby U.S. Marine training facility means it is possible you may see groups dressed in camo outfits running along the road. They do not fire their weapons here and they almost never enter the forest.

User Groups: Hikers, dogs, horses, and mountain bikes. No wheelchair facilities.

Permits: No day-use permits are required. Campfire permits required for overnight use. Parking and access are free.

Maps: For a map, ask the U.S. Forest Service for Humboldt-Toiyabe National Forest, Bridgeport District. For a topographic map, ask the USGS for Pickel Meadow.

Directions: From the junction of U.S. 395 and Highway 108, take Highway 108 west for seven miles to Leavitt Meadows Campground, on the south side of the road. If you are coming from the west, the camp is eight miles east of Sonora Pass. Day hikers may park inside the campground; backpackers must park 0.25 mile west of the camp on Highway 108.

Contact: Humboldt-Toiyabe National Forest, Bridgeport Ranger District, HCR1 Box 1000, Bridgeport, CA 93517, 760/932-7070, www.fs.fed.us/htnf.

Index

Tahoe Camping

Tahoe Hiking

**MOON TAHOE
CAMPING & HIKING**

Avalon Travel
a member of the Perseus Books Group
1700 Fourth Street
Berkeley, CA 94710, USA
www.moon.com

Editor and Series Manager: Sabrina Young
Copy Editor: Michelle Peters
Graphics Coordinator: Kathryn Osgood
Production Coordinator: Elizabeth Jang
Cover Designer: Kathryn Osgood
Interior Designer: Darren Alessi
Map Editor: Kevin Anglin
Cartographers: Kat Bennett, Suzanne Service
Proofreader: Erika Howsare

ISBN: 978-1-59880-275-7

Front cover photo: Tahoe tree and lake,
© Kathryn Osgood.
Title page photo: Man on rock looking out onto
Lake Tahoe, © Vernon Wiley/istockphoto.com

Printed in the United States of America

ABOUT THE AUTHOR

Tom Stienstra

For 30 years, Tom Stienstra's full-time job has been to capture and communicate the outdoor experience. This has led him across California – fishing, hiking, camping, boating, biking, and flying – searching for the best of the outdoors and then writing about it.

Tom is the nation's top-selling author of outdoors guidebooks. He has been inducted into the California Outdoor Hall of Fame and has twice been awarded National Outdoor Writer of the Year, newspaper division, by the Outdoor Writers Association of America. He has also been named California Outdoor Writer of the Year five times, most recently in 2007. Tom is the outdoors columnist for the *San Francisco Chronicle;* his articles appear on www.sfgate.com and in newspapers around the country. He broadcasts a weekly radio show on KCBS-San Francisco and hosts an outdoor television show on CBS/CW San Francisco.

Tom lives with his wife and sons in Northern California. You can contact him directly via the website www.tomstienstra.com. His guidebooks include:

Moon California Camping
Moon California Hiking (with Ann Marie Brown)
Moon California Fishing
Moon California Recreational Lakes & Rivers
California Wildlife
Moon Northern California Cabins & Cottages
Moon Northern California Camping
Moon Oregon Camping
Moon Pacific Northwest Camping
Moon Washington Camping
Moon West Coast RV Camping
Tom Stienstra's Bay Area Recreation